KT-408-760

# The
# Official
# *Fahrenheit 9/11*
# Reader

## MICHAEL MOORE

Simon & Schuster

NEW YORK • LONDON • TORONTO • SYDNEY

SIMON & SCHUSTER
Rockefeller Center
1230 Avenue of the Americas
New York, NY 10020

Copyright © 2004 by Michael Moore

All rights reserved,
including the right of reproduction
in whole or in part in any form.

First Simon & Schuster mass market paperback export edition 2005

SIMON & SCHUSTER and colophon are registered trademarks
of Simon & Schuster, Inc.

For information about special discounts for bulk purchases,
please contact Simon & Schuster Special Sales at
1-800-456-6798 or business@simonandschuster.com.

Manufactured in the United States of America

10   9   8   7   6   5   4   3   2   1

ISBN 0-7432-7292-7
ISBN 0-7432-7359-1

*To Elmer Bernstein*

# Contents

# Foreword:
# "The Work of
# a Patriot"

## John Berger

*Fahrenheit 9/11* is astounding.

Michael Moore's film profoundly moved the artists on the Cannes Film Festival jury, and they voted unanimously to award it the Palme d'Or. Since then it has touched many millions of people. During the first six weeks of its showing in the United States the box office takings amounted to over 100 million dollars, which is, astoundingly, about half of what *Harry Potter and the Sorcerer's Stone* made during a comparable period.

People have never seen another film like *Fahrenheit 9/11*. Only the so-called opinion-makers in the press and media appear to have been put out by it.

The film, considered as a political act, may be a historical landmark. Yet to have a sense of this, a certain perspective for the future is required. Living only close up to the latest news, as most opinion-makers do, reduces one's perspectives: everything is a hassle, no more. The film by contrast believes it may be making a very small contribution toward the changing of world history. It is a work inspired by hope.

What makes it an event is the fact that it is an effective and independent intervention into immediate world politics. Today it is rare for an artist (Moore is one) to succeed in making such an intervention, and in interrupting the prepared, prevaricating statements of politicians. Its immediate aim is to make it less likely that President Bush will be reelected next November. From start to finish it invites a political and social argument.

To denigrate this as *propaganda* is either naive or perverse, forgetting (deliberately?) what the last century taught us. Propaganda requires a permanent network of communication so that it can systematically stifle reflection with emotive or utopian slogans. Its pace is usually fast. Propaganda invariably serves the long-term interests of some elite.

This single maverick movie is often reflectively slow and is not afraid of silence. It appeals to people to think for themselves and make thought-out connections. And it identifies with, and pleads for, those who are normally unlistened to.

Making a strong case is not the same thing as saturating with propaganda. FOX TV does the latter, Michael Moore the former.

Ever since the Greek tragedies, artists have, from time to time, asked themselves how they might influence ongoing political events. A tricky question because two very different types of power are involved. Many theories of aesthetics and ethics revolve around this question. For those living under political tyrannies, art has frequently been a form of hidden resistance, and tyrants habitually look for ways to control art. All this, however, is in general terms and over a large terrain. *Fahrenheit 9/11* is something different. It has succeeded in intervening in a political program on the program's own ground.

For this to happen a convergence of factors were needed. The Cannes award and the misjudged attempt to prevent the film being distributed played a significant part in creating the *event*.

To point this out in no way implies that the film as such doesn't deserve the attention it is receiving. It's simply to remind ourselves that within the realm of the mass media a breakthrough (a smashing-down of the daily wall of lies and half-truths) is bound to be rare. And it is this rarity which has made the film exemplary. It is setting an example to millions—as if they'd been waiting for it.

The film proposes that the White House and Pentagon were taken over in the first year of the millennium by a gang of thugs—plus their Born-Again Frontman—so that U.S. power should henceforth serve, as a priority, the global interests of the Corporations. A stark scenario that is closer to the truth than most nuanced editorials. Yet more important than the scenario is the way the movie speaks out. It demonstrates that, despite all the manipulative power of communications experts, lying presidential speeches, and vapid press conferences, a single independent voice, pointing out certain home truths that countless Americans are already discovering for themselves, can break through the conspiracy of silence, the manufactured atmosphere of fear, and the solitude of feeling politically impotent.

It's a movie that speaks of obstinate faraway desires in a period of disillusion. A movie that tells jokes whilst the band plays the Apocalypse. A movie in which millions of Americans recognize themselves and the precise ways in which they are being cheated. A movie about surprises, mostly bad but some good, being discussed together. *Fahrenheit 9/11* reminds the spectator that when courage is shared one can fight against the odds.

In over a thousand cinemas across the country Michael Moore becomes with this film a People's Tribune. And what do we see? Bush is visibly a political cretin, as ignorant of the world as he is indifferent to it. Whilst the Tribune, informed by popular experience, acquires political credibility, not as a politician himself but as the voice of the anger of a multitude and its will to resist.

There is something else that is astounding. The aim of *Fahrenheit 9/11* is to stop Bush fixing the next election as he fixed the last. Its focus is on the totally unjustified war in Iraq. Yet its conclusion is larger than either of these issues. It declares that a political economy that creates colossally increasing wealth surrounded by disastrously increasing poverty, needs—in order to survive—a continual war with some invented foreign enemy to maintain its own internal order and security. It requires ceaseless war.

Thus, fifteen years after the fall of Communism, decades after the declared End of History, one of the main theses of Marx's interpretation of history again becomes a debating point and a possible explanation of the catastrophes being lived.

It is always the poor who make the most sacrifices, *Fahrenheit 9/11* announces quietly during its last minutes. For how much longer?

There is no future for any civilization anywhere in the world today that ignores this question. And this is why the film was made and became what it became. It's a film that deeply wants America to survive.

# Introduction

As I write this, my film *Fahrenheit 9/11* is still playing in hundreds of theaters across America. Though I have often heard the overused cliché of "being in the eye of a hurricane," I never really knew what that meant until I made this movie.

And it is far too early for me to possess the insight necessary to explain the fever that has erupted over *Fahrenheit 9/11*. The records started falling in the first hours of the film's release:

> Biggest opening day ever for *any* film at both New York theaters
> First documentary ever to debut at No. 1
> Largest grossing documentary ever, beating the previous record holder (*Bowling for Columbine*) by 600 percent

A Gallup poll showed that more than half of the American public said they planned on seeing the film, either in the theater or on home video. No one could remember when a film posted those kinds of numbers.

The intense desire to see *Fahrenheit 9/11* grew out of a series of events that began in late April of 2004 when our distributor was told by its parent company, the Walt Disney Company, that they would not distribute our film. Michael Eisner, the head of Disney, said that he didn't want his studio putting out a partisan political film that might offend the families who go to their amusement parks. Of course, he didn't mention that he had a problem with Disney syndicating the Sean Hannity radio show (which they do) or carrying Rush Limbaugh on their ABC-owned stations (which they do) or broadcasting Pat Robertson's *700 Club* on the Disney Family Channel (which . . . well, you get the point. What Eisner meant to say was that if my movie had been a piece of right-wing, hate-filled propaganda that supported the Bush administration's every move, then that would be OK).

When the story broke, Disney tried their best to spin it, but it didn't work and only made people want to see the film more.

We then went to the Cannes Film Festival without a distributor. As only the third documentary in the history of the festival to be placed in competition (the other two were Louis Malle and Jacques Cousteau's *The Silent World* and *Bowling for Columbine*), *Fahrenheit* went on to win the top prize, the Palme d'Or.

But we came home without a distributor. The White House went into overdrive, with Karl Rove's office making calls to encourage reporters to trash a film they hadn't seen. A Republican group began a campaign to harass any theater owners who said they were going to show *Fahrenheit 9/11*. At least three movie chains, and scores of other individual theaters, were scared off and announced they would not show our movie on any of their screens. Another group filed a complaint with the Federal Elections Commission (FEC) to have them stop us from advertising our film on TV, claiming the spots were "political ads" that violated the law. By the time the FEC ruled in our favor, our distributor had already pulled all the ads.

Rove sent the attack dogs out to denounce the movie—the official White House statement was that "we don't need to see it to know that it is wrong." Bush's dad called me a bunch of names, and their mouthpiece pundits in the media went on all the talk shows to trash me and the movie.

But none of it worked. They only made people want to see the movie. And when these millions of Americans emerged from movie theaters, they were shaken to the core. Theater managers across the country reported crowds in tears, audiences standing and cheering a blank screen at the end of the movie. So many people stayed in the theater to talk to the strangers around them that the theaters had to schedule more time between screenings.

Thousands of emails poured in to our website, an average of 6,000 a day. On some days, over 20 million people went to our website. Viewer after viewer told us their stories of watching the movie. So many letters began with one of these two lines: "I have never voted, but I am now going to vote this year" or "I'm a Republican and I just don't know what to do now."

In an election year where the presidency could be decided by a few thousand votes, these comments were profound—and frightening to the Bush White House. According to the Harris poll, about 10 percent of the people seeing the movie were Republican and 44 percent of them said they would recommend the film to other Republicans. Thirty percent of them said that they felt the movie treated Mr. Bush "fairly."

Another poll showed that over 13 percent of the undecided voters had seen the movie. One Republican pollster told me, after conducting his own informal poll by watching the movie with audiences in three separate cities, that "perhaps eighty percent of the people going into *Fahrenheit 9/11* are Kerry voters—but one hundred percent of the people coming out of *Fahrenheit 9/11* are Kerry voters. I was not able to find anyone who would say 'I am absolutely voting for Bush' after they had sat through the two hours of your movie."

In Pennsylvania, a key swing state, a Keystone poll showed that 4 percent of Kerry's vote was due to people swayed or motivated by *Fahrenheit 9/11* (and 2 percent was credited to the nonstop attacks on Bush by Howard Stern, who also strongly advocated our film).

As I write this a few months before Election Day, no one knows what all this will mean. What we do know is that *Fahrenheit 9/11* has rocked the country in a way that films rarely have a chance to do. For that privilege all of us who made the film are extremely grateful. Fifty percent of this nation does not vote. If we have something to do with bringing that number down just a few percentage points, then all will be worth it.

In the end, while we hope that *Fahrenheit 9/11* makes its contribution, we are, first and foremost, filmmakers and artists. We worked hard on creating a work of cinema that would move people not just politically but on an emotional and visceral level. I hope we have made a contribution to this art form we love so much. Who among us doesn't love to go to the movies and split a gut laughing; be surprised, shocked, reduced to tears, swept away, blown away; leave the theater wanting to go back in again? For those of us who make movies, that is why we do so. That is what I hope we have done here.

Because so many of you have asked us to publish the film's screenplay—and all the supporting evidence we have—we have decided to provide you with this book. *Screenplay* seems like an odd word for a documentary, but nonfiction may be a form of screenwriting, just like fiction (the Writers Guild in 2002, for the first time, made that point by voting *Bowling for Columbine* the best original screenplay of the year). Besides the fact that documentaries generally don't use actors, they are a style of filmmaking that is different from fiction features in that they are written after the movie is shot. You enter the editing room with hundreds of hours of footage, and then you must decide what your story is and construct—write—it. It's definitely a cart-before-the-horse system, which in some ways makes it much more challenging than fiction films, where the writer just tells everyone what to say. We can't tell George Bush what to say or John Ashcroft what to sing. But what we do with what *is* said requires a lot of noodling—to determine where it all fits into the basic story we are trying to tell. This is then all woven together with the narration that I write. It is a painstaking process that takes months, sometimes years.

So, on these pages I have published the screenplay so that you can read the film and rediscover the mountain of information and facts that *Fahrenheit 9/11* presents. It's hard to take it all in at one screening, so I hope having this screenplay will help you find the treasure that might have been buried by all those great shots of eggs hitting the presidential limo.

For those of you who have been hectored by your conservative brother-in-law who has repeated to you the talking points he has been given by FOX News about *Fahrenheit 9/11*, this book gives you all the ammo you need to refute any and all of his crazy comments about the movie. It's hard for conservatives to believe that their leader may be in bed with the wrong people, so contained herein is all the evidence you need to help sober them up. After all, friends don't let friends vote Republican.

I have also reprinted some of the best essays and reviews of the movie by people smarter than me who figured out what I was up to before I did. They will give you some good insight into what the movie means and the place it now holds in the annals of cinema.

Another chapter gives you a series of writings related to the issues in the film. I have personally chosen them because I want the discussion to go beyond just the movie and into where do we go from here. These pieces give you a more in-depth look into the

Bush-Saudi connection (including new information on the bin Laden post-9/11 flights), the reasons we were conned into going into Iraq, and why the media failed to do its job. And a ten-year-old article from the *L.A. Times* perhaps provides the real story behind why Disney didn't want to distribute *Fahrenheit 9/11.*

Finally, I wanted to share with you some of those emails I received from people after they saw the film. I am still moved by them when I read them and I think you will be, too. Included also are photos from the opening week around the country and some of our favorite editorial cartoons that ran in the major daily papers.

I don't think any of us who worked on *Fahrenheit 9/11* had a clue that it would become a pivotal moment in this historic election year. We just wanted to make a good movie. I hope we have succeeded. And I hope you enjoy this companion book to our film. Someday, after all this has passed and I have time to reflect on what it all meant, I will share that story with you. But that can't be done right now. Right now, it's a movie that in some ways, though finished, is still a work in progress, its true ending to be written on November 2, 2004, and the months that follow. That makes all of you my cowriters.

MICHAEL MOORE
*New York City*
*August 2004*

# PART I

*Fahrenheit 9/11—*
**The Screenplay**

# Narrated by Michael Moore

*Fireworks and confetti fly through the air as a triumphant Al Gore cheers at a podium with FLORIDA VICTORY sign in background—he is flanked by celebrities*

### NARRATION

Was it all just a dream?

### AL GORE

God bless you, Florida! Thank you.

### NARRATION

Did the last four years not really happen? Look, there's Ben Affleck, he's often in my dreams. And the *Taxi Driver* guy, he was there, too, and Little Stevie Wonder, he, he seemed so happy, like, like a miracle had taken place. Was it a dream?

Or was it real?

It was election night 2000, and everything seemed to be going as planned.

*News clip montage*

### TOM BROKAW (NBC NEWS)

In New York, Al Gore is our projected winner.

### DAN RATHER (CBS NEWS)

The Garden State is green for Gore.

We project that Mr. Gore is the winner in Delaware. This state has voted with the winner.

Excuse me one second, I'm so sorry to interrupt you. Mike, you know I wouldn't do this if it weren't big. Florida goes for Al Gore.

### JUDY WOODRUFF (CNN NEWS)

CNN announces that we call Florida in the Al Gore column.

### NARRATION

Then something called the FOX News Channel called the election in favor of the other guy.

### BRIT HUME (FOX NEWS)

I interrupt you, FOX News now projects George W. Bush the winner in Florida and thus it appears the winner of the presidency of the United States.

### NARRATION

All of a sudden, the other networks said, "Hey! If FOX said it, it must be true!"

**TOM BROKAW**

All of us at the networks made a mistake, and projected Florida in the Al Gore column. It was our mistake.

*Shot of John Ellis working at phones and TV monitors on Election Night*

**NARRATION**

Now, what most people don't know is that the man who was in charge of the decision desk at FOX that night, the man who called it for Bush, was none other than Bush's first cousin John Ellis. How does someone like Bush get away with something like this.

*News clip of Bush cackling*

**NARRATION**

*Bush brothers sitting on plane*

Well, first, it helps if your brother is the governor of the state in question.

**GEORGE W. BUSH**

You know something, we are gonna win Florida. Mark my words. You can write it down.

### NARRATION

*Shots of Katherine Harris, Database Technologies, and voters at polls*

Second, make sure the chairman of your campaign is also the vote countin' woman and that her state has hired a company that's gonna knock voters off the rolls who aren't likely to vote for you. You can usually tell them by the color of their skin. Then make sure your side fights like it's life or death.

### JAMES BAKER (FORMER SECRETARY OF STATE, BUSH LAWYER)

I think all this talk about legitimacy is way overblown.

### CROWD PROTESTING FLORIDA RECOUNT

President Bush! President Bush!

### NARRATION

*Democratic Leaders of Congress, Congressman Richard Gephardt, and Senator Tom Daschle sitting at desk looking at phone*

And hope that the other side'll just sit by and wait for the phone to ring.

And even if numerous independent investigations prove that Gore got the most votes . . .

### JEFF TOOBIN (CNN NEWS CONSULTANT)

If there was a statewide recount, under *every* scenario, Gore won the election.

### NARRATION

It won't matter, just as long as all your daddy's friends on the Supreme Court vote the right way.

### AL GORE

*Concession speech to Bush*

While I strongly disagree with the court's decision, I accept it.

### SENATOR TOM DASCHLE

*Addressing media with Democratic response to court's decision*

What we need now is acceptance. We have a new President-elect.

### NARRATION

*Back to Florida victory footage—Al and Tipper Gore waving*

It turns out none of this was a dream. It's what really happened.

*FADE TO BLACK*

*Al Gore presiding over Joint Session of Congress—
certifying election results*

On the day the joint session of both the House
of Representatives and the Senate was to certify
the election results, Al Gore, in his dual role as
outgoing Vice President and President of the
Senate, presided over the event that would officially anoint George W. Bush as the new
President.

*Members of Congressional Black Caucus approach the
session with objections to the Florida election results*

If any Congressman wanted to raise an objection
the rules insisted that he or she had to have the
signed support of just one Senator.

### CONGRESSMAN ALCEE HASTINGS

Mr. President—and I take great pride in calling
you that—I must object because of the overwhelming evidence of official misconduct,
deliberate fraud, and an attempt to suppress
voter turnout . . .

### AL GORE

The chair must remind members that under
Section 18 of Title 3 United States Code, no
debate is allowed in the joint session.

## CONGRESSMAN ALCEE HASTINGS

Thank you, Mr. President. To answer your question, Mr. President, the objection is in writing, signed by a number of members of the House of Representatives, but not by a member of the Senate.

*Ominous music—as various black Congressmen and -women are shunned by every member of the Senate*

## CONGRESSWOMAN CORRINE BROWN

Uh, Mr. President, it is in writing and signed by several House colleagues on behalf—and myself— of the twenty-seven thousand voters of Duval County, in which sixteen thousand of them are African-Americans that was disenfranchised in this last election.

## AL GORE

Is the objection signed by a member of the Senate?

## CONGRESSWOMAN CORRINE BROWN

Not signed by a member of the Senate. The Senate is missing.

### CONGRESSWOMAN BARBARA LEE

Mr. President, it is in writing and signed by myself, on behalf of many of the diverse constituents in our country, especially those in the Ninth Congressional district, and all American voters who recognize that the Supreme Court—not the people of the United States—decided this election.

### AL GORE

Is . . . Is the objection signed by a Senator?

### CONGRESSWOMAN BARBARA LEE

Unfortunately, Mr. President, it is not signed by one single Senator.

### CONGRESSWOMAN PATSY MINK

Unfortunately, I have no authority over the United States Senate, and no Senator has signed.

### CONGRESSWOMAN CARRIE MEEK

Mr. President, it is in writing and signed by myself and several of my constituent—constituents from Florida, a Senator is needed, but missing.

### AL GORE

Is the objection in writing and signed by a member of the House and a Senator?

### CONGRESSWOMAN MAXINE WATERS

The objection is in writing, and I don't care
that it is not, it is not signed by a member of
the Senate.

### AL GORE

The . . . the Chair will advise that the rules
do care. And . . . the . . . the signature of a
Senator . . .

### NARRATION

Not a single Senator came to the aid of the African
Americans in Congress. One after another, they
were told to sit down and shut up.

### CONGRESSMAN JESSE JACKSON JR.

It's a sad day in America, Mr. President, when we
can't find a Senator to sign an objection, new . . .
won't sign objections, I object.

### AL GORE

The gentleman . . . the gentleman will suspend . . . the gentleman will . . . the gentleman
will suspend . . .

*DISSOLVE TO RAINY INAUGURATION DAY
COVERAGE*

### PETER JENNINGS (ABC NEWS)
#### VOICEOVER

Inauguration coverage, 2001, on a nasty but it could be worse kind of day in Washington.

#### CROWD

*Protesters marching with placards and megaphones*

What do we want? Justice! When do we want it? Now!

#### NARRATION

*Huge crowds march along presidential route, police try to control*

On the day George W. Bush was inaugurated, tens of thousands of Americans poured into the streets of D.C. in one last attempt to reclaim what had been taken from them.

#### CROWD

Hail to the thief! Hail to the thief!

#### NARRATION

*Shot of Bush's limo en route to swearing-in—surrounded by protesters—being hit with eggs*

They pelted Bush's limo with eggs . . .

### POLICEMAN

Stay back, get back.


### NARRATION

And brought the inauguration parade to a halt.
The plan to have Bush get out of the limo for the
traditional walk to the White House was scrapped.

*Protesters rioting—getting carried away by police;*
*Bush's limo speeds up as security guards run to keep*
*up—escaping angry crowds*

Bush's limo hit the gas to prevent an even larger
riot. No President had ever witnessed such a thing
on his Inauguration Day.

*News clips: shots of a troubled Bush—approval ratings*
*drop almost 10 percent between May 3 and September*
*5, 2001*

And, for the next eight months, it didn't get any
better for George W. Bush. He couldn't get his
judges appointed, he had trouble getting his legislation passed, and he lost Republican control of
the Senate. His approval ratings in the polls began
to sink. He was already beginning to look like a
lame duck president. With everything going
wrong, he did what any of us would do, he went
on vacation.

*MUSIC CUE*

*Vacation, All I ever wanted*

*Vacation, Have to get away*

*Vacation, Meant to be spent alone*

*News clips: shots of George W. Bush golfing, fishing, playing with dogs*

### GEORGE W. BUSH

*As he slices a golf shot*

Oh no!

### NARRATION

In his first eight months in office before September 11, George W. Bush was on vacation, according to the *Washington Post*, forty-two percent of the time.

### GEORGE W. BUSH

*Reaction to the press corps watching his bad shot*

If I hit every shot good, people would say I wasn't working.

### NARRATION

*Over shot of Bush in cowboy hat sawing a fallen tree*

It was not surprising that Mr. Bush needed some time off. Being President is a lot of work.

## UNIDENTIFIED REPORTER

*Off camera*

*Bush, signing autographs, surrounded by reporters and kids, August 8, 2001*

What about these folks that say you're loafing here in Texas, that you're taking too long of a vacation?

## GEORGE W. BUSH

They don't understand the definition of work, then. I'm getting a lot done. Secondly, you don't have to be in Washington to work. It's uh, it's amazing, uh, what can happen with telephones and faxes and uh . . . [inaudible]

## DIFFERENT REPORTER

*Off camera*

What are you doing the rest of the day?

## GEORGE W. BUSH

Karen Hughes is coming over. We're working on some things, and uh, she'll be over here, we'll be working on a few things, a few matters. I'm working on some initiatives . . . we're uh . . . you'll see. I mean . . . I've got made while I'm here, and we'll be announcing them as time goes on.

**NARRATION**

*Michael Moore and crew at "Bush for Governor"*
*event . . .*

The first time I met him, he had some good advice
for me.

**MICHAEL MOORE**

Governor Bush . . . it's Michael Moore.

**GEORGE W. BUSH**

Behave yourself, will you? Go find real work.

**NARRATION**

*Photo op—Bush serving grits and smiling for*
*cameras*

And work was something he knew a lot
about.

**GEORGE W. BUSH**

Anybody want some grits?

**NARRATION**

*Shots of Bush at various vacation spots*

Relaxing at Camp David. Yachting off Kennebunkport.

### GEORGE W. BUSH

*To dog on the ranch*

How ya doing?

### NARRATION

Or, being a cowboy on the ranch in Texas.

### GEORGE W. BUSH

*Photo op—after sawing fallen tree, to journalists,*
*August 25, 2001*

I love the nature. I love to get in the pickup truck
with my dogs.

### GEORGE W. BUSH

*To dog, in his pickup truck, on the ranch*

Oh, hi.

### NARRATION

George Bush spent the rest of August at the ranch.
Where life was less complicated.

### GEORGE W. BUSH

*Same interview near fallen tree, August 25, 2001*

Armadillos love to dig the soil looking for bugs.
And um, so I went out there the other day and

there was Barney buried in this hole, chasing an armadillo.

### NARRATION

*Bush giggles thinking about Barney*

It was a summer to remember. And when it was over he left Texas for his second favorite place.

*George W. Bush meets Jeb Bush on Tarmac in Florida, they mug for cameras, before G. W. Bush shakes hands of men waiting in line*

On September 10, he joined his brother in Florida where they looked at files and met important Floridians. He went to sleep that night in a bed made with fine French linens.

*FADE TO BLACK*

*Credit sequence—Bush and cabinet members in makeup, moments before television addresses/interviews*

### LIONS GATE FILMS
### AND
### IFC FILMS
### AND
### THE FELLOWSHIP ADVENTURE GROUP
### PRESENT

### DONALD RUMSFELD

*Soundbite between credits—said to aide off camera*

Do you suppose he's pretty confident on those
numbers on Iraqi security forces?

A

*DOG EAT DOG FILMS*

*PRODUCTION*

FAHRENHEIT 9/11

*MUSIC: JEFF GIBBS*
*ARCHIVAL PRODUCER: CARL DEAL*
*CAMERA: MIKE DESJARLAIS*
*SOUND: FRANCISCO LATORRE*
*EDITORS: KURT ENGFEHR /*
*CHRISTOPHER SEWARD / T. WOODY RICHMAN*
*CO-PRODUCERS: JEFF GIBBS / KURT ENGFEHR*

### JOHN ASHCROFT

Make me look young! (*laughter*)

Yeah, I got a little sort of air noise. Yeah, just don't
turn it up too much so I don't want to blow my
head off.

*SUPERVISING PRODUCER: TIA LESSIN*

### VOICE OFF CAMERA

*Over shot of President Bush at desk in Oval Office,
about to make TV address*

I got a . . . I got a mic here, if they want to hear.
Testing one, two, this is the Oval Office. We're

testing, one, two. Testing one, two, this is the Oval Office. Testing one, two, three, four, five . . .

*EXECUTIVE PRODUCERS:*
*HARVEY WEINSTEIN / BOB WEINSTEIN /*
*AGNES MENTRE  •  PRODUCERS:*
*JIM CZARNECKI / KATHLEEN GLYNN*
*WRITTEN, PRODUCED, AND DIRECTED BY:*
*MICHAEL MOORE*

*BLACK SCREEN—audio of planes hitting towers*

### REPORTER

*Sound only—over black screen*

We got something that has happened here at the World Trade Center. We noticed that a plane and an awful lot of smoke.

### CROWD

*Sound only—over black screen*

Oh my God. Oh my. Let's go. Let's go. Come on. Let's go.

*FADE UP from black—as crowd watches from below in horror*

### WOMAN IN CROWD

Save their souls, Lord. Save their souls, Lord.

### CROWD

Oh, they're jumping!

*Shocked faces, people looking up and crying in disbelief,
hugging, praying. Dust fills the air as people run in
slow motion away from falling debris*

### NARRATION

*Photos of lost/missing posters, candlelight vigils*

On September 11, 2001, nearly three thousand
people, including a colleague of mine, Bill
Weems, were killed in the largest foreign attack
ever on American soil. The targets were the
financial and military headquarters of the United
States.

### UNIDENTIFIED WOMAN

*News clip: holding photo, pleading for help, crying*

If anyone has any idea, or if they've seen him or
knows where he is, to call us. He's got two little
babies. Two little babies.

### NARRATION

*Bush's limo pulling into school*

As the attack took place, Mr. Bush was on his way to
an elementary school in Florida. When informed of
the first plane hitting the World Trade Center,

where terrorists had struck just eight years prior, Mr. Bush decided to go ahead with his photo opportunity.

### TEACHER

*Bush walks into classroom*

Good morning boys and girls.

### KIDS

Good morning . . .

### GEORGE W. BUSH

Morning.

### TEACHER

Read this word the fast way. Get ready!

### KIDS

Mat.

### TEACHER

Yes, mat, get ready!

### KIDS

Cat.

## GEORGE W. BUSH

*Applauding students*

Yeah.

## TEACHER

Okay, get ready to read the words on this page
without making a mistake.

## NARRATION

*Chief of staff enters and whispers in Bush's ear*

When the second plane hit the tower, his chief of
staff entered the classroom and told Mr. Bush,
"The nation is under attack." Not knowing what to
do, with no one telling him what to do, and no
Secret Service rushing in to take him to safety, Mr.
Bush just sat there and continued to read *My Pet
Goat* with the children.

*TEXT ON SCREEN*

9:05 AM–*medium wide shot of Bush—looking past
kids*

9:07 AM–*Bush looks down at book*

9:09 AM–*Bush nervously looks at aides to the side
of room*

9:11 AM–*aide whispers in the ear of White House
Press Secretary Ari Fleischer*

9:12 AM–*Bush nodding as kids read on*

## NARRATION

*No movement from Bush, still sitting in chair, looking around room*

Nearly seven minutes passed with nobody doing anything. As Bush sat in that Florida classroom, was he wondering if maybe he should have shown up to work more often? Should he have held at least one meeting since taking office to discuss the threat of terrorism with his head of counter-terrorism? (*shot of Richard Clarke, head of Counterterrorism, testifying in Congress*)

Or maybe Mr. Bush was wondering why he had cut terrorism funding from the FBI, or perhaps he just should have read the security briefing that was given to him on August 6, 2001.

*Shots of Bush on the ranch, with aides holding the August 6 briefing*

Which said that Osama bin Laden was planning to attack America by hijacking airplanes. But maybe he wasn't worried about the terrorist threat because the title of the report was too vague.

### CONDOLEEZZA RICE
### (NATIONAL SECURITY ADVISER)

*Testifying before 9/11 Commission*

I believe the title was "Bin Laden Determined to Attack Inside the United States."

**NARRATION**

*News clip: Bush fishing, and close-up of him in Florida classroom*

A report like that might make some men jump, but as in days past, George W. Bush just went fishing. As the minutes went by, George Bush continued to sit in the classroom. Was he thinking, "I've been hanging out with the wrong crowd? Which one of them screwed me?"

Was it the guy my daddy's friends delivered a lot of weapons to? (*shot of Donald Rumsfeld shaking hands with Saddam Hussein in 1983*)

Was it that group of religious fundamentalists who visited my state when I was governor? (*Taliban leaders in Texas*)

Or was it the Saudis? (*Bush with Saudi prince*) Damn, it was them. (*Osama bin Laden shooting gun*)

I think I better blame it on this guy. (*Saddam Hussein dancing*)

**NARRATION**

*Travelers stranded at airports*

In the days following September 11, all commercial and private airline traffic was grounded.

*News clip*

**FAA CHIEF**

The FAA has taken the action to close all of the
airports in the United States.

**UNIDENTIFIED REPORTER
VOICEOVER (NBC)**

Even grounding the President's father.

*Former President Bush, on a flight forced to land in
Milwaukee*

**UNIDENTIFIED (ABC) REPORTER
VOICEOVER**

Thousands of travelers were stranded, among
them, Ricky Martin, due to appear at tonight's
Latin Grammy awards.

**NARRATION**

*Over footage of Ricky Martin shrugging to journalist*

Not even Ricky Martin could fly. But really, who
wanted to fly? No one, except the bin Ladens.

*MUSIC CUE*

*We've got to get out of this place,*
*If it's the last thing we ever do.*

*Inside office of Senator Byron Dorgan (D-North
Dakota), Senate subcommittee on aviation*

## SENATOR BYRON DORGAN

We had some airplanes authorized at the highest levels of our government to fly to pick up Osama bin Laden's family members and others from Saudi Arabia and transport them out of this country.

## NARRATION

New York Times *headline, flight logs, Osama sitting in front of map, holding rifle*

It turns out that the White House approved planes to pick up the bin Ladens and numerous other Saudis. At least six private jets and nearly two dozen commercial planes carried the Saudis and the bin Ladens out of the U.S. after September 13. In all, 142 Saudis, including twenty-four members of the bin Laden family, were allowed to leave the country.

*Interview: Craig Unger, author of* House of Bush, House of Saud, *with White House in background*

## INTERVIEW: CRAIG UNGER

Osama's always been portrayed as a bad apple, the black sheep in the family and that they cut off all relationship with him around 1994. In fact, things are much more complicated than that.

### MICHAEL MOORE

*Over footage of Osama at son's wedding*

You mean Osama has had contact with other family members?

### CRAIG UNGER

That's right, in the summer of 2001 just before 9/11, one of Osama's sons got married in Afghanistan; several family members showed up at the wedding.

### MICHAEL MOORE

Bin Ladens?

### CRAIG UNGER

That's right, so they're not cut off completely, that's really an exaggeration.

*TV clip: CNN,* Larry King Live

### LARRY KING

We now welcome to *Larry King Live*—good to see him again—Prince Bandar, the ambassador of the Kingdom of Saudi Arabia to the United States.

### PRINCE BANDAR

...d about twenty-four members of bin
...ily, and, uh . . .

## LARRY KING

Here?

## PRINCE BANDAR

In America, students, and, His Majesty felt that it's not fair for those innocent people to be subjected to any harm. On the other hand, we understood the high emotions, so, with coordination with the FBI we got them all out.

## NARRATION

*Jack Cloonan being interviewed by Michael Moore*

This is retired FBI agent Jack Cloonan. Before 9/11, he was a senior agent on the joint FBI-CIA al Qaeda task force.

## JACK CLOONAN

I, as an investigator, would not want these people to have left. I think in the case of the bin Laden family I think it would have been prudent, hand the subpoenas out, have them come in, get on the record, you know, get on the record.

## MICHAEL MOORE

That's the proper procedure.

## JACK CLOONAN

Yeah.

Yeah, how many people were pulled off of airlines after that, coming into the country who were what? They were from the Middle East or they fit a very general picture.

**MICHAEL MOORE**

We held hundreds of people.

**JACK CLOONAN**

We held hundreds, and I . . .

**MICHAEL MOORE**

For weeks and months at a time . . .

Did the authorities do anything when the bin Ladens tried to leave the country?

**CRAIG UNGER**

No, they were identified at the airport. They looked at their pass . . . passports and they were identified.

**MICHAEL MOORE**

Well, that's what would happen to you or I if we were to leave the country.

**CRAIG UNGER**

Exactly, exactly.

### MICHAEL MOORE

So a little interview, check the passport, what else?

### CRAIG UNGER

Nothing.

### NARRATION

*Over clips from TV show* Dragnet, *detectives looking for answers*

I don't know about you but usually when the police can't find a murderer, don't they usually want to talk to the family members to find out where they think he might be?

Dragnet *clips*

You have no idea where your husband might be?

### MAN #1

Well, if you should hear anything, let us know, will you? You willing to come downtown and give us a statement?

### MAN #2

This going to take long?

### MAN #1

You got the time.

### MAN #2

Mine's worth money, yours isn't.

### MAN #1

Send in a bill.

### MAN #2

I asked you a question.

### MAN #1

You're here to answer 'em, not to ask 'em.

### MAN #2

Now you listen to me, cop, I pay your salary.

### MAN #1

All right, sit down, I'm gonna earn it.

### NARRATION

*More shots from* Dragnet

Yeah, that's how cops do it. What was going on here?

## INTERVIEW: SENATOR
### BYRON DORGAN

I think we need to know a lot more about that. That needs to be the subject of a significant investigation. What happened? How did it happen? Why did it happen? And who authorized it?

## INTERVIEW: JACK CLOONAN

Try to imagine what those poor bastards were feeling . . . when they were jumping out of that building . . . to their death . . . those . . . those . . . those young guys, and cops and firemen that ran into that building, never asked a question . . . and they're dead. And families' lives are ruined. And they'll never . . . they'll never have peace.

### MICHAEL MOORE

That's right.

### JACK CLOONAN

And, if I had to inconvenience a, uh, a member of the bin Laden family with a subpoena or a grand jury, do you think I'd lose any sleep over it? Not for a minute, Mike.

### MICHAEL MOORE

And no one would question it.

#### JACK CLOONAN

No, it's right . . .

#### MICHAEL MOORE

Not even the biggest civil libertarian . . .

#### JACK CLOONAN

No, no . . .

#### MICHAEL MOORE

. . . no one would question . . .

#### JACK CLOONAN

It's just . . . it's just you know, you got a lawyer? Fine. Counselor? Fine. Mr. bin Laden, this is why I'm asking you, it's not because I think that you're anything, I just want to ask you the questions that I would anybody . . .

#### MICHAEL MOORE

Right.

#### JACK CLOONAN

. . . and that's all.

## NARRATION

*Shots of White House, Oklahoma City bombing, Bill Clinton, Timothy McVeigh, and a private jet*

None of this made any sense. Can you imagine in the days after the Oklahoma City terrorist bombing, President Clinton helping to arrange a trip out of the country for the McVeigh family? What do you think would have happened to Clinton if that had been revealed?

*FILM FOOTAGE (of men burning someone at the stake)*

Burn him! Burn him!

*TV clip: CNN, Larry King Live*

## LARRY KING

Prince Bandar, do you know the bin Laden family?

## PRINCE BANDAR (SAUDI AMBASSADOR TO THE U.S.)

I do, very well.

## LARRY KING

What are they like?

## PRINCE BANDAR

They're really lovely human beings. Uh, he is the only one I never . . . I don't know him well, I met him only once.

## LARRY KING

What was the circumstance under which you met him?

## PRINCE BANDAR

This is ironic. In mid-eighties, if you remember, we and the United States were supporting the Mujahadeen, to, uh, liberate Afghanistan from the Soviets. He came to thank me for my efforts to bring the Americans, our friends, to help us against the atheists, he said, the Communists.

## LARRY KING

How ironic.

## PRINCE BANDAR

Isn't that ironic?

## LARRY KING

Now, in other words he came to thank you for helping bring America to help him.

**PRINCE BANDAR**

Uh-hem.

**LARRY KING**

And now he may be responsible for bombing
America.

**PRINCE BANDAR**

Absolutely.

**LARRY KING**

What did you make of him when you met him?

**PRINCE BANDAR**

I was not impressed, to be honest with you . . .

**LARRY KING**

Not impressed.

**PRINCE BANDAR**

No, he was, I thought he was a simple and very
quiet guy.

*Bush in classroom—still thinking*

**NARRATION**

*Back to footage of Bush in the Florida classroom, not
looking happy*

Hmmm, a simple and quiet guy whose family just happened to have a business relationship with the family of George W. Bush. Is that what he was thinking about? Because if the public knew this, it wouldn't look very good. Was he thinking, "You know, I need a big black marker"? *(footage of Michael Moore giving speech accusing Bush of being a deserter)* In early 2004, in a speech during the New Hampshire primary, I called George W. Bush a deserter from his time in the Texas Air National Guard. In response, the White House released his military records in the hopes of disproving the charge.

*Shot of the military records*

What Bush didn't know is that I already had a copy of his military records, uncensored, obtained in the year 2000, and there is one glaring difference between the records released in 2000 and those he released in 2004. *(close-up of black magic marker over text)* A name had been blacked out. In 1972, two airmen were suspended for failing to take their medical examination. One was George W. Bush *(MUSIC CUE: guitar riff from* Cocaine*)* and the other was James R. Bath. In 2000 the documents show both names. But in 2004, Bush and the White House had Bath's name blacked out. Why didn't Bush want the press and the public to see Bath's name on his military records? Perhaps he was worried that the American people would find out that at one time James R. Bath was the Texas money manager for the bin Ladens. Bush and Bath had become good friends when they both served in the Texas Air National Guard. After they were discharged, when Bush's dad was head of the CIA, Bath opened up his own aviation business, after selling a plane to a man by the name of Salem bin Laden, heir to the second largest fortune in Saudi Arabia, the Saudi bin Laden Group.

### JIM MOORE (INVESTIGATIVE REPORTER AND AUTHOR)

"W." at that time was just starting off in the world as a businessman. Because he's a guy who's always tried to emulate his father, he decided to go into the oil business. *(historical footage and photos of George W. Bush)* He founded an oil company, a drilling company, out in west Texas called Arbusto, which was very, very good at drilling dry holes that nothing came out of. But the question has always been, "Where did this money come from?" Now his dad, his dad was rich, his dad could have done this for him but his dad didn't do this for him. There is no indication that daddy wrote a check to start him off in this company.

## NARRATION

*Over historical footage of George Bush*

So where did George W. Bush get his money?

## GEORGE W. BUSH

*Old footage of him shaking someone's hand*

I'm George Bush.

## NARRATION

*Photo of James Bath, and agreement between Bath and Salem bin Laden*

One person who did invest in him was James R. Bath. Bush's good friend James Bath was hired by the bin Laden family to manage their money in Texas and invest in businesses. And James Bath himself, in turn, invested in George W. Bush. *(financial records verifying a $50,000 investment in Bush's company Arbusto)*

Bush ran Arbusto into the ground, as he did every other company he was involved in, until finally one of his companies was bought by Harken Energy and they gave him a seat on their board.

## INTERVIEW: JIM MOORE

A lot of us have suspected through the years that . . . that there has been Saudi oil money involved in all of these companies—Harken, Spectrum 7, Arbusto

Drilling, all of the Bush companies. Whenever they got into trouble there were these angel investors who flowed money into the companies.

### INTERVIEW: CRAIG UNGER

So the question is: Why would Saudis, who had all the oil in the world, go around the . . . around the globe to invest in this lousy oil company. And the thing is it had one big asset, Harken had one thing going for it, which is that George W. Bush was on its board of directors at a time when his father was President of the United States.

### GEORGE W. BUSH

*Television interview, August 1992*

When you're the President's son, and you've got unlimited access, combined with some credentials from a prior campaign, in Washington, D.C., people tend to respect that. And, access is power. And, uh, I can find my dad and talk to him any time of the day.

### NARRATION

*Photos of George Bush at Harken Energy*

Yes, it helps to be the President's son. Especially when you're being investigated by the Securities and Exchange Commission.

*News clip*

## BILL PLANTE (CBS REPORTER)
## VOICEOVER

In 1990, when Mr. Bush was a director of Harken
Energy, he received this memo from company
lawyers, warning directors not to sell stock if they
had unfavorable information about the company.
One week later, he sold $848,000 worth of Harken
stock. Two months later, Harken announced losses
of more than $23 million.

## NARRATION

*Shot of Robert Jordan and map of Saudi Arabia*

The James Baker law partner who helped Bush
beat the rap from the SEC was a man by the name
of Robert Jordan, who, when George W. became
president, was appointed ambassador to Saudi
Arabia. After the Harken debacle, the friends of
Bush's dad got him a seat on another board, of a
company owned by the Carlyle Group.

## INTERVIEW: DAN BRIODY (AUTHOR
## OF *THE HALLIBURTON AGENDA*)

We wanted to look at which companies actually
gained from September 11. We turned up this
company, Carlyle Group. (*graphics showing many
of the companies owned by the Carlyle Group*)

The Carlyle Group is a multinational conglomerate that invests in heavily government-regulated
industries like telecommunications, health care,
and, particularly, defense. Both George W. Bush
and George H. W. Bush worked for the Carlyle
Group, the same company that counted the bin
Laden family among its investors. *(both Bushes in
a private box at a sporting event)* Carlyle Group
was holding its annual investor conference on the
morning of September 11 in the Ritz-Carlton
Hotel in Washington, D.C. At that meeting were
all of the Carlyle regulars, James Baker, likely John
Major, definitely George H. W. Bush, though he
left the morning of September 11. Shafiq bin
Ladin, who is Osama bin Laden's half-brother, and
was in town to look after his family's investments
in the Carlyle Group. All of them, together in one
room, watching as the, uh, the planes hit the
towers and then in fact the bin Laden family was
invested in one of their defense funds, which ironically meant that, um, as the United States started
increasing its defense spending, um, the bin
Laden family stood to gain from those investments, uh, through the Carlyle Group.

## ANNOUNCER

*Footage of Bush being introduced at United Defense
company event—subsidiary of Carlyle Group*

Our commander in chief, President George W.
Bush.

## NARRATION

*Bush at United Defense*

With all the weapons companies it owned, the
Carlyle Group was in essence, the eleventh largest
defense contractor in the United States. It owned
United Defense, makers of the Bradley armored
fighting vehicle. September 11 guaranteed that
United Defense was going to have a very good year.
(Los Angeles Times *headline*) Just six weeks after
9/11, Carlyle filed to take United Defense public
and in December made a one-day profit of $237
million. But, sadly, with so much attention focused
on the bin Laden family being important Carlyle
investors, the bin Ladens eventually had to withdraw. Bush's dad, though, stayed on as senior adviser to Carlyle's Asia Board for another two years.

## DAN BRIODY

As unseemly as it seems to . . . to know that
George H. W. Bush was meeting with the bin
Laden family while Osama was a wanted terrorist,
well before September 11th, it's very discomfort-
ing for Americans to know that.

(*shots of G. H. W. Bush meeting with Saudis*)
George H. W. Bush is a man who has, obviously,
incredible reach into the White House. He
receives daily CIA briefings, which is the right of
any ex-president. But very few ex-presidents actually exercise that right; he does. And I think in a

very real way they are benefiting from the confusion that arises when George H. W. Bush visits Saudi Arabia, on behalf of Carlyle, and meets with the royal family and meets with the bin Laden family. Is he representing the United States of America, or is he representing an investment firm in the United States of America or is he representing both? This company is about money. It's not about conspiracies to run the world or you know engineer political maneuvering and things like that. It's about making money and it's about making a lot of money and they've done very very well.

*News clip*

### HELEN THOMAS (MEMBER OF WHITE HOUSE PRESS CORPS)

*Off camera, at White House press briefing questioning spokesman Ari Fleischer*

Get you on the record on this question. In the White House view, there's no ethical conflict in former President Bush and former Secretary of State Jim Baker using their contacts with world leaders to represent one of the most well-known military arms dealers, the Carlyle Group?

### ARI FLEISCHER

The President has full faith that his family will conform with all proper ethics laws, all ethics laws, and will act properly in their conduct.

*Bush with Saudi Royals and associates*

### NARRATION

*Americana shots of normal U.S. citizens, juxtaposed
with shots of Saudi Royals and Bush confidants*

Okay, so let's say one group of people, like the
American people, pay you $400,000 a year to be
President of the United States, but then another
group of people invest in you, your friends, and
their related businesses $1.4 billion over a number
of years *(number flashes on screen: $1.4 billion)*,
who you gonna like? Who's your daddy? Because
that's how much the Saudi Royals and their associates have given the Bush family, their friends, and
their related businesses in the past three decades.

*News clip*

### GEORGE H. W. BUSH

*Greeting Saudis*

Good morning, everybody. We've had a very nice
reunion with friends.

### NARRATION

Is it rude to suggest that when the Bush family
wakes up in the morning they might be thinking
about what's best for the Saudis instead of what's
best for you or me? Because 1.4 billion just doesn't

buy a lot of flights out of the country. It buys a lot
of love.

*MUSIC CUE*

*Bush and cabinet members with Saudi elite—holding*
*hands and smiling for photo ops*

> *Shiny happy people holding hands*
>
> *Shiny happy people holding hands*
>
> *Shiny happy people laughing*
>
> *Everyone around, love them, love them*
>
> *Put it in your hands*
>
> *Take it, take it*
>
> *There's no time to cry*
>
> *Happy, happy*
>
> *Put it in your heart*
>
> *Where tomorrow shines*
>
> *Gold and silver shine*

### NARRATION

Sooner or later, this special relationship with a
regime that Amnesty International condemns as a
widespread human rights violator, would come
back to haunt the Bushes. (*footage of a public*
*beheading in Jeddah, Saudi Arabia*) Now, after
9/11, it was an embarrassment and they preferred
that no one ask any questions.

*News clip*

### CAROL ASHLEY (MOTHER OF 9/11 VICTIM)

The investigation should have begun on September 12, um, there's no reason why it shouldn't have. Three thousand people were dead. It was a murder. And it should have gotten started immediately.

### NARRATION

Washington Post *headline "Bush Seeks to Restrict Hill Probes of Sept 11"*

First, Bush tried to stop Congress from setting up its own 9/11 investigation.

### NEWS CLIP: GEORGE W. BUSH

It's important for us to, uh, not reveal how we collect information. That's what the enemy wants. And we're fighting an enemy.

### NARRATION

*Newspaper headline "Bush Opposes 9/11 Panel"*

When he couldn't stop Congress, he then tried to stop an independent 9/11 commission from being formed.

*News clip*

## NORAH O'DONNELL (NBC REPORTER)

The President's position was a break from history. Independent investigations were launched within days of Pearl Harbor and President Kennedy's assassination.

## NARRATION

*Member of Congress holding "Report of 9/11 Investigation"*

But when Congress did complete its own investigation, the Bush White House censored 28 pages of the report.

*News clip*

## ANDREA MITCHELL (NBC REPORTER) VOICEOVER

The President is being pressed by all sides to declassify the report. U.S. officials tell NBC News most of the secret sources involve Saudi Arabia.

## GEORGE W. BUSH

*Interviewed on* Meet the Press

We have uh, given, uh, extraordinary cooperation with, uh, Chairman Kean and Hamilton.

### GOVERNOR THOMAS KEAN
### (CHAIRMAN, 9/11 COMMISSION)

We haven't gotten the materials we needed, and we certainly haven't gotten them in a timely fashion. The deadlines we set have passed.

### TIM RUSSERT (HOST, *MEET THE PRESS*)

Will you testify before the commission?

### GEORGE W. BUSH

This commission? You know, I don't . . . I . . . testify? I mean, I'd be glad to visit with them.

### INTERVIEW: ROSEMARY DILLARD
### (WIDOW OF 9/11 VICTIM)

What it would do, is, the hole that's in my heart, and has been in my heart since September 11. I lost my husband of fifteen years. I am now by myself. I need to know what happened to him. I know what I got back, from the aut . . . got the autopsy. That man was my life, and I have no plan. I took a . . . I was taking a class, and they asked me what was I going to do in the next five years. And if I'm not doing something with this, I don't know what reason I have to live. So, it's very important. Very important. Okay?

### NARRATION

*Over footage of 9/11 family protest on Washington*

Ignored by the Bush Administration, more than 500 relatives of 9/11 victims filed suit against Saudi royals and others. The lawyers the Saudi Defense Minister hired to fight the 9/11 families? The law firm of Bush family confidant James A. Baker.

*Michael Moore and Craig Unger on the streets of Washington, D.C.*

#### MICHAEL MOORE

So, we're right here in the center of three important American landmarks, uh, the Watergate hotel and office building. The Kennedy Center over there. And, uh, the embassy of Saudi Arabia.

#### CRAIG UNGER

Yeah.

#### MICHAEL MOORE

How much money do the Saudis have invested in America, roughly?

#### CRAIG UNGER

Uh, I've heard figures as high as $860 billion.

#### MICHAEL MOORE

860 billion.

### CRAIG UNGER

Billion.

### MICHAEL MOORE

That's a lot of money.

### CRAIG UNGER

A lot.

### MICHAEL MOORE

And, uh, what, what percentage of our economy does that represent, I mean, that seems like a lot.

### CRAIG UNGER

*As they talk, Secret Service cars begin to pull up in front of embassy, and approach the interview*

Well, in terms of in . . . investments on Wall Street, American equities, it's roughly six or seven percent of America. They own a fairly good slice of America.

And most of that money goes into the great blue-chip companies. You, uh, Citigroup, Citibank, is, uh, the largest stockholder is a Saudi. Uh, AOL TimeWarner has big Saudi investors. (*Secret Service agents are talking with one another and watching interview from afar*)

#### MICHAEL MOORE

So, I read where, like, the Saudis have a trillion dollars in our banks, their money. What would happen if, like, one day they just pulled that trillion dollars out?

#### CRAIG UNGER

A trillion dollars? That would be an enormous blow to the economy.

#### MICHAEL MOORE

Right, right.

#### SECRET SERVICE AGENT

*Walks up and interrupts interview*

Mr. Moore, can I speak to you for a moment, please, sir?

#### MICHAEL MOORE

Yeah. Sure.

#### SECRET SERVICE AGENT

How are you doing?

#### MICHAEL MOORE

I'm good. How are you doing?

### SECRET SERVICE AGENT

Steve Kimball, Secret Service. How are you doing, sir?

### MICHAEL MOORE

How are you doing, sir? Yes.

### SECRET SERVICE AGENT

Uh, we're just ascertaining information. You're doing a documentary regarding the Saudi Arabia embassy? Or chancellery?

### MICHAEL MOORE

Uh, no. I'm doing a documentary and part of it is about Saudi Arabia.

### NARRATION

*Michael Moore and Secret Service agent continue to talk*

Even though we were nowhere near the White House for some reason the Secret Service had shown up to ask us what we were doing standing across the street from the Saudi embassy.

### MICHAEL MOORE

*(to Secret Service agent)* We're not here to cause any trouble or anything, you know. Is that . . .

### SECRET SERVICE AGENT

Yeah, that's fine. We just wanted to make sure, to get some information as far as what was actually going on.

### MICHAEL MOORE

What's going on, yeah, yeah, yeah. I didn't realize the Secret Service guards foreign embassies.

### SECRET SERVICE AGENT

Uh, not usually. No sir.

### MICHAEL MOORE

No, no. Do they give you any trouble? The Saudis?

### SECRET SERVICE AGENT

No comment on that, sir.

### MICHAEL MOORE

Oh, okay. Well, I'll take that as a yes. All right, good. Thank you very much. Thanks for the work that you do.

### NARRATION

*Agents walking away and on the steps of embassy*

It turns out that Saudi Prince Bandar is perhaps the best protected ambassador in the U.S. The

U.S. State Department provides him with a six-man security detail. Considering how he and his family and the Saudi elite own seven percent of America, it's probably not a bad idea.

*Intimate photos of George W. Bush and Prince Bandar*

Prince Bandar was so close to the Bushes, they considered him a member of the family. And they even had a nickname for him, "Bandar Bush." Two nights after September 11, George Bush invited Bandar Bush over to the White House for a private dinner and a talk. Even though bin Laden was a Saudi *(Osama bin Laden)* and Saudi money had funded al Qaeda, and fifteen of the nineteen hijackers were Saudis *(photos of high-jackers)*, here was the Saudi ambassador casually dining with the President on September 13. What were they talking about?

*(splitscreen photos of Bush and Bandar)* Were they commiserating? Or comparing notes?

*(footage of Saudi police, and* Houston Chronicle *headline "U.S. Reluctant to Upset Flawed, Fragile Saudi Ties")* Why would Bandar's government block American investigators from talking to the relatives of the fifteen hijackers? Why would Saudi Arabia become reluctant to freeze the hijackers' assets?

The two of them walked out on the Truman Balcony so that Bandar could smoke a cigar and have a drink. In the distance, across the Potomac was the Pentagon partially in ruins. (*Pentagon burning*) I wonder if Mr. Bush told Prince Bandar not to worry because he already had a plan in motion.

*News clip*

## CHARLES GIBSON (HOST OF ABC NEWS' *GOOD MORNING AMERICA*)

*Interviewing Richard Clarke, Bush's counterterrorism chief*

You come in September 12 ready to plot what response we take to al Qaeda. Let me talk to the . . . about the response that you got from top administration officials. On that day, what did the president say to you?

### RICHARD CLARKE

The president, in a very intimidating way, left us, me and my staff, with the the clear indication that he wanted us to come back with the word that there was an Iraqi hand behind 9/11. Because they had been planning to do something about Iraq from before the time they came into office.

### CHARLES GIBSON

Did he ask about any other nations other than Iraq?

**RICHARD CLARKE**

No. No, no, no. No, not at all. It was Iraq,
Saddam. Find out, get back to me.

**CHARLES GIBSON**

And were his questions more about Iraq than
about al Qaeda?

**RICHARD CLARKE**

Absolutely. Absolutely. He didn't ask me about al
Qaeda.

**CHARLES GIBSON**

And the reaction you got that day from the
Defense Secretary, Donald Rumsfeld, from his
assistant Paul Wolfowitz?

**RICHARD CLARKE**

Well, Donald Rumsfeld said, when we talked
about bombing the al Qaeda infrastructure in
Afghanistan, he said there were no good targets
in Afghanistan. Let's bomb Iraq. And we said, but
Iraq had nothing to do with this. And that didn't
seem to make much difference.

And the reason they had to do Afghanistan first
was it was obvious that al Qaeda had attacked
us. And it was obvious that al Qaeda was in
Afghanistan. The American people wouldn't

have stood by if we had done nothing on
Afghanistan.

*Burning map of Afghanistan . . . Opening sequence
from* Bonanza *with leaders' faces superimposed.
George W. Bush, Donald Rumsfeld, Dick Cheney,
and Tony Blair.*

### NARRATION

*Over news footage from Afghanistan invasion*

The United States began bombing Afghanistan
just four weeks after 9/11. Mr. Bush said he was
doing so because the Taliban government of
Afghanistan had been harboring bin Laden.

*Various news clips*

### GEORGE W. BUSH

I'll smoke them out of their holes.

We're gonna smoke 'em out.

Smoke him out.

Smoke him out of his cave.

### UNIDENTIFIED ACTOR

*Footage from western film from the 1930s*

Let's rush him and smoke him out.

### NARRATION

For all his tough talk, Bush really didn't do much.

*News clip*

### RICHARD CLARKE

*On* Good Morning America

Well, what they did was slow and small. They put only eleven thousand troops into Afghanistan. There are more police here in Manhattan—more police here in Manhattan—than there are U.S. troops in Afghanistan.

Basically the President botched the response to 9/11. He should have gone right after bin Laden. U.S. Special Forces didn't get into the area where bin Laden was for two months.

### NARRATION

*Photo op with press: Footage of Bush hunting*

Two months? A mass murderer who attacked the United States was given a two-month head start? Who in their right mind would do that?

### GEORGE W. BUSH

Anybody say nice shot?

## OFF CAMERA

Nice shot, helluva shot.

## NARRATION

Or was the war in Afghanistan really about something else? Perhaps the answer was in Houston, Texas.

*Oil rigs, map of pipeline, shots of Taliban in Texas*

In 1997, while George W. Bush was governor of Texas, a delegation of Taliban leaders from Afghanistan flew to Houston to meet with Unocal executives to discuss the building of a pipeline through Afghanistan, bringing natural gas from the Caspian Sea. And who got a Caspian Sea drilling contract the same day Unocal signed the pipeline deal? A company headed by a man named Dick Cheney. Halliburton.

## INTERVIEW: MARTHA BRILL OLCOTT
### (UNOCAL PROJECT CONSULTANT)

From the point of view of the U.S. government, this was kind of a magic pipeline, um, because it could serve so many purposes.

## NARRATION

*Shots of Kenneth Lay and Enron*

And who else stood to benefit from the pipeline?

Bush's number one campaign contributor, Kenneth Lay, and the good people of Enron. Only the British press covered this trip. Then in 2001, just five and a half months before 9/11, the Bush administration welcomed a special Taliban envoy to tour the United States to help improve the image of the Taliban government.

*Footage from Taliban's visit to U.S., with Sayed Rahmatullah Hashimi, the Taliban minister, being confronted at a press conference by a female protester dressed up in a burka*

### PROTESTER

*Whipping burka off her head, yells at minister*

You have imprisoned the women. It's a horror, let me tell you.

### SAYED RAHMATULLAH HASHIMI (TALIBAN MINISTER)

And I'm really sorry to your husband. He must have a very difficult time with you.

### NARRATION

*News clip from March 19, 2001, of Hashimi leaving State Department*

Here is the Taliban official visiting our State Department to meet with U.S. officials. Why on earth would the Bush administration allow a

Taliban leader to visit the United States knowing that the Taliban were harboring the man who bombed the USS *Cole* and our African embassies? Well, I guess 9/11 put a stop to that. *(photos of Osama bin Laden and USS* Cole *and African embassy rubble)*

When the invasion of Afghanistan was complete, we installed its new president, Hamid Karzai. Who was Hamid Karzai? *(photo op of Bush and Hamid Karzai)* He was a former adviser to Unocal. Bush also appointed as our envoy to Afghanistan Zalmay Khalilzad, who was also a former Unocal adviser. *(photo of Khalilzad and Bush in Oval Office)* I guess you can probably see where this is leading.

*Footage of Karzai signing agreement*

Faster than you can say "Black Gold, Texas Tea," Afghanistan signed an agreement with their neighboring countries to build a pipeline through Afghanistan carrying natural gas from the Caspian Sea. Oh, and the Taliban? They mostly got away, as did Osama bin Laden and most of al Qaeda.

### GEORGE W. BUSH

*Speaking to the press at the White House, referring to Osama bin Laden*

Terror is bigger than one person. And, uh, he's just . . . he's . . . he's, uh, he's a person who's now been marginalized, so I don't know where he is, nor . . .

you know I just don't spend that much time on him, hell to even be honest with you.

### NARRATION

Didn't spend much time on him? What kind of President was he?

*TV clip:* Meet the Press *interview*

### GEORGE W. BUSH

I'm a "War President." I make decisions here in the Oval Office, uh, in foreign policy matters, with war on my mind.

### NARRATION

*Bush walking with General Tommy Franks*

With the war in Afghanistan over and bin Laden forgotten the "war president" had a new target— the American people.

*Big dramatic FOX graphics: "War on Terror"*

*Various news clips*

### DAVID ASMAN (FOX NEWS ANCHOR)

We've got an unusual terror warning from the Feds to tell you about. FOX News has obtained an FBI bulletin that warns terrorists could use pen guns, just like in James Bond, filled with poison, as weapons.

### JOHN SIEGENTHALER (NBC ANCHOR)

Good evening everyone, America is on high alert tonight, just four days before Christmas.

### WOLF BLITZER (CNN ANCHOR)

. . . a possible terror threat.

### JOHN ROBERTS (CBS ANCHOR)

As bad as or worse than 9/11.

### JOIE CHEN (CBS REPORTER)
### VOICEOVER

But where? How? There's nothing specific to report.

### PIERRE THOMAS (ABC REPORTER)
### VOICEOVER

Be on the lookout for model airplanes, packed with explosives.

### MIKE EMMANUEL
### (FOX NEWS REPORTER)

The FBI is warning ferries may be considered particularly at risk for hijacking.

### LOCAL NEWS REPORTER
### (CONUS ARCHIVES) VOICEOVER

Could these cattle be a target for terrorists?

*Interview: Congressman Jim McDermott
(D-Washington), Psychiatrist and Member
of Congress*

### MICHAEL MOORE

Fear works.

### CONGRESSMAN JIM MCDERMOTT

Fear does work, yes. You can make people do anything if they're afraid.

### MICHAEL MOORE

And how do you make them afraid?

### CONGRESSMAN JIM MCDERMOTT

Well, you make them afraid by creating an aura
of endless threat. They played us like an organ.
(*shots of terror alert color chart*) They raised
the . . . the orange, and then up to red, and
they dropped it back to orange. I mean, they
gave these mixed messages, which were crazy
making.

*News clips of speeches*

## GEORGE W. BUSH

The world has changed after September the 11th.
It's changed because we're no longer safe.

## GEORGE W. BUSH

Fly and enjoy America's great destination spots.

## DONALD RUMSFELD

We have entered what may very well prove to be
the most dangerous security environment the
world's known.

## GEORGE W. BUSH

Take your families and enjoy life.

## DICK CHENEY

Terrorists are doing everything they can to gain
even deadlier means of striking us.

## GEORGE W. BUSH

Get down to Disney World in Florida.

## CONGRESSMAN JIM MCDERMOTT

It's like training a dog. You tell him, "Sit down,"
and you tell him to roll over at the same time, dog
doesn't know what to do. Well, the American people were being treated like that. It was really very,

very skillfully and . . . and ugly in . . . in what they did.

*News clip*

## GEORGE W. BUSH

*Photo op: press on golf course*

We must stop the terror. I call upon all nations to do everything they can to stop these terrorist killers. Thank you. Now watch this drive. *(swings golf club)*

## CONGRESSMAN JIM MCDERMOTT

They will continue, in my view, as long as this administration is in charge, of every once in a while stimulating everybody to be afraid. Just in case you forgot. *(more shots of terror alert color chart)* It's not going to go down to green or blue. It's never going to get there. There clearly is no way that anyone can live constantly on edge like that.

## PROMOTIONAL VIDEO FOR ZYTECH ENGINEERING

*Spokesman talks directly to camera in a concerned tone*

The harsh reality facing American families today is that they're not as safe as they used to be. Drug dealers and users looking for their next fix. Gangs who roam the streets in search of their next victim and the growing threat of terrorists means the need for protection is ever greater. And now, that protection is here. *(shot of "safe room"—looks like a large Porta Potti)*

Zytech Engineering LLC has developed and tested a safe room, finally affordable to the average American citizen. The kind of protection formerly obtainable only by the wealthy or powerful.

### CEO OF ZYTECH CORP

*Sitting inside "safe room" showing audience how comfortable this metal box is*

Heck, you can be sitting in here drinking your finest Bordeaux and enjoying life while chaos is erupting outside.

*Public service announcement*

### TOM RIDGE (HOMELAND SECURITY CHIEF)

Every family in America should prepare itself for a terrorist attack.

*News clip: The* Today *show*

### MATT LAUER (NBC *TODAY* SHOW HOST)

Now to escaping from a skyscraper. John Rivers is the CEO of the Executive Chute Corporation. Good morning to you John.

### JOHN RIVERS

*Talking to Matt Lauer from his showroom in Three Rivers, Michigan*

Good morning, Matt.

### MATT LAUER

Tell me about the product you're bringing to the market.

### JOHN RIVERS

It's a, uh, emergency escape chute. It's an option of last resort.

### MATT LAUER

How high do you have to be in the building for that chute to actually take effect?

### JOHN RIVERS

You only have to be on the tenth floor or above.

**MATT LAUER**

They can put this on themselves?

**JOHN RIVERS**

Right, they can put this on themselves in as easy as about 30 seconds. It's real easy to put on . . . here. *(woman modeling the parachute is having trouble getting her foot into the harness)*

**JOHN RIVERS**

It's okay . . . real easy to put on, but, uh . . . when you first get the chute, you're gonna want to put it on and try it on a few times yourself . . . *(he is bending down, trying to help her get foot into loop—no luck)*

**MATT LAUER**

Jamie's having a little trouble putting that thing on, I want to mention. I mean, is this something that . . . that you honestly think in a moment of panic that someone can operate properly?

**JOHN RIVERS**

*Jamie continues to struggle with the chute—now it's the buckle across her waist*

Oh yeah, yeah, it is. It's . . . it's, this is actually, uh, Jamie's probably never put this thing on before in her life, so . . .

It's okay. Don't worry about it. It's something that when you get it you're going to want to put it on several times. (*Jamie looks dejected into the camera*)

*News clip*

### DAVE BONDY (NEWS REPORTER, WNEM, MICHIGAN)

Well, despite the raising of the terror alert level, residents here in Saginaw are continuing with their Christmas errands. Frances Stroik and her family do some last minute holiday shopping knowing that al Qaeda is planning to attack America. She says being in Saginaw doesn't make her feel any safer than if she was in New York City.

### FRANCES STROIK

*From WNEM newscast*

Midland is close-by. And I said, "Detroit's not far, that far away." I said, "they could be something, and Flint could be some . . . be concerns for people around here."

### MEL STROIK

*From WNEM newscast*

You never know where they're gonna hit. You never know where they're gonna hit.

*News clip*

### JIM MIKLASZEWSKI (NBC NEWS REPORTER) VOICEOVER

But one potential target specifically mentioned by the terrorists has security officials baffled. It's tiny Tappahannock, Virginia, population 2,016. Such an attack could generate widespread fear, that even here, in rural small-town America, no one is entirely safe.

### INTERVIEW: MAYOR ROY GLADDING

Oh, on the six o'clock news there was something about a terrorist alert in Tappahannock.

### MICHAEL MOORE

*To Sheriff Clarke*

What did the FBI tell you?

### SHERIFF STANLEY CLARKE

Well, they contacted me by phone, basically let me know about this word "Tappahannock," and that's how it started.

### MAYOR ROY GLADDING

In their so-called chatter that they pick up, they wasn't sure. Tappahannock, there's a Rappahannock county. This is the Rappahannock River. *(map of the area)*

*Quick interviews with residents of Tappahannock*

### FRANCES WILMORE

There is a Rappahannock . . . a place called
Rappahannock, and they got it mixed up.

### MALE RESIDENT

This is Tappahannock, not Rappahannock.

### MICHAEL MOORE

Is there any terrorist target around here?

### MAYOR ROY GLADDING

Not that we can really think of.

### SHERIFF STANLEY CLARKE

It can happen anywhere.

### MAYOR ROY GLADDING

We have a Wal-Mart here.

### FRANCES WILMORE

We're having a big spaghetti supper in here.

### MALE RESIDENT

Wal-Mart, probably.

### MICHAEL MOORE

Do you feel extra suspicious of outsiders?

### ROBERT ROYAL

Oh, everybody does that. It's just something that happens.

### FEMALE RESIDENT

When I look at certain people, I wonder, "Oh my goodness! Do you think they could be a terrorist?"

### WILLIAM J. JACKSON

You never know what's going to happen.

### MALE RESIDENT

That's right, you never know what's going to happen.

### WILLIAM J. JACKSON

You never know what's going to happen. It could happen right now, you know.

### ROBERT ROYAL

Never trust nobody you don't know. And even if you do know them, you really can't trust them then.

## NARRATION

*Shots of scared Americans*

From Tappahannock to Rappahannock to every town and village in America, the people were afraid. And they turned to their leader to protect them. But, protect them from what?

*John Ashcroft singing at podium: "Let the Eagle Soar," words and music by John Ashcroft*

### JOHN ASHCROFT

*(singing) Let the eagle soar,*

*Like she's never soared before.*

*From rocky coast, to golden shore,*

*Let the mighty eagle soar . . .*

*Text on screen*

*Footage from Senate race of 2000*

### NARRATION

*Footage from Missouri Senate race of 2000*

Meet John Ashcroft. In 2000, he was running for reelection as Senator from Missouri against a man who died the month before the election. *(Senator Carnahan's portrait—draped in black)* The voters preferred the dead guy. So, George

W. Bush made him his attorney general.
(*Ashcroft being sworn in on three Bibles*) He
was sworn in on a stack of Bibles, 'cause when
you can't beat a dead guy, you need all the help
you can get.

*Footage from 9/11 Commission hearings*

## NARRATION

During the summer before 9/11, Ashcroft told
acting FBI director Thomas Pickard that he
didn't want to hear anything more about terrorist
threats.

## 9/11 COMMISSIONER
## RICHARD BEN-VENISTE

*Questioning Thomas Pickard*

Mr. Watson had come to you and said that the
CIA was very concerned that there would be an
attack. You said that you told the Attorney General
this fact repeatedly in these meetings. Is that
correct?

## THOMAS PICKARD (ACTING FBI
## DIRECTOR, SUMMER 2001)

(*answers Ben-Veniste*) I told him on, uh, at least
two occasions.

### RICHARD BEN-VENISTE

And you told the staff, according to this statement, that Mr. Ashcroft told you that he did not want to hear about this anymore. Is that correct?

### THOMAS PICKARD

That is correct.

### NARRATION

*Close-ups of FBI documents, July 10, 2001, noting that students of Osama bin Laden were attending civil aviation universities*

His own FBI knew that summer that there were al Qaeda members in the U.S., and that bin Laden was sending his agents to flight schools around the country. But Ashcroft's Justice Department turned a blind eye and a deaf ear. But after 9/11, John Ashcroft had some brilliant ideas for how to protect America.

*News clip*

### ELIZABETH HASHAGEN
### (NEWS 12, LONG ISLAND)

The U.S.A. Patriot Act adopted by Congress and signed by Bush six weeks after the attacks has changed the way the government does business. The U.S.A. Patriot Act allows for searches of medical and financial records, computer and telephone conversations, and even for the books you take out of the library. But most of the people we spoke to say they're willing to give up some liberties to fight terrorism.

### MAN (FROM NEWSCAST)

Maybe that's a good thing.

### WOMAN (FROM NEWSCAST)

It's definitely sad, but it has to be done.

### NARRATION

*Footage of members of Peace Fresno, gathering in living room, looking harmless*

Yes. Something needed to be done. These are the good people who make up Peace Fresno, a community group in Fresno, California. Unlike the rest of us, they've received an early lesson in what the Patriot Act is all about.

Each week they meet to discuss matters of . . . peace. They sit around, they share stories, they eat cookies. *(group passing cookies—woman takes two)* Some have more than one. This is Aaron Stokes, a member of Peace Fresno. *(photo of Aaron Stokes at Peace Fresno protest)* The other members liked him.

### INTERVIEW: EUGENIE BARANOFF
### (MEMBER OF PEACE FRESNO)

He had come to the meetings. He went with us. We'd go out on Friday nights and stand on a very busy corner in Fresno and he had gone with us, he had handed out flyers, he went with us in June to a WTO protest.

### NARRATION

Then one day Aaron didn't show up to the meeting.

### INTERVIEW: CAMILLE RUSSELL
### (MEMBER OF PEACE FRESNO)

My friend Dan and I were reading the Sunday newspaper and when I picked up the paper, in the local section Aaron's picture caught my eye. The article said that a sheriff's deputy had been killed and I saw it had a name that wasn't the right name. It said that he was a member of the Sheriff's Anti-Terrorism Unit.

### NARRATION

*Close-up of paper*

That's right, the photo of the man in the newspaper was not the Aaron Stokes they had come to know. He was actually Deputy Aaron Kilner. And he had infiltrated their group.

## CATHERINE CAMPBELL

*Imposing shot of Sheriff Pierce*

Sheriff Pierce made it very clear that yes, in fact, Aaron Kilner was assigned to infiltrate Peace Fresno, that he was able to infiltrate organizations that are open to the public.

### NARRATION

*Shots of smiling peace activists at meeting*

You could understand why the police needed to spy on a group like Peace Fresno. Just look at them. A gathering of terrorists if I ever saw one.

### NARRATION

*Older man walking across park—and in gym*

This is Barry Reingold, a retired phone worker from Oakland, California. Barry likes to work out in the gym. Somewhere between his cardio and his strength training, Barry got political.

### INTERVIEW: BARRY REINGOLD

We were up in the gym and it was after we were working out and a number of us were talking about 9/11 and Afghanistan and bin Laden and someone said "Bin Laden's a real asshole for murdering those people," and I said, "Yeah that's

true, but he will never be as big an asshole as
Bush who bombs all over the world for oil profits."

### NARRATION

Barry didn't have to worry about the police spying
on him. His fellow weight lifters were more than
willing to turn him in.

### BARRY REINGOLD

I was taking a nap and I guess it was one thirty,
two o'clock in the afternoon and they came to my
place and I said: "Well, who's there?" And they
said: "The FBI." I said: "The FBI? I mean, why
are they here?"

### NARRATION

Yes, the FBI had come to see Barry, and they
weren't there to Jazzercize.

### BARRY REINGOLD

The FBI said, "Have you been talking to people
about 9/11 and about bin Laden and oil profits and
Afghanistan?" I said, "A lot of people are talking
about these things."

I feel my rights have been, you know, trampled on.
I mean, if you have something to say to me in the
gym, well then fine, don't tell the FBI and they
come to my apartment while I'm taking a nap.

### INTERVIEW: CONGRESSMAN PORTER GOSS [(R-FLORIDA), CHAIR, HOUSE INTELLIGENCE COMMITTEE]

There is nothing to be ashamed of here. There is full transparency. There is nothing about the . . . the, uh, Patriot Act that I am ashamed of in any way, shape, or form. I have a 1-800 number, call me. *(words flash on screen: NOT REALLY TRUE)* I'm the guy you call, if there is a violation or abuse. *(words flash on screen: BUT, HERE'S HIS PRIVATE OFFICE LINE . . .)* If you got a poster child on this, I wanna see it, that's what I do. *(numbers flash on screen: 202-225-2536)* I am hired by the people of the United States to provide oversight. I provide oversight.

### INTERVIEW: CONGRESSMAN JIM MCDERMOTT (D-WASHINGTON)

Trent Lott said, the day the bill was introduced, "Maybe now we can do things we've wanted to do for the last ten years."

*News clip*

### GEORGE W. BUSH

Now, I've always . . . you know a dictatorship would be a heck of a lot easier, there's no question about it.

### INTERVIEW: CONGRESSMAN
### JIM MCDERMOTT

I mean, they had . . . they had all this on the shelf somewhere, ideas of things they would like to do. And they got 9/11 and they said, "That's our chance! Go for it!"

### INTERVIEW: CONGRESSMAN
### JOHN CONYERS [(D-MICHIGAN),
### HOUSE JUDICIARY COMMITTEE]

There was an immediate assumption on the part of the administration that there had to be a surrender of certain of our rights.

### INTERVIEW: CONGRESSWOMAN
### TAMMY BALDWIN [(D-WISCONSIN),
### HOUSE JUDICIARY COMMITTEE]

There's several definitions in the bill that are quite troubling. First of all, the definition of "terrorist" . . . and . . . and it's so expansive that it could include people who . . .

### MICHAEL MOORE

Like me?

*She laughs*

### CONGRESSMAN JIM MCDERMOTT

No one read it. That's the whole point. They wait till the middle of the night, they drop it in the middle of the night, it's printed in the middle of the night, and the next morning when we come in, it passes.

### MICHAEL MOORE

Um, how could Congress pass this Patriot Act without even reading it?

### CONGRESSMAN JOHN CONYERS

Sit down, my son. We don't read most of the bills. Do you really know what that would entail if we were to read every bill that we pass? Uh, well the good thing, it would slow down the legislative process.

### NARRATION

*Michael Moore approaches huge ice cream truck in D.C.*

I couldn't believe that virtually no member of Congress had read the Patriot Act before voting on it. So I decided the only patriotic thing to do was for me to read it to them.

*Truck traveling around Capitol—Michael Moore reading Patriot Act on loudspeaker*

## MICHAEL MOORE

Members of Congress, this is Michael Moore.
I would like to read to you the U.S.A. Patriot
Act. Section 1, Section 210 of this code reads as
follows . . . Section 2703 C . . .

*News clip: photo op at a diner*

## GEORGE W. BUSH

My job is to secure the homeland, and that's
exactly what we're going to do. But I'm here to
take somebody's order. That would be you,
Stretch, what would you like?

## STRETCH (REPORTER)

Right behind you.

## GEORGE W. BUSH

I'm gonna order some ribs.

## NARRATION

We all know you can't secure the homeland on
an empty stomach. And in order to remain
secure, everyone needs to sacrifice. *(footage
of baby and mother)* Especially little Patrick
Hambleton. I'm sure each of us has our own
personal airport security horror story. But here's
my favorite: the terrorist threat that was posed
by his mommy's breast milk.

## INTERVIEW: SUSAN HAMBLETON

*In her home*

> I thought, well, if I just put a little bit on my lips, then that would be sufficient because obviously I'm tasting it. And, she looked at me and I felt like she was telling me, "You need to chug that." She goes, "No, you need to drink more." And of a four-ounce bottle, I wound up drinking two more ounces of breast milk that then, because it's touched my lips, has to be tossed.

## NARRATION

*Airport security shots*

> While Homeland Security was making sure breast milk was kept off our planes, they were also doing everything possible to ensure no one could light a fire bomb on board.

## WOMAN

*Dropping five matchbooks and two lighters into airport security container*

> I can bring that on the plane?

## AIRPORT SECURITY

Actually, you can. Yes, you're fine. Whoops . . . one too many books of matches. You can have four books of matches and two lighters.

### INTERVIEW: SENATOR BYRON DORGAN
### [(D-NORTH DAKOTA), SENATE
### SUBCOMMITTEE ON AVIATION]

When we already have the experience of Richard Reid, the shoe bomber, who would have blown up an airplane with his shoe bomb had he had a butane lighter, according to the FBI, why would the Transportation Security Agency say it's okay to take four books of matches and two butane lighters in your pockets as you board an airplane?

*Footage of cigarette manufacturing—with the word "SOMEBODY" flashing over it*

I'm guessing that somebody put pressure on them to say, you know, "When an airplane lands people want to light up pretty quickly so don't take their lighters away."

### NARRATION

*Clips from various stories*

Okay, let me see if I got this straight . . . old guys in the gym, bad. Peace groups in Fresno, bad. Breast milk, really bad. But matches and lighters on the plane? Oh, hey, no problem! Was this really about our safety. Or was something else going on?

## NARRATION

*See the expansive Shores of Oregon coastline*

This is where the Pacific Ocean meets the shores of Oregon. Over one hundred miles of beautiful, open coastline on our border. And, thanks to the budget cutbacks, the total number of State Police protecting it? One. *(shot of solitary trooper)* Part time. Meet Trooper Brooks.

## INTERVIEW: STATE TROOPER
## JOSHUA BROOKS

I maybe get a chance to hit this stretch of highway once maybe twice a week during my shifts. You know, just to even drive up here and look. You know, I mean, as far as I know, somebody could . . . there's a lot of things they could do. I don't even want to suspect, because it just makes me ill inside.

## NARRATION

Back at the State Trooper patrol office, thanks to the budget cuts, Trooper Kenyon had to come in on his day off to catch up on some paperwork.

## INTERVIEW: STATE TROOPER
## ANDY KENYON

*At shuttered office*

For the most part, especially during the summer-time, when people show up here, this is exactly what they get. They closed the door, they can read the sign about the office closure, and, just basically explains that, uh, due to our cutbacks that our office is not open for administrative business. And there's a little sign down at the bottom that explains when the office is closed that they can use the phone booth to get in touch with our dispatch. Ironically enough, that phone is a piece of junk, it doesn't work very well. So, half the time when they pick up the phone and dispatch gets a bunch of static and they don't hear anything.

For Tuesday, there'll be no troop on patrol. Wednesday there'll be no troop on patrol. Thursday there'll be no troop on patrol.

You get calls all the time, people will call in a suspicious vehicle, or somebody looking suspicious, you know . . . and I don't hardly ever respond to that anymore. I just don't have the time to do it.

One night I asked, "How many people do we have in this state of Oregon on duty tonight?" And we had eight troopers . . . on . . . for the entire state of Oregon . . . working.

I think, you know, Oregon is a prime example that homeland security is not as secure as what, I think, people would like to believe.

## STATE TROOPER JOSHUA BROOKS

Nobody's sent me any manual that says here's how you catch a terrorist, you know. If I had that manual, I'd read it. But I don't. So . . . yeah.

## NARRATION

*Shots of troopers on patrol*

Of course, the Bush administration didn't hand out a manual on how to deal with the terrorist threat because the terrorist threat wasn't what this was all about. They just wanted us to be fearful enough so that we'd get behind what their real plan was.

*News clips: warheads being loaded onto ship intercut with Bush—in makeup—sitting at his desk before addressing the nation on TV*

## WOMAN'S VOICE

*Off camera, giving Bush the four-minute warning before TV address on March 19, 2003*

Four minutes.

## WOMAN

*Off camera—as we see more warheads being loaded*

Three minutes.

### WOMAN

*Off camera—aircraft carriers getting ready for battle,
Bush practices faces before going "live"*

Thirty seconds.

### WOMAN

*Off camera—Bush looks uncomfortable as clock ticks
down*

Fifteen seconds. Ten, nine, eight, seven . . .

### WOMAN

*Off camera*

Six . . . five . . . four . . . three . . . two . . . one . . .

*TV address*

### GEORGE W. BUSH

My fellow citizens . . .

*Cut to shots of Baghdad, March 2003—kids playing,
weddings, people laughing, etc.*

### GEORGE W. BUSH

*Over footage of Iraq in early March 2003*

At this hour, American and coalition forces are
in the early stages of military operations to
disarm Iraq, to free its people, and to defend

the world from grave danger. On my orders,
coalition forces have begun striking selected
targets of military importance to undermine
Saddam Hussein's ability to wage war. (*just as
little girl lands at end of slide—massive
explosions land all over Baghdad*)

### NARRATION

*Over footage of U.S. shock and awe carpet bombings
over Baghdad*

On March 19, 2003, George W. Bush and
the United States military invaded the
sovereign nation of Iraq—a nation that had
never attacked the United States. A nation
that had never threatened to attack the United
States. A nation that had never murdered a
single American citizen.

*News clip: Iraqi man holding dead baby, standing by a
pickup truck full of dead Iraqi bodies*

### TRANSLATION OF INTERVIEW

What's this baby's crime?

Was he going to fight the soldiers?

Cowards! I went out with a bat

and asked the soldier to hit me.

I swear on the Koran.

Those who don't fear death

don't die.

### INTERVIEW: IRAQI YOUNG MAN
### DIGGING THROUGH RUBBLE

We are going to find this, I think, piece of my
neighbor, young girl, age 20, Shams, I think is
other part of her body. That's all.

### INTERVIEW: U.S. SOLDIER
### ON THE STREET IN IRAQ

There is a lot of innocent civilians that were killed.
And, I think that is because, uh, the U.S. Army,
you know, we came in, and we knew it wasn't
gonna be easy, and they pretty much at first shot
anything that moved.

### INTERVIEW: U.S. SOLDIER
### ON THE STREET IN IRAQ

When war happens and the fighting starts, you
know, it's kinda like we're pumped up and motivated and ready to go.

### INTERVIEW: U.S. SOLDIER
### ON THE STREET IN IRAQ

It's the ultimate rush. 'Cause you know you're
going into the fight to begin with and then you
got a good song playing in the background . . . and,

uh, that gets you real fired up. Ready to do the job.

*Two U.S. soldiers at tank*

You can hook your CD player up to the tank's internal communications system . . .

**SOLDIER**

To the Charlie Box.

**SOLDIER**

. . . so that way when you put your helmet on you can hear it through the helmet.

**SOLDIER IN TANK**

This is the one we listen to the most, this is the one we travel, when we kill the enemy, Drowning Pool, "Let the Bodies Hit the Floor," is just fitting for the job we were doing.

*Dead and maimed Iraqi civilians*

**SOLDIER**

We picked, uh . . . "The Roof Is on Fire," because, uh, basically it symbolized Baghdad being on fire, and uh, at the time we wanted it to burn to get Saddam and his regime out.

*Same soldier singing to camera*

"The roof, the roof, the roof is on fire, we don't need no water, let the motherfucker burn, burn motherfucker, burn . . ."

*Shots of Baghdad on fire*

". . . we don't need no water, let the motherfucker burn, burn motherfucker, burn . . ."

**SOLDIER**

*Looking scared on street*

This is a whole totally different picture here, being pushed into the city, urban warfare, in a tank, you know, civilians . . .

*U.S. tanks rumble through streets of Baghdad*

**SOLDIER**

*Iraqi man being taken away*

Yeah, the civilians, it gets you . . .

**SOLDIER**

*Little Iraqi boy crying*

You don't know who's friendly, who's enemy . . .

**SOLDIER**

*Footage of operation on Iraqi toddler whose left arm is
in pieces on an operating table*

This was a lot more real and true than just a video
game. A lot of people thought it was just gonna be
"Ah, yeah, look through the sight and shoot!" Nah.
A lot of this is face-to-face, and especially riding
by after the . . . some of the bombs that went off
and seeing all the people on the side of the road
bloated up *(dead rotting Iraqi bodies),* and just all
the smells around you, I mean, from the people
lying dead, rotted, it's a lot more gruesome than
you think. *(bloodied body being carried onto
stretcher)*

**SOLDIER**

*Women and children in hospital, faces disfigured from
napalm*

We called in with some artillery and some napalm
and things like that; some innocent women and
children got hit. We met them on the road and
they had little girls with noses blown off and . . .
and, uh, and like husbands carrying their dead
wives and things like that. That was extremely difficult to deal with 'cause you're like, you know,
"Shoot, what the hell do we do now."

*News clip*

### DONALD RUMSFELD

*Intercut with carpet bombing of an area*

The targeting capabilities and the care that goes into targeting is as impressive as anything anyone could see. *(Iraqi baby's head being sewn up with no anesthesia)*

*Nightscope footage and audio of soldier killing an Iraqi walking across an area*

### SOLDIER

Got him, good. The second one, get the other one.

### DONALD RUMSFELD

The care that goes into it, the humanity that goes into it.

*News clip*

### IRAQI WOMAN

*Standing in rubble—hysterical with grief*

#### Translation

They have no conscience!

They know nothing!

They slaughtered us!

They destroyed our houses!

God will destroy their houses!

God is great!

God destroy their houses!

Victory to Iraq!

### AL JAZEERA REPORTER

*Off camera*

You mean, they killed civilians?

### IRAQI WOMAN

Yes, civilians!

It's our uncle's house!

We're all civilians.

There is no militia here.

I pray to God to avenge us!

I can only count on you, God!

We've had five funerals because of the bombings.

Oh God!

Oh God!

God save us from them!

Where are you, God?

Where are you?

### INTERVIEW: BRITNEY SPEARS

*Looking bored and obnoxiously chewing gum—from interview with CNN's Tucker Carlson*

Honestly, I think we should just trust our President in every decision that he makes and we should just support that, you know, and, uh, be faithful in what happens.

### TUCKER CARLSON

*Off camera*

Do you trust this president?

### BRITNEY SPEARS

Yes, I do.

### NARRATION

*Over footage of Bush taking podium for State of the Union address—to large cheers*

Britney Spears was not alone. The majority of the American people trusted the President, and why shouldn't they? He had spent the better part of the last year giving them every reason why we should invade Iraq.

*Montage of various news clips*

### GEORGE W. BUSH

Saddam Hussein has gone to elaborate lengths, spent enormous sums, taken great risks to build and keep weapons of mass destruction.

### COLIN POWELL

Saddam Hussein is determined to get his hands on a nuclear bomb.

### GEORGE W. BUSH

Nuclear weapon.

Nuclear weapon.

Nuclear weapon.

### COLIN POWELL

*Over satellite photographs*

Active chemical munitions bunkers . . . Mobile production facilities.

### GEORGE W. BUSH

We know he's got chemical weapons.

### GEORGE W. BUSH

He's got 'em.

He's got 'em.

He's got 'em.

### NARRATION

*Slow motion footage of Colin Powell addressing media*

Huh . . . that's weird. Because that's not
what Bush's people said when he first took
office.

### COLIN POWELL

*Press conference, February 2001*

He has not developed any significant capability
with respect to weapons of mass destruction. He
is unable to project conventional power against
his neighbors.

*News clip*

### CONDOLEEZZA RICE

*July 2001*

We are able to keep arms from him. His military
forces have not been rebuilt.

### GEORGE W. BUSH

*State of the Union Address*

Saddam Hussein aids and protects terrorists,
including members of al Qaeda.

## DICK CHENEY

*From interview on* Meet the Press

There was a relationship between Iraq and al Qaeda.

*Various news clips of George W. Bush repeating the stump speech*

Saddam

Al Qaeda

Saddam

Al Qaeda

Saddam

The al Qaeda

Saddam

Saddam

Saddam

Al Qaeda.

## DONALD RUMSFELD

*Testifying before Congress*

It is only a matter of time before terrorist states armed with weapons of mass destruction develop the capability to deliver those weapons to U.S. cities.

## COLIN POWELL

*At the United Nations*

What we are giving you are facts and conclusions based on solid intelligence.

*Drawings of possible weapons sites in Iraq*

## GEORGE W. BUSH

*Various speeches*

This is a man who hates America.

This is a man who cannot stand what we stand for.

His willingness to terrorize himself.

He hates the fact—like al Qaeda does—that we love freedom.

After all, this is the guy that tried to kill my dad at one time.

## INTERVIEW: CONGRESSMAN
## JIM MCDERMOTT

They simply got people to believe that there was a real threat out there when in fact, there wasn't one.

## DONALD RUMSFELD

*Pentagon briefing*

You get told things every day that don't happen. It doesn't seem to bother people.

### NARRATION

*Over Senate session of Congress*

Of course, the Democrats were there to put a stop to all these falsehoods.

### SENATOR TOM DASCHLE [(D-SOUTH DAKOTA), SENATE DEMOCRATIC LEADER]

*Speaking in session*

I will vote to give the President the authority he needs.

### COLIN POWELL

*Testifying*

The United States is prepared to lead a Coalition of the Willing that will do it.

### GEORGE W. BUSH

*Talking to reporters*

When I say we will lead a Coalition of the Willing to disarm him if he chooses not to disarm, I mean it.

### REPORTER

*Off camera*

Who is in that Coalition of the Willing now, are . . . ?

### GEORGE W. BUSH

*Not appreciative of the question*

You will find out who's in the Coalition of the Willing.

### ANNOUNCER

*Spinning globe—over shots from each country*

The Coalition of the Willing . . . roll call!

*Young girls hula dancing*

The Republic of Palau!

*Guy driving a cart with two oxen*

The Republic of Costa Rica!

*Black-and-white film footage of a Viking ship*

The Republic of Iceland.

### NARRATION

Of course, none of these countries has an army, or, for that matter, weapons, so it looked like we'd be doing most of the invading stuff ourselves.

But then there was also . . .

### ANNOUNCER

*Film footage of vampires waking from their coffins*

Romania!

*Musicians playing*

The Kingdom of Morocco!

### NARRATION

*Snake charmers and wild monkeys flying across a field*

Morocco wasn't officially a member of the Coalition, but according to one report, they did offer to send two thousand monkeys to help detonate land mines.

### GEORGE W. BUSH

These are men of vision.

### ANNOUNCER

*Someone smoking a huge pipe*

The Netherlands!

### GEORGE W. BUSH

*Monkeys at a boardroom table*

And I'm proud . . . I'm proud to call them allies.

### ANNOUNCER

Afghanistan!

### NARRATION

*Our troops in Afghanistan*

Afghanistan? Oh yeah, they had an army . . . our army! I guess that's one way to build a coalition—just keep invading countries. Yes, with our mighty coalition intact, we were ready.

### DONALD RUMSFELD

One could almost say it's the mother of all coalitions.

### MILITARY CHOIR

*From FOX News*

> (*Singing*) America, America . . .

### NARRATION

Fortunately, we have an independent media in this country who would tell us the truth.

*Montage of various news clips—reporters being biased*

### SHEPARD SMITH (FOX NEWS ANCHOR)

The rallying around the President, around the flag, and around the troops clearly has begun.

### SOLDIER

*From FOX News*

And we're gonna win!

### LINDA VESTER (FOX NEWS ANCHOR)

You really have to be with the troops to understand that kind of adrenaline rush that they get.

### KATIE COURIC (NBC *TODAY* SHOW HOST)

I just want you to know, I think Navy SEALS rock!

### CNN REPORTER

The pictures you're seeing are absolutely phenomenal.

### DAN RATHER (CBS NEWS ANCHOR)

When my country's at war, I want my country to win.

### PETER JENNINGS (ABC NEWS ANCHOR)

Iraqi opposition has faded in the face of American power.

**REPORTER**

What you're watching here is truly historic television and journalism.

**CNN REPORTER**

It was absolutely electrifying, they actually had to strap me in with my camera at the back of the plane . . .

**TED KOPPEL (ABC NEWS ANCHOR, *NIGHTLINE*)**

. . . an awesome synchronized killing machine.

**DAN RATHER**

There is an inherent bias in the coverage of the American press in general.

**NEIL CAVUTO (FOX NEWS HOST)**

Am I slanted and biased? You damn well bet I am!

**NARRATION**

*Soldiers praying over dead American soldier, coffins, funeral*

But one story the media wasn't covering was the personal story of each and every soldier who was killed in the war. The government would not allow any cameras to show the coffins coming home.

That kind of story is a downer, especially when you are getting ready for a party on a boat.

*MUSIC CUE*

*Bush flying in on jet—to aircraft carrier—interacting with troops*

> *Look at what's happened to me*
>
> *I can't believe it myself*
>
> *Suddenly I'm up on top of the world*
>
> *It should've been somebody else.*
>
> *Believe it or not,*
>
> *I'm walking on air.*
>
> *I never thought I could feel so free—*
>
> *Flying away on a wing and a prayer.*
>
> *Who could it be?*
>
> *Believe it or not, it's just me.*

### GEORGE W. BUSH

*On carrier with MISSION ACCOMPLISHED sign in background*

My fellow Americans, major combat operations in Iraq have ended. In the battle of Iraq, the United States and our allies have prevailed.

*News clip Iraq—bomb going off near soldiers—U.S.*
*casualties being loaded off trucks—chaos—soldiers*
*yelling*

## SOLDIERS

*Barely audible in background*

Get out of the way . . . let's go . . . move it . . .
move it . . . move it . . . move it . . . move it . . . get
another one . . . come on buddy . . . come on
buddy . . . hang in there . . . hang in there buddy.

*Various news clips—over footage of Arlington Cemetery*

## REPORTER

162, the number of troops killed by hostile fire.

## REPORTER

244 U.S. troops . . .

## REPORTER

384 U.S. troops have lost their lives.

## REPORTER

Total killed 484.

## REPORTER

Died in the line of duty, 500.

**REPORTER**

631 American troops.

**REPORTER HAROLD MOSS**

More than 825 troops have been killed in Iraq.

**REPORTER**

Largest number of American military deaths since Vietnam.

**GEORGE W. BUSH**

*Press conference in White House*

There are some who feel like, that, uh, if they attack us, that we may decide to leave prematurely. They don't understand what they're talking about, if that's the case. Let me finish. There are some who feel like that, you know, the conditions are such that they can attack us there. My answer is, "Bring 'em on!"

*Footage of mutilated U.S. bodies in Fallujah—beaten with sticks, dragged from cars, and hung from the bridge*

**INTERVIEW: U.S. SOLDIER**

The United States was planning on, uh, just walking through here like it was going to be easy and all, but, it's not that easy to conquer a country, is it? (*footage of Iraqis marching in the streets*)

### DAN RATHER

The renewed battle for control of Iraq raged for a fourth day today with street clashes in nearly every corner of the country.

Iraq could become, quote, "Another Vietnam."

### REPORTER

*Footage of men with guns in Iraqi streets*

Officials say they see evidence that Sunni and Shiite extremists might be joining forces.

### GEORGE W. BUSH

*At press conference*

They're not happy they're occupied. I wouldn't be happy if I were occupied either.

*MUSIC CUE*

*Iraqi fighters marching and carrying weapons*

*Everybody here we go—ooh ooh*

*Come on party people—ooh ooh*

*Throw your hands in the air—ooh ooh*

*Come on party people—ooh ooh*

*Wave 'em like you don't care*

**REPORTER**

*Over footage of Japanese aid workers with knives at their throats*

Two Japanese aid workers and a journalist kidnapped by men calling themselves the Mujahadeen Squadrons. They threatened to burn the hostages alive if Japan does not withdraw its troops from Iraq within three days.

*News clip: footage of Thomas Hamill being held by captors, as his convoy burns on highway*

**REPORTER**

What's happened?

**THOMAS HAMILL**
**(HALLIBURTON EMPLOYEE)**

They attacked our convoy.

**REPORTER**

You want to give us your name?

**HOSTAGE**

Hamill. Thomas.

**CBS REPORTER**

The Pentagon might keep up to 24,000 troops in combat beyond their tour.

### INTERVIEW: SOLDIER

I know our numbers in the military have gone down, you know they talk about retention.

### INTERVIEW: SOLDIER

You know, I never really expected to be deployed this long. I don't think anybody did.

### SOLDIER

I don't have any clue as to why we're still in Iraq.

### SOLDIER

*Surrounded by other soldiers*

If Donald Rumsfeld was here, I'd ask him for his resignation.

### NARRATION

*Clashes in Baghdad*

With the war not going as planned, and the military in need of many more troops, where would they find the new recruits?

### BILL PLANTE (CBS REPORTER)

Military experts say three times the 120,000 U.S. troops now deployed would be needed to pacify and rebuild the country.

# NARRATION

*Shots of depressed downtown Flint, Michigan*

They would find them all across America. In the places that had been destroyed by the economy. Places where one of the only jobs available was to join the army. Places like my hometown of Flint, Michigan.

*Interview with a group of young African American men in a "Boys Club" gym in Flint*

## INTERVIEW: TORIAN BILLINGS

And, I was watching TV one day and they showed like some of the buildings and areas that had been hit by bombs and things like that, and while watching I got to thinking, like, there's parts of Flint that look like that, and we ain't been in a war.

*Shuttered neighborhood in Flint*

## INTERVIEW: GREGORY FITCH

Look at the neighborhood I live in. Most of them are abandoned. I mean, you know, that's not right, you want to talk about terrorism? Come right here. President Bush, right here. Come right here. He knows about this corner. I emailed him.

*Career Alliance office, Flint, Michigan*

## LILA LIPSCOMB (EXECUTIVE
## ASSISTANT, CAREER ALLIANCE)

At the end of January of '04, the unemployment rate in Flint was actually 17 percent, but you have to take into consideration as well, that when your unemployment runs out, you're no longer counted. I would say that we're probably close to at least 50 percent. Not working or under-employed, because being underemployed is just as dangerous.

So my family has gone through the welfare system. When it was Jobs Central, in the mid-80s, I came through the job training partnership program here at Jobs Central and I went to a secretary school. Years later, I'm the executive assistant to the president of the agency. Interesting.

My mother used to tell me all the time that "Why do you always go for the underdog?" It was because the underdog is who needed me. People that don't have anything, that's who I have to fight for. And that's who I have fought for my entire life.

I started taking my children, and telling my children, "The military is a good option. I can't afford to have you go to college, I cannot pay your way. Financial aid will not help you." So, I, as a mother, started teaching my children about the options that the military could do, that would take them around the world, they would see all the things that I, as a mother, could not let them see.

It would pay for their education that I as their mother, and their father, could not pay for.

**MICHAEL MOORE**

The military's a good option for kids in Flint?

**LILA LIPSCOMB**

Military's an excellent option for the people in the city of Flint.

*Interior, gym—training center—group of African American boys*

**MICHAEL MOORE**

How many of you have a friend or a family member in the service? *(almost every hand gets raised)* Anybody currently serving overseas?

**MARTRES BROWN**

A brother of mine.

**ADRIAN WALKER**

My cousin.

**STUDENT**

*Off camera*

My brother.

**MICHAEL MOORE**

Where is your brother?

**MARTRES BROWN**

Iraq.

**ADRIAN WALKER**

Germany.

**JORDAN POLK**

My cousin got shipped off to Iraq, like, three days ago.

**TORIAN BILLINGS**

There's like a Army or Navy recruiter or Marines recruiter up there almost every week, in the lunchroom, recruiting students from uh . . . the lunchroom.

**ARMY RECRUITING AD**

*Very over the top animation and music, like a video game*

There are people with a calling. Most serve one weekend a month and two weeks a year. Earning money for college. Protecting their community. In the Army National Guard, you can!

### INTERVIEW: RANDY SUTTON

I'm going into the air force myself. I'm going to take the year off, probably, after high school, and then just go and make a career, I want to be an aircraft maintenance technician.

### INTERVIEW: HARRY WILLIAMS

I ran into a recruiter and, uh, there was something I noticed about it, and this is kinda on another . . . I just . . . I noticed it was odd, it was more like he was hiring me for a job than recruiting me for the army. It was the way he approached me. He approached a friend of mine. I was in Borders Books and Music, he just came up, it was like he was handing us a business card. He had business cards made for the army and everything.

### NARRATION

*Marine recruiters on the prowl for recruits in Flint*

Meet Marine Staff Sergeant Dale Kortman and Sergeant Raymond Plouhar. They are two of the many recruiters assigned to Flint, Michigan. They're very busy these days.

### SERGEANT RAYMOND PLOUHAR

*In car, talking to each other about someone going for a run*

Look it, he's running away already . . . He's seen us coming.

### SERGEANT DALE KORTMAN

*In car, talking about young African American crossing their path*

What we got here? He's a little gangsta, yeah.

### SERGEANT RAYMOND PLOUHAR

We're heading over to the Courtland mall right now.

### NARRATION

*As we follow them in car*

They decided not to go to the wealthier Genesee Valley mall in the suburbs. They have a hard time recruiting young people there. Instead, they went to the other mall.

### SERGEANT DALE KORTMAN

*Two of them discussing a plan of attack*

Let's go in through Mervyn's . . .

### SERGEANT RAYMOND PLOUHAR

In through Mervyn's . . .

### SERGEANT DALE KORTMAN

And then we'll walk straight down . . .

### SERGEANT RAYMOND PLOUHAR

Straight down . . .

### SERGEANT DALE KORTMAN

. . . and straight back and then go down to the . . .

*They approach their first recruits*

Gents! You know we're looking at ya, right! You guys ever thinking about joining up?

### JOHN KINGSTON

I thought about going to college and playing basketball.

### SERGEANT DALE KORTMAN

Okay, okay. You any good?

### JOHN KINGSTON

Yeah. Especially basketball.

### SERGEANT DALE KORTMAN

Good. You can play ball for the Marine Corps as well, you know, travel around the world, get on the

Marine Corps basketball team. Um, David
Robinson was in the military as well . . .

### JOHN KINGSTON

Oh, was he?

### SERGEANT DALE KORTMAN

So, yeah, so, you can definitely hook it up so.

### INTERVIEW: SERGEANT
### RAYMOND PLOUHAR

*Says to camera*

Right now there is somebody out there who wants
to be a marine but has no idea how to do it.

### SERGEANT DALE KORTMAN

*To different recruit*

Where you work at?

### MONTREY BOWLES

I work at KFC.

### SERGEANT DALE KORTMAN

Sweet!

**MONTREY BOWLES**

Dort and Lapeer.

**SERGEANT DALE KORTMAN**

You can hook us up with some deals.

**MONTREY BOWLES**

Yes.

**INTERVIEW: SERGEANT
RAYMOND PLOUHAR**

*To camera*

They're waiting to get recruited.

**MONTREY BOWLES**

I don't know, I was probably gonna start with a
career in music or something.

**SERGEANT DALE KORTMAN**

A career in music?

Maybe we can get you a career in music, you
know, let the marines go for it. I'm sure you know
who Shaggy is, right?

**MONTREY BOWLES**

Yeah.

**SERGEANT DALE KORTMAN**

You know anything about him?

**MONTREY BOWLES**

Yeah. He, uh, the Jamaican, uh, something.

**SERGEANT DALE KORTMAN**

Yeah.

**MONTREY BOWLES**

Yeah.

**SERGEANT DALE KORTMAN**

How about a former marine? Did you know it?

You definitely need to know discipline if you're gonna get into music.

**MONTREY BOWLES**

Yeah, I understand that.

**SERGEANT DALE KORTMAN**

Especially discipline with the money. If you make a million you need to manage that money. So, come in the office, we can sit down and talk, and show you everything we know about the marines. Sound like a plan?

### SERGEANT RAYMOND PLOUHAR

What have you got going on later this afternoon?

How about tomorrow?

Say right around ten o'clock Monday morning?

### MONTREY BOWLES

Yeah, that sounds pretty good.

### SERGEANT RAYMOND PLOUHAR

You want me to come pick you up?

### INTERVIEW: SERGEANT RAYMOND PLOUHAR

*To camera*

It's better to get them when they're ones and twos. And work on them that way.

### SERGEANT DALE KORTMAN

Ladies, you ready to join up?

Green hat right behind us. Looks . . . young. He's young.

### SERGEANT RAYMOND PLOUHAR

Yeah.

### SERGEANT DALE KORTMAN

*Sees possible recruits*

> We got two over here. Right over by the red van.

> You go that way, I go this way, we corner 'em.

*Talking to young man*

> You're in the ninth grade?

### BOY

Yes sir.

### SERGEANT DALE KORTMAN

Man, you look older than ninth grade, so . . .

### BOY

Yes, sir.

### SERGEANT DALE KORTMAN

All right. Here's my card.

### SERGEANT RAYMOND PLOUHAR

*To a young guy entering mall with his wife and baby*

> You ever thought about being a marine man?

## CLIFFTON E. WALKER

Uh . . . I thought about it. I got a wife and kid now, so . . .

## SERGEANT RAYMOND PLOUHAR

Even more reason to join up.

## SERGEANT DALE KORTMAN

*To a young African American kid who said he wasn't interested in joining up*

What I want to do, man, real quick, is, uh, just get some information from you, so I can scratch you off my list saying I've already talked to you, you know, you're not interested. Is that cool? All right? What's your name? What's your phone number?

What's your address, Mario?

Add another one to the list.

*Interview—interior—gym*

## MARTRES BROWN

However, you know, one would love to have that chance to experience college life, you know, stuff young people can do without having the risk of dying in the process, I guess I could say, candidly.

*Iraq, 2003 Christmas Eve raid—command post*

### INTERVIEW: SOLDIER IN CHARGE

The holidays do add a little bit more friction as opposed to just another night, in the fact that we want to give our guys a little bit time off, a little bit time to relax; however, we are in a combat zone, my soldiers do recognize that fact.

### SOLDIER

*Looking nervous before raid*

Everybody's a little bit nervous about it, I guess. But . . .

### SOLDIER

*Older soldier behind him—making fun of his fear*

We're professionals. We're going to take care of you. I promise.

*Off-camera laughter*

### SOLDIER

Every house here has the right to have weapons. Maximum—excuse me—one AK 47. We always expect the targets to be armed.

### SOLDIER

*All suited up and ready to go—cocks his gun*

Rock 'n' roll.

## TWO SOLDIERS

*Showing their tools for the raid*

> Fuckin' bolt cutters. He's got everything to crack
> doors open. Pop this in there . . .

*MUSIC CUE*

*Soldiers in tanks—out on nighttime patrol*

> *You better watch out, you better not cry*
>
> *You better not pout, I'm telling you why. Why?*
>
> *Santa Claus is coming to town. Gather round.*
>
> *He's making a list, checking it twice.*
>
> *He's gonna find out who's naughty and nice.*
>
> *Santa Claus is coming to town.*
>
> *He sees you when you're sleeping.*
>
> *He knows when you're awake.*
>
> *He knows if you've been bad or good*
>
> *So be good for goodness sake*
>
> *You better watch out.*

*Soldiers kick in door of residence in Baghdad*

## SOLDIER

Where's the guy at? Hey, just hold up.

### SOLDIER

*To interpreter—wondering where crying, older Iraqi woman is going*

No, no, no . . . where's she going?

### WOMAN

I'll go with her?

### SOLDIER

Where's she going?

### WOMAN

She's going to call him.

### SOLDIER

*Chaotic, dark house, hear voices calling out*

She's going to call him? No, no, no, no, no . . . just where is he at right now? Not on the phone . . . Not on the phone. Is he in the house? Is he in the house? He is? He is in the house? Where?

### SOLDIER

Get up there! Second floor! Second floor!

### SOLDIER

Watch out, watch out!

**SOLDIER**

Go! Go! Go!


**SOLDIER**

Watch out, Adele. Watch out. Watch out!


**SOLDIER**

One coming up!


**SOLDIER**

*Young Iraqi man on his stomach on the floor with flashlight in his face*

He's al Douri? That's Suheib al Douri? Suheib al Douri. What's your name?


**MAN**

Suheib. Suheib.


**SOLDIER**

This is Suheib?


**IRAQI WOMAN**

*(subtitles)*

What has he done?

He is just a college student?

### SOLDIER

Calm down, calm down, please.

### SOLDIER

All right . . . up to the roof.

### SOLDIER

We appreciate your cooperation.

### SOLDIER

This is the target.

### SOLDIER

So he's about to bring him out . . .

### SOLDIER

Go!

### SOLDIER

Move out!

## INTERVIEW: SOLDIER AT COMMAND POST

We have to . . . as you go back to the old saying,
win the hearts and minds of the people. That's
our job. We have to . . . we have to bring the
ideal of democracy and freedom to the country

and show them that the American people are not here to . . . to rule Iraq.

### IRAQI WOMEN

*Back in the apartment—Christmas Eve raid, women are on the couch—young girl is crying with fear*

(subtitles)

Don't be afraid.

He's not going to hit you.

What did he do?

Why don't you tell us? God keep you, what did he do?

### INTERVIEW: SOLDIER

I start doing evidence turn in. That process takes about three hours. So, uh, that's going to be it for the night and that concludes Christmas Eve.

*MUSIC CUE*

*He's making a list, checking it twice.*

*He's gonna find out who's naughty and nice.*

*Santa Claus is coming to town*

### SOLDIER AS SANTA

Merry Christmas PRT, Merry Christmas. Santa came to Iraq just for you guys.

### SOLDIER

Trying to keep the skies clear for you Santa . . .

*Interview: Lila Lipscomb's house in Flint, Michigan—as we see Lila putting flag outside her house*

### MICHAEL MOORE

Do you consider yourself a proud American?

### LILA LIPSCOMB

Absolutely. I'm an extremely proud American. I think I'm probably more proud than the average Joe. When I put my flag out, I can't allow it to touch the ground, because I know the lives that were lost and the blood that was shed so that I could be here and have a flag.

### MICHAEL MOORE

Right . . . how often do you put the flag out?

### LILA LIPSCOMB

Every single day, every single day. I started when my daughter was in Desert Storm. I had the same flag flying on my front porch and the same yellow ribbons, praying and hoping every single day that my child would come home safe and that everybody's child would come home safe.

### MICHAEL MOORE

And she did.

### LILA LIPSCOMB

And she did.

### MICHAEL MOORE

Do you have other family members that have been in the military?

### LILA LIPSCOMB

Absolutely. Uncles, aunts, cousins, brothers, father . . .

### MICHAEL MOORE

Very strong military family . . .

### LILA LIPSCOMB

Very strong. My family was . . . my family is what I consider part of the backbone of America. It's families like mine, and it's not just my family, there's hundreds of families, millions of families out here, that this country was founded on their backs.

I have been known to be a conservative
Democrat.

**MICHAEL MOORE**

That's what you consider yourself, yeah?

**LILA LIPSCOMB**

Mm-hmm. Yeah.

**MICHAEL MOORE**

Yeah. It's a great country.

**LILA LIPSCOMB**

It's a great country. It's a great country.

*Shows the cross around her neck*

The cross that I choose to wear, if you notice, it's a
multicultural, a multicolor cross. That's because I
believe that all God's people come in many colors.
And my family itself is multicultural.

**MICHAEL MOORE**

You have a daughter who went into the military?

**LILA LIPSCOMB**

Into the military.

**MICHAEL MOORE**

Then, your firstborn son in the military?

**LILA LIPSCOMB**

Into the military.

**MICHAEL MOORE**

Well, that's, uh, you know, that's quite a gift to the country . . .

**LILA LIPSCOMB**

Exactly right.

**MICHAEL MOORE**

. . . from your family.

**LILA LIPSCOMB**

Exactly right.

**MICHAEL MOORE**

Uh-huh. So, having a son in the army . . . pretty proud thing.

**LILA LIPSCOMB**

*Shot of Michael Pedersen, in fatigues, saluting*

Oh . . . you know what . . . he made it . . .

## MICHAEL MOORE

What was your reaction to protesters during, say, the Gulf War or Vietnam, or . . .

## LILA LIPSCOMB

*Over protest footage*

I always hated the protesters. I always hated the protesters. It was just a slap in my face. It was just, like, they were dishonoring my son. And I burned in my soul to tell them, "You don't understand, they're not there because they want to be there." But then I came to understand that they weren't protesting the men and the women that were there, they were protesting the concept of the war.

*Iraq—interview with U.S. soldier*

## SOLDIER

I know I'm a soldier and I'm here to do a job and I've been a soldier for a while. Once you have to go and do your job and you see the things that you see, I was saying that there's some disillusionment in that.

## U.S. SOLDIER BY TANK

*Scared voice shaking*

Battalion commander fully expects us to, um, be

attacked in some type of way, before we get to
[*inaudible*]. I know that so far it's been pretty
calm, not much has happened. But, be aware that
it can and it probably will.

### U.S. SOLDIER IN FIELD

They're beginning to organize themselves, just in
neighborhoods. The kids get together a lot—well,
can't say kids—but, uh, guys about 17, 18, starting
to come together and they hate us. Just why? I'm
not really sure.

### NARRATION

*Footage of abuse of Iraqi detainees by U.S. soldiers,
hoods over their heads, taking photos of them*

Immoral behavior breeds immoral behavior. When
a president commits the immoral act of sending
otherwise good kids to war based on a lie, this is
what you get.

### SOLDIER

*Soldiers taunting prisoners, wounded Iraqis lying on
stretcher*

Is he ticklish? Ali Baba still has a hard-on.

### SOLDIER

Why are you touching someone else's?

### SOLDIER

He touched his dick.

### INTERVIEW: U.S. SOLDIER IN IRAQ

To have these people shoot at us, kill us, blow us up, whatever means they can, and, I don't understand it, we're trying to help these people and it seems they don't want our help, "get out of here," but the minute something goes wrong with them, "oh, why weren't you here? Why didn't you do this?" You know, it's . . . I hate this country.

### U.S. SOLDIER IN IRAQ

You know, you . . . you . . . I feel that a part of your soul is destroyed in taking another life. And yeah, that statement is very true. You cannot kill someone without killing a part of yourself.

*Capitol Hill—interview with Corporal Abdul Henderson USMC, served in Iraq*

### MICHAEL MOORE

If you get called up, would you go back to Iraq?

### ABDUL HENDERSON

*In uniform*

No.

**MICHAEL MOORE**

You're not.

**ABDUL HENDERSON**

No.

**MICHAEL MOORE**

What repercussions do you face, if you don't?

**ABDUL HENDERSON**

There's possible jail time. That's one possible thing.

**MICHAEL MOORE**

Are you willing to risk that?

**ABDUL HENDERSON**

Yes. Yes. I will not let my person . . . I will not let anyone send me back over there to kill other poor people, especially when they pose no threat to me and my country. I won't do it.

*Footage of Bush in tails, addressing crowd at a fund-raiser*

## GEORGE W. BUSH

This is an impressive crowd. The haves, and the have mores! Some people call you the elite. I call you my base.

## NARRATION

*Various shots of Bush at photo ops with soldiers and vets*

While Bush was busy taking care of his base and professing his love for our troops, he proposed cutting combat soldiers' pay by 33 percent and assistance to their families by 60 percent. He opposed a $1.3 billion increase in veterans' benefits, $1.3 billion in veterans' health care, and closing seven veterans' hospitals, and he tried to double the prescription drug costs for veterans and opposed full benefits for part-time reservists.

*Photo and grave of Brett Petriken*

And when Staff Sergeant Brett Petriken from Flint was killed in Iraq on May 26, the army sent his last paycheck to his family. But they docked him for the last five days of the month that he didn't work because he was dead.

## INTERVIEW: CONGRESSMAN
## JIM MCDERMOTT

They say they're not going to leave any veterans behind, but they're leaving all kinds of veterans behind.

*Interview—Walter Reed Army Medical Hospital*

*Interviews with wounded vets*

### WOUNDED SOLDIER (LOST BOTH LEGS)

To say that we're forgotten, no, I know we're not forgotten . . . but missed? Yes. Yes. You know, there are a lot of soldiers that have been missed, you know that have been skipped over, that didn't get the proper coverage that they deserved.

### TEXT ON SCREEN

Nearly 5,000 wounded in the first 13 months of the war.

### WOUNDED SOLDIER (LOST BOTH LEGS)

They have a death toll, but they're not showing the amount of people that are being injured or are being amputated because of their injuries you know.

## WOUNDED SOLDIER

*Prepped for surgery—lost both hands*

Like, I still feel like I have hands . . .

## BRIAN WILLIAMS (NBC NEWS REPORTER)

*Off camera*

Yeah?

## WOUNDED SOLDIER

. . . and the pain is like . . . my hands are, like,
being crushed in a vise. But they do a lot to help it,
and they take a lot of the edge off it, it . . . it makes
it a lot more tolerable.

*Interviews: Blanchfield Army Community Hospital,
Fort Campbell, Kentucky*

## WOUNDED SOLDIER

*Talking in a group of wounded soldiers*

I was injured in late April, on patrol in Baghdad.
Couple of guys come out and ambushed us. Um . . .
I've got nerve damage and stuff like that; I've got
a lot of pain. I'm constantly in pain. Take a lot of
morphine to help with that stuff. Uh . . . doing,
doing . . . you know, just readjusting, getting life
back on . . . track. You know what I'm saying? I'm
not going to do what it is that I did before.

Um, I was a Republican for quite a few years . . .
and um . . . it . . . for some reason, they uh, they
conduct business in a very dishonest way. I'm
going to be incredibly active in the Democratic
Party down where I live once I get out. So, I'm
going to definitely do my best to ensure that the
Democrats win control.

*Interview: interior—Lila Lipscomb's house—sur-*
*rounded by family*

## LILA LIPSCOMB

*Lila and Howard Lipscomb, parents of Sergeant*
*Michael Pedersen*

Iraq, Baghdad, I didn't know anything of those
things.

*Photos of Michael before he left for Iraq*

And, he . . . we were in the hallway in the upstairs
of our house and he was crying and he said that he
was really scared and he didn't want to have to go
to Iraq. So we were able to have a whole conversa-
tion about sometimes some fear is healthy because
it keeps our senses about us. And that's when he
told me that he had not told anybody else but he
knew he was going to Baghdad.

We were, as everybody, we were glued to the TV,
just glued, completely glued to the television, in
hopes of seeing a glimpse of him.

Can't you please go over to where the helicopters
are? Can't you please let us see him? Then, that
night, it was about 10 something, I went upstairs
to the bedroom, and I was laying in bed, and I was
flipping the channels with the remote . . . all I
heard was "Black Hawk down, south central Iraq."

*News clip*

### PHIL ITTNER (CBS REPORTER)

*On camera*

All I can tell you at this hour is that last night the
army did indeed lose a Black Hawk helicopter. We
are being told by officers on the ground that there
were six occupants inside the Black Hawk.

### INTERVIEW: LILA LIPSCOMB

The next morning I got up and I said, "You push
those thoughts out of your mind. Okay Jesus, I
need you to come in, I need you, Jesus, you gotta
help me through this."

The army called me and I remember getting on
the phone and him saying, asking me, was I Lila
Lipscomb, and I said, "Yes." And he said, "Mother
of Sergeant Michael Pedersen?" And I remember
dropping the telephone. *(Lila begins to cry)* And
all I can honestly say that I remember is, "Ma'am,
the United States Army, the Secretary of Defense
regretfully informs you . . ." That's all I know.

The grief grabbed me so hard that I literally fell on the floor and I was alone, I didn't have anybody to pick me up, so I literally crawled over to my desk, and was hanging on, and I remember screaming, "Why does it have to be Michael? Why did you have to take my son? Why is it my son that you had to take? He didn't do anything! He wasn't a bad guy, he was a good guy, why did you have to take my son?"

*News clip*

## GEORGE W. BUSH

*Interviewed for ABC by Diane Sawyer*

I . . . I . . . I'm . . . uh . . . uh . . . I can't imagine what it must be like to lose a son or a daughter, or a husband, and or a wife, for that matter, and I . . . it pains me.

*Lipscomb home—interview continues*

## MICHAEL MOORE

You have his last letter?

## LILA LIPSCOMB

Yeah. It was mailed March 16, but I didn't get it until probably a week before he was killed.

"Hello. Hey mama, well, sorry I haven't been able

to call. They took the phone seven days ago. I got the letter and box, that is so cool, your first grandson came the same day your oldest son did. (*Lila cries*)

"How is everyone? I'm doing fine. We are just out here in the sand and windstorms, waiting. What in the world is wrong with George 'trying to be like his dad' Bush? He got us out here for nothing whatsoever. I am so furious right now, Mama. I really hope they do not reelect that fool, honestly.

"I am in good spirits and I am doing okay. I really miss you guys. Thanks for the Bible . . . (*Lila cries*) and books and candy. I really look forward to letters from you guys. Well, tell all the family hello and that I am doing fine. We don't expect anything to happen any time soon. I cannot wait to get home and get back to my life. Tell Sputnik congrats. And I'll see my first nephew soon, as soon as I get back to the States. Hope you guys are doing okay. And keep sending the mail. It makes getting through the days easier. Well, I am on my way to bed, so I will write you guys soon. I love and miss . . . all of you guys . . ." (*Lila is overcome with emotion*)

(*crying*) I want him to be alive. And I can't make him alive. But your flesh just aches. You want your child. It's out of sync. A parent is not supposed to bury their child.

## HOWARD LIPSCOMB SR.

*Over shot of Michael in church as an altar boy*

I feel ... I ... I ... I feel sad for my family
because we lost our son. But, I really feel sorry for
the other families that is losing their kids as we
speak. And for what? I don't ... That's the, I
guess, sickening part. For what?

*CUT TO: Halliburton PSA*

## DAVID LESAR (HALLIBURTON CEO)

*On Halliburton commercial*

You've heard a lot about Halliburton lately.
Criticism is okay. We can take it. Criticism is not
failure. Our employees are doing a great job.
We're feeding the soldiers, we're rebuilding Iraq.
Will things go wrong? Sure they will ... it's a war
zone. We're serving the troops because of what we
know, not who we know.

*Cut to Bush and Cheney addressing press on campaign
trail, July 2000*

## DICK CHENEY

Well, let me tell you about Halliburton, the company I ran ... I'm very proud of what I did at
Halliburton, and the people of Halliburton are
very proud of what they've accomplished. And uh,
I, frankly, uh, don't feel any need to apologize for

the way I've spent my time over the last five years as the CEO and chairman of a major American corporation.

### GEORGE W. BUSH

*Interrupts*

Yeah, this is also an attempt to divert attention away from the fact they have no energy policy, and as the Secretary of Energy said, "We were caught unawares!"

### NARRATION

*Scene of economic conference hotel ballroom—lots of white men mingling around buffet table*

In the middle of the war, Microsoft, DHL, and other corporations invited Halliburton to a conference to figure out how much money could be made in Iraq.

### MICHAEL MELE
### (U.S. ARMY CORPS OF ENGINEERS)

*At podium addressing conference*

Having worked this, uh, effort even since before the invasion, the liberation of Iraq started. You, industry, are definitely a vital part of that effort. We appreciate your interest in this. We need you.

### YOUSSEF SLEIMAN
### (IRAQ INITIATIVES
### HARRIS CORPORATION)

*At podium*

Now, lots of you are small businesses and you are struggling, "How do we get a piece of this big action? All of you big guys are going to get it and the rest of us that have subcontracting capability or none at all." USTDA is for you. Once that oil starts flowing and money coming, it's going to be lots of money. It's the second largest reserve of oil in the world, there's no question about how much money is there.

### INTERVIEW: DR. SAM KUBBA
### (AMERICAN IRAQI CHAMBER
### OF COMMERCE)

I've been getting complaints from Iraqi firms, and from American firms, uh, the lack of transparency, the corruption . . . I think the profits that American companies are making, the major, the main companies, uh, are so overwhelming. I mean, like when you have a line item for a million dollars and you subcontract it out for fifty or sixty or seventy thousand dollars, that's a huge profit. And it's the American taxpayer that's going to pay for that.

### YOUSSEF SLEIMAN

*Still at podium addressing conference*

. . . and it's going to get better! Start building relationships, because it's going to get much better as the oil flows and their budget increases, and the good news is, whatever it costs, the government will pay you.

### DR. SAM KUBBA

War is always good for certain companies, I mean that are in the war, the business of war.

### INTERVIEW: GEORGE SIGALOS
### (VICE PRESIDENT, HALLIBURTON)

We're very proud of the work we're doing, again it's supporting the U.S. government and the U.S. military, and the real heroes of the campaign, the real heroes of the reconstruction are the men and women of the U.S. Armed Forces, and we're very proud of being any part of that we can in supporting them.

### ANNOUNCER

*Clips from melodramatic Halliburton commercial*

Halliburton delivers hot meals, supplies, clean clothing, and communications to our soldiers so they can be a little closer to home.

## SOLDIER IN COMMERCIAL

*On the phone listening as his wife gives birth back in the States*

Yeah. Yeah. It's a girl? It's a girl!

## ANNOUNCER
## (HALLIBURTON COMMERCIAL)

Halliburton, proud to serve our troops.

*Women in Florida retirement home—talking about Halliburton*

### BERTHA OKOSKIN

I just read in the paper, Halliburton got another contract. Halliburton got another contract. Which is not being contested at all.

### EVELYN STROM

Because nobody knows.

### BERTHA OKOSKIN

Well, it's in the paper, so somebody knows.

### EVELYN STROM

But that's after it happens. It's after the fact. It's too late.

*News clip*

### HAROLD MOSS

The United States is now a major player in the Iraqi oil business. American troops guard the oil fields as Texas oil workers assess their potential.

### WORKER

So it's a safe environment to work in. We don't feel any risk at all. We feel we're being well protected here or we wouldn't be here.

*Interview with U.S. soldier in Iraq*

### SOLDIER

It's no secret . . . I mean, I make, anywheres, I don't know, between two and three thousand a month. A Halliburton employee out here driving a bus can make all between eight and ten thousand a month. Explain that one to me. For forty hours a week. Driving the same two-and-a-half-mile route. Go figure. Where do you . . . where's the justification in that?

*CUT TO: economic conference—interior hotel*

### GORDON BOBBIT (KALMAR RT CENTER)

There's no other single area of the world today with the opportunity for business, new business, similar to the opportunity that's available today in Iraq.

### INTERVIEW: GRANT HABER
### (AMERICAN INNOVATIONS, INC.)

The President went in and did what he did and we're all supporting him and our troops and we want to make sure that, you know, the efforts and the lost lives and . . . it wasn't for no reason.

### INTERVIEW: DR. SAM KUBBA

If it wasn't for the oil, nobody would be there. Nobody would worry about it.

### INTERVIEW: BLAINE OBER
### (HIGH PROTECTION COMPANY)

Unfortunately, at least for the near term, we think it's going to be a good situation . . . err, a dangerous situation. Good for business, bad for the people.

*Interview of Florida retirees*

### BERTHA OKOSKIN

Today on the news, Rumsfeld was saying . . . and Wolf, Wolf, Wolf-owitz, was saying, "Oh, the Iraqi people are much, much better off. Isn't it better that we got rid of Saddam and now the Iraqi people can do what they want to do and really be

free?" Will they ever be free? No, they'll not be
free. And where are the . . . are the weapons of
mass destruction? It was a . . . We were duped.
We were really duped. And these poor people,
the young men and women who are being killed
there . . . it's unnecessary. I . . . I . . . I . . . that's
it . . .

### EVELYN STROM

That's the disgrace.

### BERTHA OKOSKIN

No more.

### EVELYN STROM

That's the disgrace.

*President Bush at podium—giving speech*

### GEORGE W. BUSH

They died in a just cause for defending freedom
and they will not have died in vain.

### NARRATION

*Exterior: Washington, D.C.—Lila walking to White
House*

Lila had called to tell me that she was coming
down from Flint to Washington, D.C., to attend a

jobs conference. On her break, she said she was going to go and pay a visit to the White House.

*Lila is crying in front of the White House, she approaches a protester [Concepcion Picciotto] who has photos and a sign calling Bush a terrorist*

Bush killed children, Iraqi children, Iraqi children . . .

### LILA LIPSCOMB

My son killed . . .

### PROTESTER AT WHITE HOUSE

. . . killed my people in the Spain yesterday. His lies kill people, your children, too.

### LILA LIPSCOMB

Yes. My son.

### PROTESTER AT WHITE HOUSE

. . . business to do Iraq now. And they killing all these young Americans . . .

### LILA LIPSCOMB

Yes.

### PROTESTER AT WHITE HOUSE

. . . for what? For oil. Bush is a terrorist.

*Woman approaches and confronts Lila*

### WOMAN PASSERBY

No he isn't. This is all staged. This is all staged.

### PROTESTER

Yes, yes, he's the butcher of Iraq. He's the butcher of Iraq.

### LILA LIPSCOMB

*Turns angrily to the woman, gets in her face and says*

My son.

### WOMAN PASSERBY

Where was he killed?

### LILA LIPSCOMB

You tell me my son . . .

### WOMAN PASSERBY

Where was he killed?

### LILA LIPSCOMB

. . . is not a stage . . .

### WOMAN PASSERBY

Where was he killed?

### LILA LIPSCOMB

He was killed in Karbala. April 2. It's not a stage.
My son is dead.

### WOMAN PASSERBY

Well, a lot of other people, too.

Blame al Qaeda!

*Lila walks away upset*

### MICHAEL MOORE

What did that woman yell at you?

### LILA LIPSCOMB

*Lila is crying, and having trouble catching her breath*

That I'm supposed to blame the al Qaeda. The al
Qaeda didn't make a decision to send my son to
Iraq. Ignorance . . . that we deal with . . . with
everyday people. 'Cause they don't know. People
think they know, but you don't know. I thought I
knew, but I didn't know.

*Lila breaks down in tears*

I need my son.

God, it's tougher than I thought it was gonna be to be here, but it's freeing also, because I finally have a place to put all my pain and all my anger and to release it.

### NARRATION

*Michael Moore and Corporal Henderson walking on Capitol Hill*

I guess I was tired of seeing people like Lila Lipscomb suffer. Especially when, out of the 535 members of Congress, only one had an enlisted son in Iraq.

I asked Corporal Henderson of the United States Marine Corps to join me on Capitol Hill to see how many members of Congress we could convince to enlist *their* children to go to Iraq.

### MICHAEL MOORE

*Approaching John Tanner*

Congressman, I'm Michael Moore.

### CONGRESSMAN JOHN TANNER

Hey Michael, how you doin'?

### MICHAEL MOORE

Good, good, I'm good.

### CONGRESSMAN JOHN TANNER

Good.

### MICHAEL MOORE

Good.

### CONGRESSMAN JOHN TANNER

John Tanner.

### MICHAEL MOORE

Nice to meet you. Very nice to meet you.

### CONGRESSMAN JOHN TANNER

What are you all doing?

### MICHAEL MOORE

Well, I'm here with Corporal Henderson, United States Marine Corps.

### CONGRESSMAN JOHN TANNER

Well, Corporal, I was in the Navy years ago, 1968 to '72. We had marines guarding the base.

### MICHAEL MOORE

You have kids?

### CONGRESSMAN JOHN TANNER

Yeah.

### MICHAEL MOORE

Any way we can get them to enlist? And go over there and help out with the effort? We got all the brochures . . .

### CONGRESSMAN JOHN TANNER

One of 'em's got two children . . .

### MICHAEL MOORE

Oh yeah, well, see, there's not that many Congressmen that've got kids over there . . . and in fact, only one. You know, so we just thought maybe they, you know, you guys should send your kids there first you know. What do you think about that idea?

### CONGRESSMAN JOHN TANNER

*At the same time as Moore*

I know, I know, I know.

### CONGRESSMAN JOHN TANNER

I don't disagree with it.

### MICHAEL MOORE

Oh, you don't, oh good, well, here, take some
brochures then, at least take a marine brochure . . .
and pass it around. Encourage fellow members,
you know, if they're for the war, to get behind it,
you know. And send their own.

### CONGRESSMAN JOHN TANNER

Thank you, Mike.

### MICHAEL MOORE

Thank you, sir, thank you very much.

### MICHAEL MOORE

*Approaching another Congressman*

Congressman? I'm Michael Moore.

### CONGRESSMAN

What do you need?

### MICHAEL MOORE

I'm trying to get members of Congress to get
their kids to enlist in the army and go over to
Iraq. (*Congressman looks dumbfounded at
Michael Moore*)

Congressman? Congressman? (*chasing down
other congressman*)

Congressman Castle? Congressman Castle?

Congressman? Congressman? Congressman
Doolittle, Michael Moore . . .

### CONGRESSMAN DOOLITTLE

Uhhhh . . .

### MICHAEL MOORE

I'm wondering if, uh . . . uh, is there any way to . . .

### NARRATION

Of course, not a single member of Congress
wanted to sacrifice their child for the war in Iraq,
and who could blame them? Who would want to
give up their child? Would you? Would he? (*shot
of White House and Bush with kids*) I've always
been amazed that the very people forced to live in
the worst parts of town, go to the worst schools,
and who have it the hardest (*inner-city shots,
poverty*), are always the first to step up to defend
that very system. They serve so that we don't have
to. (*Americans enlisting*) They offer to give up
their lives so that we can be free. It is, remarkably,
their gift to us. And all they ask for in return is that
we never send them into harm's way unless it's
absolutely necessary. (*soldiers in Iraq—smiling
and hopeful*) Will they ever trust us again?

*Various news clips*

### GEORGE W. BUSH

He had used weapons.

### DONALD RUMSFELD

We know where they are, they're in the area around Tikrit, and Baghdad, and . . . and east, west, south, and north.

### CONDOLEEZZA RICE

There is a tie between Iraq and what happened on 9/11.

### DICK CHENEY

The struggle can only end with their complete and permanent destruction.

### GEORGE W. BUSH

We waged a war to save a civilization itself. We did not seek it, but we will fight it, and we will prevail.

*Shots of leaders exiting frame after soundbites, fund-raisers, juxtaposition between rich elite who control the war and working class who die in it*

### NARRATION

George Orwell once wrote that it's not a matter of whether the war is not real or if it is. Victory is not possible. The war is not meant to be won, it is meant to be continuous. A hierarchical society is only possible on the basis of poverty and ignorance. This new version is the past and no different past can ever have existed. In principle, the war effort is always planned to keep society on the brink of starvation. The war is waged by the ruling group against its own subjects and its object is not the victory over either Eurasia or East Asia, but to keep the very structure of society intact.

### GEORGE W. BUSH

*At podium—stumbling with words*

There's an old saying in Tennessee, I know it's in Texas, probably in Tennessee, that says: Fool me once, shame on . . . shame on you . . . Fool me, you can't get fooled again.

### NARRATION

For once, we agreed.

## CREDITS

# PART II

---

# *Fahrenheit 9/11—* The Backup and Evidence

# November 2, 2000, to September 11, 2001: How Did We Ever End Up Here?

**FOX was the first network to call Florida for Bush. Before that, some other networks had called Florida for Gore, and they changed after FOX called it for Bush.**

SOURCE: "With information provided from the Voter News Service, NBC was the first network to project Gore the winner in Florida at 7:48 PM. At 7:50 PM, CNN and CBS project Gore the winner in Florida as well." By 8:02 PM, all five networks and the Associated Press had called Gore the winner in Florida. Even the VNS called Gore the winner at 7:52 PM. At 2:16 AM, FOX calls Florida for Bush, NBC follows at 2:16 AM. ABC is the last network to call Florida for Bush, at 2:20 AM, while AP and VNS never call Florida for Bush. CNN: http://www.cnn.com/2001/ALLPOLITICS/stories/02/02/cnn.report/cnn.pdf.

SOURCE: Ten minutes after the top of the hour, network excitement was again beginning to build. At 2:16 AM, the call was made: FOX News Channel, with Bush's first cousin John Ellis running its election desk, was the first to project Florida—and the presidency—for the Texas governor. Within minutes, the other networks followed suit. "George Bush, Governor of Texas, will become the 43rd President of the United States," CNN's Bernard Shaw announced atop a graphic montage of a smiling Bush. "At 18 minutes past two o'clock Eastern time, CNN declares that George Walker Bush has won Florida's 25 electoral votes and this should put him over the top." PBS: http://www.pbs.org/newshour/media/election2000/election_night.html.

**The man who was in charge of the decision desk at FOX on election night was Bush's first cousin, John Ellis.**

SOURCE: "John Ellis, a first cousin of George W. Bush, ran the network's 'decision desk' during the 2000 election, and FOX was the first to name Bush the winner. Earlier, Ellis had made six phone calls to Cousin Bush during the vote-counting." William O'Rourke, "Talk Radio Key to GOP Victory," *Chicago Sun-Times*, December 3, 2002.

SOURCE: A FOX News consultant, John Ellis, who made judgments about presidential "calls" on Election Night admits he was in touch with George W. Bush and Florida governor Jeb Bush by telephone several times during the night, but denies breaking any rules. CNN, November 14, 2000; http://www.cbsnews.com/stories/2000/11/14/politics/main249357.shtml.

SOURCE: John Ellis, the FOX consultant who called Florida early for George Bush, had to stop writing about the campaign for the *Boston Globe* because of family "loyalty" to Bush. *CBS News,* http://www.cbsnews.com/stories/2000/11/14/politics/main249357.shtml, November 14, 2000.

**"Make sure the chairman of your campaign is also the vote countin' woman and that her state has hired a company that's gonna knock voters off the rolls who aren't likely to vote for you. You can usually tell them by the color of their skin."**

SOURCE: "The vote total was certified by Florida's secretary of state, Katherine Harris, head of the Bush campaign in Florida, on behalf of Gov. Jeb Bush, the candidate's brother." Mark Zoller Seitz, "Bush Team Conveyed an Air of Legitimacy," *San Diego Union-Tribune,* December 16, 2000.

SOURCE: The Florida Department of State awarded a $4 million contract to the Boca Raton–based Database Technologies Inc. (subsidiary of ChoicePoint). They were tasked with finding improperly registered voters in the state's database, but mistakes were rampant. "At one point, the list included as felons 8,000 former Texas residents who had been convicted of misdemeanors." *St. Petersburg Times* (Florida), December 21, 2003.

SOURCE: Database Technologies, a subsidiary of ChoicePoint, "was responsible for bungling an overhaul of Florida's voter registration records, with the result that thousands of people, disproportionately black, were disenfranchised in the 2000 election. Had they been able to vote, they might have swung the state, and thus the presidency, for Al Gore, who lost in Florida." Oliver Burkeman, Jo Tuckman, "Firm in Florida Election Fiasco

Earns Millions from Files on Foreigners," *The Guardian*, May 5, 2003. http://www.guardian.co.uk/usa/story/0,12271, 949709,00.html. See also, *Atlanta Journal-Constitution*, May 28, 2001.

SOURCE: In 1997, Rick Rozar, the late head of the company bought by ChoicePoint, donated $100,000 to the Republican National Committee. Melanie Eversley, "Atlanta-Based Company Says Errors in Felon Purge Not Its Fault," *Atlanta Journal-Constitution*, May 28, 2001.

SOURCE: Frank Borman of Database Technologies Inc. has donated extensively to New Mexico Republicans, as well as to the presidential campaign of George W. Bush. Opensecrets.org, "Frank Borman."

**If there were a statewide recount, under *every* scenario, Gore would have won the election.**

SOURCE: "[A] consortium [Tribune Co., owner of the *Times;* Associated Press; CNN; the *New York Times;* the *Palm Beach Post;* the *St. Petersburg Times;* the *Wall Street Journal;* and the *Washington Post*] hired the NORC [National Opinion Research Center, a nonpartisan research organization affiliated with the University of Chicago] to view each untallied ballot and gather information about how it was marked. The media organizations then used computers to sort and tabulate votes, based on varying scenarios that had been raised during the post-election scramble in Florida. Under any standard that tabulated all disputed votes statewide, Mr. Gore erased Mr. Bush's advantage and emerged with a tiny lead that ranged from 42 to 171 votes." Donald Lambro, "Recount Provides No Firm Answers," *Washington Times*, November 12, 2001.

SOURCE: "The review found that the result would have been different if every canvassing board in every county had examined every undervote, a situation that no election or court authority had ordered. Gore had called for such a statewide manual recount if Bush would agree, but Bush rejected the idea and there was no mechanism in place to conduct one." Martin Merzer, "Review of Ballots Finds Bush's Win Would Have Endured Manual Recount," *Miami Herald,* April 4, 2001.

SOURCE: See also, the following article by one of the *Washington Post* journalists who ran the consortium recount. The relevant point is made in Table I of the article. http://www.aei.org/docLib/20040526_KeatingPaper.pdf.

**Congressional Black Caucus members tried to object to the election outcome on the floor of the House; no Senator would sign the objections.**

SOURCE: "While Vice President Al Gore appeared to have accepted his fate contained in two wooden ballot boxes, Democratic members of the Congressional Black Caucus tried repeatedly to challenge the assignment of Florida's 25 electoral votes to Bush. . . . More than a dozen Democrats followed suit, seeking to force a debate on the validity of Florida's vote on the grounds that all votes may not have been counted and that some voters were wrongly denied the right to vote." Susan Milligan, "It's Really Over: Gore Bows Out Gracefully," *Boston Globe,* January 7, 2001.

SOURCE: The Congressional Black Caucus effort failed for "lack of the necessary signature by any senator." Senate Minority Leader Tom Daschle (D-SD) had previously advised Democratic senators not to cooperate. "They did not." Robert Novak, "Sweeney Link Won't Help Chaos," *Chicago Sun-Times*, January 14, 2001.

**"On the day George W. Bush was inaugurated, tens of thousands of Americans poured into the streets of D.C. . . . They pelted Bush's limo with eggs."**

SOURCE: "Shouting slogans like 'Hail to the Thief' and 'Selected, Not Elected,' tens of thousands of protesters descended on George W. Bush's inaugural parade route yesterday to proclaim that he and Vice President Dick Cheney had 'stolen' the election." Michael Kranish and Sue Kirchhoff, "Thousands Protest 'Stolen' Election," *Boston Globe*, January 21, 2001.

SOURCE: "Scuffles erupted between radicals and riot police while an egg struck the bullet-proof presidential limousine as it carried Mr. Bush and wife Laura to the White House." Damon Johnston, "Bush Pledges Justice as Critics Throw Eggs," *The Advertisers*, January 22, 2001.

See also film footage.

**The inauguration parade was brought to a halt and the traditional walk to the White House was scrapped.**

SOURCE: Bush made one concession to the weather—or to security concerns: he stayed in his limousine nearly the entire length of the mile-long inaugural parade, waving through a slightly foggy window. He got out to walk only for a brief distance when his motorcade reached the VIP grandstands in front of the Treasury Department and the White House. Doyle McManus, et al., "Bush Vows to Bring Nation Together," *Los Angeles Times*, January 21, 2001.

SOURCE: Bush's limo, which traveled most of the route at a slow walking pace, stopped dead just before it reached the corner of 14th Street and Pennsylvania Avenue, where most of the protesters had congregated. Then it sped up dramatically, and Secret Service agents protecting the car on foot had to follow at a full run. When they reached a section of the parade route where the sidewalks were restricted to official ticketholders, Bush and his wife, Laura, who wore a flattering electric turquoise suit, got out of the limo to walk and greet supporters. Helen Kennedy, "Bush Pledges a United US," New York *Daily News*, January 21, 2001.

## "[F]or the next eight months, it didn't get any better for George W. Bush."

SOURCE: In a poll conducted September 5 to September 9, 2001, *Investor's Business Daily* and the *Christian Science Monitor* showed President Bush's approval rating at 45 percent, down from 52 percent in May (*Investor's Business Daily/Christian Science Monitor* Poll, conducted by TIPP, 9/5 to 9/9, 2001). Zogby's polling had Bush at 47 percent in late July 2001, down from 57 percent in February (Zogby, 7/26 to 7/29, 2001).

SOURCE: In June 2001, a *Wall Street Journal/NBC News* poll showed President Bush's approval rating at 50 percent, which was the lowest presidential approval rating in five years. Richard L. Berke, "G.O.P. Defends Bush in Face of Dip in Poll Ratings," *New York Times*, June 29, 2001.

SOURCE: On July 26, 2001, in an article entitled "Bush Lacks the Ability to Force Action on Hill," Dana Milbank of the *Washington Post* wrote, "It may be premature to conclude that Bush has lost control of his agenda, but lawmakers and strategists in both parties said that Bush's next year is much more likely to look like the fractious month of July than like the orderly march toward Bush's tax cut this spring. . . . The troubles began, of course, with Vermont Sen. James M. Jeffords' departure from the GOP, giving control of the Senate to the Democrats. But the problems are nearly as bad in the House, where moderates who supported Bush's tax cut are proving recalcitrant on other issues. They rebelled against GOP leaders on campaign finance reform and held up Bush's "faith-based" legislation over concerns about discrimination. Next week, they're likely to oppose Bush's proposal to drill in the Arctic National Wildlife Refuge."

SOURCE: California's energy crisis also took a toll on Bush's approval ratings. Due to rolling blackouts and rising utility bills, Bush's ratings took a toll among Californians. The poll showed that almost as many Californians disapproved of the President's job as approved of it with an approve/disapprove of 42/40. "Calif. Governor Says He'll Sue to Force Government Action," *Houston Chronicle,* May 30, 2001.

**"In his first eight months in office before September 11, George W. Bush was on vacation, according to the *Washington Post,* forty-two percent of the time."**

SOURCE: "News coverage has pointedly stressed that W.'s month-long stay at his ranch in Crawford is the longest presidential vacation in 32 years. *Washington Post* supercomputers calculated that if you add up all his week-ends at Camp David, layovers at Kennebunkport, and assorted to-ing and fro-ing, W. will have spent 42 percent of his presidency 'at vacation spots or en route.'" Charles Krauthammer, "A Vacation Bush Deserves," *Washington Post*, August 10, 2001.

## Bush relaxes at Camp David, Kennebunkport, and his ranch in Crawford, Texas.

SOURCE: As of April 2004, President Bush had made 33 trips to Crawford during his presidency, bringing his total to more than 230 days at the ranch in just over three years. "Add his 78 trips to Camp David and five to his family's compound at Kennebunkport, Maine, and Bush has spent all or part of 500 days—or about 40 percent of his presidency—at one of these his three retreats." "Bush Retreats to a Favorite Getaway: Crawford Ranch," *Houston Chronicle*, April 11, 2004.

## On September 10, 2001, Bush joined his brother in Florida where he slept the night in "a bed made with fine French linens."

SOURCE: Bush has not been bashful about visiting Florida, ground zero in the vote-recount battle that followed the 2000 election. On this trip, he was spending a good deal of time with his brother, Governor Jeb Bush. "President to Push Congress on Education in Fourth Florida Visit," Associated Press, September 10, 2001; see also, CNN Inside Politics, September 10, 2001.

SOURCE: Two individuals prepared the president's room "and made the bed with some of the family's fine French linens." Tom Bayles, "The Day Before Everything

Changed, President Bush Touched Locals' Lives,"
*Sarasota Herald-Tribune,* September 10, 2002.

**"As the attack took place, Mr. Bush was on his way to
an elementary school in Florida. When informed of
the first plane hitting the World Trade Center, where
terrorists had struck just eight years prior, Mr. Bush
decided to go ahead with his photo opportunity."**

*Note:* It should be emphasized that at the time Bush was
notified of the first plane attack, he (unlike the rest of
America) was already aware that Osama bin Laden was
planning to attack America by hijacking airplanes, per the
August 6, 2001, Presidential Daily Brief (PDB). He was
also aware, of course, that the World Trade Center had
been historically a target for terrorist attacks. He nonetheless went ahead with this photo opportunity in a school full
of children.

SOURCE: "Mr. Bush arrived at the school, just before 9
AM, expecting to be met by its motherly principal, Gwen
Rigell. Instead he was pulled sharply aside by the familiar,
bulky figure of 51-year-old Karl Rove, a veteran political
fixer and trusted aide of both Mr. Bush and his father,
George Sr. Mr. Rove, a fellow Texan with an expansive
manner and a colorful turn of phrase, told the President
that a large commercial airliner (American Flight 11) had
crashed into the North Tower of the World Trade Center.
Mr. Bush clenched his teeth, lowered his bottom lip and
said something inaudible. Then he went into the school."
William Langley, "Revealed: What Really Went on During
Bush's 'Missing Hours,'" *The Telegraph,* December 16,
2001.

SOURCE: "The airborne attack on the World Trade Center was at least the second terrorist attempt to topple the landmarks. In 1993, terrorists sought to bomb one building so that it would explode and fall into the other. The plot did not succeed, but six people were killed and more than 1,000 injured." Cragg Hines, "Terrorists Strike from Air; Jetliners Slam into Pentagon, Trade Center," *Houston Chronicle*, September 11, 2001.

SOURCE: August 6, 2001, Presidential Daily Brief (PDB), "Bin Ladin Determined to Strike Inside US": "Al-Qa'ida members—including some who are US citizens—have resided in or traveled to the US for years, and the group apparently maintains a support structure that could aid attacks. . . . FBI information since that time indicates patterns of suspicious activity in this country consistent with preparations for hijackings or other types of attacks, including recent surveillance of federal buildings in New York." August 6, 2001, "Bin Ladin Determined to Strike Inside US," http://www.cnn.com/2004/images/04/10/white house.pdf.

**"When the second plane hit the tower, his chief of staff entered the classroom and told Mr. Bush, 'The nation is under attack.' "**

SOURCE: "At 9:05 AM, the White House chief of staff, Andrew H. Card Jr., stepped into the classroom and whispered into the president's right ear, 'A second plane hit the other tower, and America's under attack.' " David E. Sanger and Don Van Natta Jr., "After The Attacks: The Events; In Four Days, A National Crisis Changes Bush's Presidency," *New York Times*, September 16, 2001.

## "Mr. Bush just sat there and continued to read *My Pet Goat.*"

SOURCE: "It was while attending a second-grade reading class at Emma E. Booker Elementary School in Sarasota, Fla., to promote his education reforms that President Bush learned America was under attack. In the presence of her VIP guest, teacher Sandra Kay Daniels, 45, conducted the day's lesson, which centered on a story about a pet goat." "9/11: A Year After," *Los Angeles Times*, September 11, 2002.

SOURCE: President Bush listened to eighteen Booker Elementary School second-graders read a story about a girl's pet goat Tuesday before he spoke briefly and somberly about the terrorist attacks. "Bush Hears of Attack While Visiting Booker," *Sarasota Herald-Tribune*, September 12, 2001.

See also film footage.

## "Nearly seven minutes passed with nobody doing anything."

SOURCE: "[H]e lingered in the room for another six minutes [after being informed of the second plane]. . . . [At] 9:12, he abruptly retreated, speaking to Mr. Cheney and New York officials." David E. Sanger and Don Van Natta Jr., "After The Attacks: The Events; In Four Days, A National Crisis Changes Bush's Presidency," *New York Times*, September 16, 2001.

SOURCE: "Mr. Bush remained in the elementary school for nearly a half an hour after Andy Card whispered in his ear." Michael Kranish, "Bush: US to Hunt Down Attackers," *Boston Globe*, September 11, 2001.

# George W. Bush Lets Osama—and Lots of Others—Get Away

**"Should he have held at least one meeting since taking office to discuss the threat of terrorism with his head of counterterrorism?"**

SOURCE: "[T]hey didn't allow me to brief him on terrorism. You know, they're saying now that when I was afforded the opportunity to talk to him about cybersecurity, it was my choice. I could have talked about terrorism or cybersecurity. That's not true. I asked in January to brief him, the president, on terrorism, to give him the same briefing I had given Vice President Cheney, Colin Powell, and Condi Rice. And I was told, 'You can't do that briefing, Dick, until after the policy development process.'" Richard Clarke interview with Tim Russert on NBC's *Meet the Press,* March 28, 2004.

SOURCE: "Clarke asked on several occasions for early Principals Committee meetings on these issues [outlined in his January 25, 2001, memo] and was frustrated that no early meeting was scheduled. He wanted principals to accept that al Qaeda was a 'first order threat' and not a routine problem being exaggerated by 'chicken little' alarmists. No Principals Committee meetings on al Qaeda were held until September 4, 2001." National Commission on Terrorist Attacks Upon the United States, Threats and

Responses in 2001, Staff Statement No. 8, "National Policy Coordination," pp. 9–10; http://www.9-11commission.gov/ hearings/hearing8/staff_statement_8.pdf.

SOURCE: See Testimony of Richard A. Clarke before the National Commission on Terrorist Attacks Upon the United States, March 24, 2004:

MR. ROEMER: Okay. Let's move into, with my 15 minutes, let's move into the Bush administration. On January the 25th, we've seen a memo that you had written to Dr. Rice, urgently asking for a principals review of al Qaeda. You include helping the Northern Alliance, covert aid, significant new '02 budget authority to help fight al Qaeda—

MR. CLARKE: Uh-huh.

MR. ROEMER: —and response to the U.S.S. *Cole*. You attached to this document both the Delenda Plan of 1998 and a strategy paper from December 2000. Did you get a response to this urgent request for a principals meeting on these, and how does this affect your time frame for dealing with these important issues?

MR. CLARKE: I did get a response. The response was that in the Bush administration I should, and my committee, the counter-terrorism security group, should report to the deputies committee, which is a subcabinet level committee, and not to the principals, and that therefore it was inappropriate for me to be asking for a principals meeting. Instead, there would be a deputies meeting.

MR. ROEMER: So, does this slow the process down to go to the deputies rather than to the principals or a small group, as you had previously done?

MR. CLARKE: It slowed it down enormously, by

months. First of all, the deputies committee didn't meet urgently in January or February. Then, when the deputies committee did meet, it took the issue of al Qaeda as part of a cluster of policy issues, including nuclear proliferation in South Asia, democratization in Pakistan, how to treat the problems, the various problems, including narcotics and other problems in Afghanistan, and launched on a series of deputies meetings extending over several months to address al Qaeda in the context of all of those interrelated issues. That process probably ended, I think, in July of 2001, so we were readying for a principals meeting in July, but the principals' calendar was full, and then they went on vacation, many of them, in August, so we couldn't meet in August, and therefore the principals met in September.

## "Or maybe Mr. Bush was wondering why he had cut terrorism funding from the FBI."

SOURCE: "This question of resources will also come up in the commission's questioning of Attorney General John Ashcroft, who was brand new on the job in the fall of 2001 and on September 10 cut the FBI's request for new counterterrorism money by 12 percent." John Dimsdale, "Former FBI Director Louis Freeh and Attorney General John Ashcroft to appear before 9/11 commission tomorrow," NPR Radio: Marketplace, April 12, 2004. See also, 2001 budget documents including Attorney General John Ashcroft FY 2003 budget request to Office of Management and Budget, September 10, 2001, showing $65 million offset in the FBI budget for counter-terrorism equipment grants: http://www.americanprogress.org/atf/cf/%7BE9245FE4-9A2B-43C7-A521-5D6FF2E06E03%7D/FY03ASHCROFT.pdf.

**The security briefing that was given to him on August 6, 2001, said that Osama bin Laden was planning to attack America by hijacking airplanes.**

SOURCE: August 6, 2001, Presidential Daily Brief (PDB): "Al-Qa'ida members—including some who are US citizens—have resided in or traveled to the US for years, and the group apparently maintains a support structure that could aid attacks. Two al-Qa'ida members found guilty in the conspiracy to bomb our Embassies in East Africa were US citizens, and a senior EIJ member lived in California in the mid-1990s. A clandestine source said in 1998 that a Bin Ladin cell in New York was recruiting Muslim-American youth for attacks. We have not been able to corroborate some of the more sensational threat reporting, such as that from a . . . [redacted portion] . . . service in 1998 saying that Bin Ladin wanted to hijack a US aircraft to gain the release of 'Blind Shaykh' 'Umar 'Abd al-Rahman and other US-held extremists. Nevertheless, FBI information since that time indicates patterns of suspicious activity in this country consistent with preparations for hijackings or other types of attacks, including recent surveillance of federal buildings in New York." August 6, 2001, "Bin Ladin Determined to Strike Inside US," http://www.cnn.com/2004/images/04/10/whitehouse.pdf.

SOURCE: "The Aug. 6, 2001, document, known as the President's Daily Brief, has been the focus of intense scrutiny because it reported that bin Laden advocated airplane hijackings, that al-Qaida supporters were in the United States and that the group was planning attacks here." Clarke J. Scott, "Clarke Gave Warning on Sept. 4,

2001; Testimony Includes Apology to Families of Sept. 11 Victims," Associated Press, March 25, 2004.

## On August 6, 2001, George W. Bush went fishing.

SOURCE: "President Bush swung into vacation mode Monday, fishing for bass in his pond, strolling the canyons on his 1,600-acre ranch, taking an early-morning run." Associated Press, "President Bush Vacationing in Texas," August 6, 2001.

## "Was it the guy my daddy's friends delivered a lot of weapons to?"

SOURCE: In 1995, a member of Reagan's National Security Council and co-author of his National Security Directives, Howard Teicher, signed a sworn affidavit stating: "From early 1982 to 1987, I served as a Staff Member to the United States National Security Council. . . . In June 1982, President Reagan decided that the United States could not afford to allow Iraq to lose the war to Iran. President Reagan decided that the United States would do whatever was necessary and legal to prevent Iraq from losing the war with Iran. Pursuant to the secret NSDD, the United States actively supported the Iraqi war effort by supplying the Iraqis with billions of dollars of credits, by providing U.S. military intelligence and advice to the Iraqis, and by closely monitoring third-country arms sales to Iraq to make sure that Iraq had the military weaponry required.

"This message was delivered by Vice President Bush who communicated it to Egyptian President Mubarak, who in turn passed the message to Saddam Hussein. Under CIA Director Casey and Deputy Director Gates, the CIA made sure that non-U.S. manufacturers manufactured and sold to Iraq the weapons needed by Iraq. In certain instances where a key component in a weapon was not readily available, the highest levels of the United States government decided to make the component available, directly or indirectly, to Iraq. I specifically recall that the provision of anti-armor penetrators to Iraq was a case in point. The United States made a policy decision to supply penetrators to Iraq." Affidavit of former National Security Council official Howard Teicher, *United States of America* v. *Carlos Cardoen et al.*, January 31, 1995. http://www.information clearinghouse.info/article1413.htm.

SOURCE: "Questions have been raised about whether the United States not only ignored foreign arms shipments to Iraq, but actually encouraged or even arranged them. A former National Security Council official, Howard Teicher, said in a 1995 court affidavit that the CIA made sure Iraq received weapons from non-U.S. manufacturers." Ken Guggenheim, "War Crimes Trial for Saddam Could Reveal Details of Past U.S. Help," Associated Press, January 24, 2004.

SOURCE: "There is ample documentation demonstrating that the Reagan and Bush administrations supplied critical military technologies that were put directly to use in the construction of the Iraqi war machine. There is also strong evidence indicating that the executive branch's failure to crack down on illegal weapons traffickers or keep track of third party transfers of U.S. weaponry allowed a substantial flow of U.S.-origin military equipment and military components to make their way to Iraq." William D. Hartung, "Weapons at War; A World Policy Institute Issue

Brief," May 1995. See also, Alan Friedman, *Spider's Web: The Secret History of How the White House Illegally Armed Iraq* (Bantam Books, 1993); Kenneth R. Timmerman, *The Death Lobby: How the West Armed Iraq* (Houghton, Mifflin, 1991).

SOURCE: "Rep. Dante Fascell (D-Fla.), chairman of the House Foreign Affairs Committee, said . . . that the United States could not 'make a claim for purity' on arms sales, since the U.S. government has sold weapons to Iran, Iraq 'and everybody else in the world.'" Robert Shepard, "Congress Approves Aid for Former Soviet Republics," United Press International, October 3, 1992.

SOURCE: "A covert American program during the Reagan administration provided Iraq with critical battle planning assistance at a time when American intelligence agencies knew that Iraqi commanders would employ chemical weapons in waging the decisive battles of the Iran-Iraq war, according to senior military officers with direct knowledge of the program. Those officers, most of whom agreed to speak on the condition that they not be identified, spoke in response to a reporter's questions about the nature of gas warfare on both sides of the conflict between Iran and Iraq from 1981 to 1988. Iraq's use of gas in that conflict is repeatedly cited by President Bush and, this week, by his national security adviser, Condoleezza Rice, as justification for 'regime change' in Iraq. The covert program was carried out at a time when President Reagan's top aides, including Secretary of State George P. Shultz, Defense Secretary Frank C. Carlucci and Gen. Colin L. Powell, then the national security adviser, were publicly condemning Iraq for its use of poison gas, especially after Iraq attacked Kurds in Halabja in March 1988." Patrick E. Tyler, "Officers Say U.S. Aided Iraq in War Despite Use of Gas," *New York Times*, August 18, 2002.

### "Was it that group of religious fundamentalists who visited my state when I was governor?"

SOURCE: "A senior delegation from the Taleban movement in Afghanistan is in the United States for talks with an international energy company that wants to construct a gas pipeline from Turkmenistan across Afghanistan to Pakistan. A spokesman for the company, Unocal, said the Taleban were expected to spend several days at the company's headquarters in Sugarland, Texas." "Taleban in Texas for Talks on Gas Pipeline," BBC News, December 4, 1997. (Sugarland is twenty-two miles outside Houston.)

### "Or was it the Saudis? Damn, it was them."

SOURCE: "The 27 classified pages of a congressional report about Sept. 11 depict a Saudi government that not only provided significant money and aid to the suicide hijackers but also allowed potentially hundreds of millions of dollars to flow to Al Qaeda and other terrorist groups through suspect charities and other fronts, according to sources familiar with the document. One U.S. official who has read the classified section said it describes 'very direct, very specific links' between Saudi officials, two of the San Diego–based hijackers and other potential co-conspirators 'that cannot be passed off as rogue, isolated or coincidental.'" Of all the hijackers, fifteen of the nineteen were Saudi. Josh Meyer, "Report Links Saudi Government to

9/11 Hijackers, Sources Say," *Los Angeles Times*, August 2, 2003.

## "In the days following September 11, all commercial and private airline traffic was grounded."

SOURCE: "On the morning of September 11, there were 4,873 instrument flight rule (IFR) flights operating in U.S. airspace. As soon as Secretary Mineta was aware of the nature and scale of the terrorist attack on New York and Washington—that we were faced with, not one, but four possible hijackings, and several other rumors of missing or unidentified aircraft—the Secretary ordered the air traffic system shut down for all civil operations." Jane F. Garvey on Aviation Security Following the Terrorist Attack on September 11, September 21, 2001; http://www.faa.gov/newsroom/testimony/2001/testimony_010921.htm; see also, "Airports to Remain Closed, Mineta Says," Department of Transportation Press Release, September 12, 2001.

## "[T]he White House approved planes to pick up the bin Ladens and numerous other Saudis."

SOURCE: Fearing reprisals against Saudi nationals, the Saudi government asked for help in getting some of its citizens out of the country. National Commission on Terrorist Attacks Upon the United States, Threats and Responses in 2001, Staff Statement No. 10, The Saudi Flights, p. 12; http://www.911commission.gov/hearings/hearing10/staff_statement_10.pdf.

SOURCE: "Now, what I recall is that I asked for flight manifests of everyone on board and all of those names need to be directly and individually vetted by the FBI before they were allowed to leave the country. And I also wanted the FBI to sign off even on the concept of Saudis being allowed to leave the country. And as I recall, all of that was done. It is true that members of the Bin Laden family were among those who left. We knew that at the time. I can't say much more in open session, but it was a conscious decision with complete review at the highest levels of the State Department and the FBI and the White House." Testimony of Richard Clarke, Former Counterterrorism Chief, National Security Council, before the Senate Judiciary Committee, September 3, 2003.

SOURCE: "I was making or coordinating a lot of decisions on 9/11 and the days immediately after. And I would love to be able to tell you who did it, who brought this proposal to me, but I don't know. Since you pressed me, the two possibilities that are most likely are either the Department of State, or the White House Chief of Staff's Office. But I don't know." Testimony of Richard A. Clarke before the National Commission on Terrorist Attacks Upon the United States, March 24, 2004.

**"At least six private jets and nearly two dozen commercial planes carried the Saudis and the bin Ladens out of the U.S. after September 13. In all, 142 Saudis, including twenty-four members of the bin Laden family, were allowed to leave the country."**

*Note:* It should be noted that even though the film does not make the allegation, strong evidence has recently come to light that at least one private plane flew to pick up Saudi nationals while private flights were still grounded. Moreover, for nearly three years, the White House has denied that this flight existed. This was reported in the June 9, 2004, *St. Petersburg Times* article cited below.

SOURCE: After the airspace reopened, six chartered flights with 142 people, mostly Saudi Arabian nationals, departed from the United States between September 14 and 24. One flight, the so-called Bin Ladin flight, departed the United States on September 20 with 26 passengers, most of them relatives of Usama Bin Ladin. National Commission on Terrorist Attacks Upon the United States, Threats and Responses in 2001, Staff Statement No. 10, The Saudi Flights, p. 12; http://www.9-11commission.gov/hearings/hearing 10/staff_statement_10.pdf.

SOURCE: It should be noted that the U.S. Customs and Border Protection document released by the Department of Homeland Security under the FOIA, February 24, 2004, lists 162 Saudi nationals who flew out of the country between September 11 and September 15, 2001, departing from New York's Kennedy Airport, Washington's Dulles, and Dallas/Fort Worth. http://www.judicialwatch.org/archive/ 2004/ homelandsecurity.pdf.

SOURCE: For an official list of Saudi passport holders (names redacted) who flew out of the country between September 11 and September 15, 2001, see U.S. Customs and Border Protection document released by the Department of Homeland Security under the FOIA, February 24, 2004; http://www.judicialwatch.org/archive/ 2004/homelandsecurity.pdf.

SOURCE: The *St. Petersburg Times* reported on June 9, 2004: "Two days after the Sept. 11 attacks, with most of the nation's air traffic still grounded, a small jet landed at Tampa International Airport, picked up three young

Saudi men and left. The men, one of them thought to be a member of the Saudi royal family, were accompanied by a former FBI agent and a former Tampa police officer on the flight to Lexington, Ky. The Saudis then took another flight out of the country."

Moreover: "For nearly three years, White House, aviation and law enforcement officials have insisted the flight never took place and have denied published reports and widespread Internet speculation about its purpose. . . . The terrorism panel, better known as the 9/11 Commission, said in April that it knew of six chartered flights with 142 people aboard, mostly Saudis, that left the United States between Sept. 14 and 24, 2001. But it has said nothing about the Tampa flight. . . . The 9/11 Commission, which has said the flights out of the United States were handled appropriately by the FBI, appears concerned with the handling of the Tampa flight. . . .

"Most of the aircraft allowed to fly in U.S. airspace on Sept. 13 were empty airliners being ferried from the airports where they made quick landings on Sept. 11. The reopening of the airspace included paid charter flights, but not private, nonrevenue flights." Jean Heller, "TIA now verifies flight of Saudis; The government has long denied that two days after the 9/11 attacks, the three were allowed to fly." *St. Petersburg Times*, June 9, 2004.

**In 2001, one of Osama's sons got married in Afghanistan; several family members attended the wedding.**

SOURCE: "Bin Laden as well as his mother, two brothers and a sister, who flew from Saudi Arabia, attended the wedding of one of his sons, Mohammad, in the Afghan

city of Kandahar on Monday, the Arabic daily *Al-Hayat*
said. . . . Another of bin Laden's sons married one of
al-Masri's daughters in January. *Al-Hayat* said several
members of the bin Laden family, who run a major construction company in Saudi Arabia, also traveled from the
kingdom to attend the wedding. Agence France Presse,
"Bin Laden Full of Praise for Attack on USS *Cole* at Son's
Wedding," Thursday, March 1, 2001.

## "We held hundreds of people" immediately after 9/11.

SOURCE: "More than 1,200 foreigners have been
detained as part of the government's investigation into the
terror attacks, some spending months in prison. Some
civil liberties advocates have complained, but government
officials insist they are simply enforcing long-standing
immigration laws." "A Nation Challenged," *New York
Times*, November 25, 2001.

SOURCE: "The Department of Homeland Security
announced new rules yesterday designed to prevent a
recurrence of the lengthy detention of hundreds of foreign nationals, many of whom were prevented from making telephone calls or contacting lawyers for months after
they were jailed in the wake of the Sept. 11, 2001, attacks.
The guidelines, made public yesterday by Asa Hutchin-
son, the department's undersecretary for border and
transportation security, were welcomed by civil rights
groups that had bitterly denounced the detention of 762
immigration violators after the attacks, based on sometimes ill-founded FBI suspicions that they had links to
terrorism. The new rules are a response to a highly critical
198-page report last June by Glenn A. Fine, the Justice

Department's inspector general. It concluded that in the chaotic aftermath of the terrorist strikes on the World Trade Center and the Pentagon, hundreds of Arab and South Asian men who had committed sometimes minor immigration violations languished in jail without timely review by U.S. officials. Guards mistreated some of them. The average detention lasted three months, and the longest was 10 months before the immigrants were cleared of terrorism ties and released from jail." John Mintz, "New Rules Shorten Holding Time for Detained Immigrants," *Washington Post*, April 14, 2004.

SOURCE: "In the days, weeks and months following the tragic events of September 11, 2001, hundreds of American immigrants were rounded up and detained, often under harsh or abusive conditions, in the name of keeping America safe. Not because of evidence (or even sound hunches) that they were involved in the terrorist attacks that brutally ended the lives of more than 3,100 people. Not because they were found to have ties to—or even knowledge of—terrorist groups who might threaten American security in the future. Instead, hundreds of immigrants were arbitrarily snared in this dragnet, marked for arrest and thrown (literally, at times) in jail. The exact number is unknown, because the government refuses to release that information. They had one thing in common: Almost all were Arab or South Asian men, and almost all were Muslim. . . . Once arrested, many immigrants were labeled 'of interest' to the September 11 investigation and thrown into legal limbo—detained for weeks or months in connection with a criminal investigation, but denied the due process rights that they would have been entitled to had they actually been charged with crimes." ACLU, "America's Disappeared: Seeking International Justice for Immigrants Detained after September 11," January 2004, aclu.org.

## The FBI conducted "a little interview, check[ed] the passport."

SOURCE: Last year, the *National Review* reported that the FBI conducted brief, day-of-departure interviews with the Saudis—in the words of an FBI spokesman, "at the airport, as they were about to leave." Experts interviewed by the *National Review* called the FBI's actions "highly unusual" given the fact that those departing were actually members of Osama bin Laden's family. "They [the FBI] could not have done a thorough and complete interview," said John L. Martin, the former head of internal security at the Justice Department. "The Great Escape: How did assorted bin Ladens get out of America after September 11?" *National Review,* September 29, 2003.

SOURCE: "Thirty of the 142 people on these flights were interviewed by the FBI, including 22 of the 26 people (23 passengers and 3 private security guards) on the Bin Ladin flight. Many were asked detailed questions. None of the passengers stated that they had any recent contact with Usama Bin Ladin or knew anything about terrorist activity." National Commission on Terrorist Attacks Upon the United States, Threats and Responses in 2001, Staff Statement No. 10, The Saudi Flights, p. 12; http://www.9-11commission. gov/hearings/hearing10/staff_ statement_10.pdf.

SOURCE: "I talked to several people who were with the FBI during the actual repatriation. And they told me there was a lot of back-and-forth between the FBI and the Saudi Embassy. And the Saudi Embassy tried to get people to leave without even identifying them. The FBI succeeded in identifying people and going through their passports. But, in many cases, you had the FBI meeting people for the first time on the tarmac or on the planes themselves as they were departing. That was not time for a serious interview or a serious interrogation." Interview with Craig Unger, CNN, September 4, 2003.

# George W. Bush and His Early Friends in Texas

**White House released records in response to Moore's charge of deserter.**

SOURCE: Left-leaning filmmaker Michael Moore got the discussion started in January, when he endorsed Clark for president and called the President a "deserter." The White House responded by releasing the President's service records, including an honorable discharge. James Rainey, "Who's the Man? They Are; George Bush and John Kerry Stand Shoulder to Shoulder in One Respect: Macho is Good. Very Good. It's Been That Way Since Jefferson's Day," *Los Angeles Times*, March 18, 2004.

"[T]here is one glaring difference between the records released in 2000 and those he released in 2004. A name had been blacked out. In 1972, two airmen were suspended for failing to take their medical examination. One was George W. Bush and the other was James R. Bath."

SOURCE: See National Guard Bureau, Aeronautical Orders Number 87, September 29, 1972: http://www.michaelmoore.com/warroom/f911notes/index.php?id=18.

"James R. Bath was the Texas money manager for the bin Ladens."

SOURCE: See Notarized Trust Agreement, Harris County, Texas, signed by Salem M. Binladen, July 8, 1976 (original document), Attachment C ("I, Salem M. Binladen, do hereby vest unto James Reynolds Bath, 2330 Belle-fontaine, Houston, Texas, full and absolute authority to act on my behalf in all matters relating to the business and operation of Binladen-Houston offices in Houston, Texas.") Notarized Trust Agreement, Harris County, Texas, July 8, 1976.

SOURCE: "According to a 1976 trust agreement, drawn shortly after [George H. W.] Bush was appointed director of the Central Intelligence Agency, Saudi Sheik Salem M. Binladen appointed Bath as his business representative in Houston. Binladen, along with his brothers, owns Binladen Brothers Construction, one of the largest construction companies in the Middle East." Jerry Urban, "Feds Investigate Entrepreneur Allegedly Tied to Saudis," *Houston Chronicle,* June 4, 1992.

**George W. Bush and James R. Bath had become good friends.**

SOURCE: "Bath, 55, acknowledges a friendship with George W. Bush that stems from their service together in the Texas Air National Guard." Jonathan Beaty, "A Mysterious Mover of Money and Planes," *Time*, October 28, 1991.

SOURCE: "In a copy of the record released by the National Guard in 2000, the man in question, James R. Bath, was listed as being suspended from flying for the National Guard in 1972 for failing to take a medical exam next to a similar listing for Mr. Bush. It has been widely reported that the two were friends and that Mr. Bath invested in Mr. Bush's first major business venture, Arbusto Energy, in the late 1970s after Mr. Bath began working for Salem bin Laden." Jim Rutenberg, "A Film to Polarize Along Party Lines," *New York Times*, May 17, 2004.

**"After they were discharged, when Bush's dad was head of the CIA, Bath opened up his own aviation business, after selling a plane to a man by the name of Salem bin Laden, heir to the second largest fortune in Saudi Arabia, the Saudi bin Laden Group."**

SOURCE: "Bath opened his own aircraft brokerage firm in 1976." Jonathan Beaty, "A Mysterious Mover of Money and Planes," *Time*, October 28, 1991. (Bush was CIA director, 1976 to 1977.)

SOURCE: "Sometime around 1974 . . . Bath was trying to sell a F-27 turboprop, a sluggish medium-range plane that was not exactly a hot ticket in those days, when he received a phone call that changed his life. The voice on the other end belonged to Salem bin Laden. . . . Bath not only had a buyer for a plane no one else seemed to want, he had also stumbled upon a source of wealth and power that was certain to pique the interest of even the brashest Texas oil baron." Craig Unger, *House of Bush, House of Saud* (Scribner, 2004), pp. 19–20.

**George W. Bush "founded an oil company, a drilling company, out in west Texas called Arbusto, which was very, very good at drilling dry holes."**

SOURCE: "After graduating from the Harvard Business School, Bush organized his first company, Arbusto Energy (Arbusto is Spanish for Bush), in 1977 on the eve of a run for Congress. According to records on file with the Securities and Exchange Commission, Arbusto didn't start active operations until March 1979. . . . According to 1984 securities filings, Bush's limited partners had invested $4.66 million in Bush's various drilling programs but they had received cash distributions of only $1.54 million. However, Bush's CFO stated, 'We didn't find much oil and gas,' adding 'We weren't raising any money.'" George Lardner Jr. and Lois Romano, "Bush Name Helps Fuel Oil Dealings," *Washington Post,* July 30, 1999.

SOURCE: "Bush eventually renamed his company Bush Exploration and later merged with a firm called Spectrum 7. Documents filed with the Securities and Exchange Commission show that the firm lost money from 1979 to 1982 and that investors who put in nearly $4.7 million got back just $1.5 million. Published reports contend that Bush Exploration was salvaged by Cincinnati oilmen Bill

DeWitt and Mercer Reynolds. Bush today says otherwise, that his company was on firm financial footing and that the merger was a strategic one. Either way, George W. drilled his fair share of dry holes. As Conaway rues to this day, the company 'never hit . . . the Big Kahuna.' " Maria La Ganga, "Bush Finesses Texas 2-Step of Privilege, Personality," *Los Angeles Times,* March 2, 2000.

**"There is no indication that daddy wrote a check to start him [Bush] off in his company."**

SOURCE: "Seed money, upward of $4 million, was largely raised between 1979 and 1982 with the help of [Bush's] uncle, financier Jonathan Bush. The Arbusto investor list is filled with family and famous friends. His grandmother, Dorothy W. Bush, chipped in $25,000. Corporate luminaries like George L. Ball, chief executive of Prudential-Bache Securities, invested $100,000. Macomber and William H. Draper III, who invested more than $125,000, were later named presidents of the U.S. Export-Import Bank during the Reagan and Bush administrations." Maria La Ganga, "Bush Finesses Texas 2-Step of Privilege, Personality," *Los Angeles Times,* March 2, 2000.

**"Bush's good friend James Bath was hired by the bin Laden family to manage their money in Texas and invest in businesses. And James Bath himself, in turn, invested in George W. Bush."**

SOURCE: See Notarized Trust Agreement, Harris County, Texas, signed by Salem M. Binladen, July 8, 1976: "I, Salem M. Binladen, do hereby vest unto James Reynolds Bath, 2330 Bellefontaine, Houston, Texas, full and absolute authority to act on my behalf in all matters relating to the business and operation of Binladen-Houston offices in Houston, Texas." Notarized Trust Agreement, Harris County, Texas, July 8, 1976.

SOURCE: Bath's business relationship with Salem bin Laden, and other wealthy Saudi businessmen, has been well documented. See, e.g., Mike Ward, "Bin Laden Relatives Have Ties to Texas," *Austin American-Statesman*, November 9, 2001; Jerry Urban, "Feds Investigate Entrepreneur Allegedly Tied to Saudis," *Houston Chronicle*, June 4, 1992; Thomas Petzinger Jr., et al., "Family Ties: How Oil Firm Linked to a Son of Bush Won Bahrain Drilling Pact," *Wall Street Journal*, December 6, 1991.

SOURCE: "[E]arly 1980s tax records reviewed by *Time* show that Bath invested $50,000 in Bush's energy ventures and remained a stockholder until Bush sold his company to Harken in 1986." Jonathan Beaty, "A Mysterious Mover of Money and Planes," *Time*, October 28, 1991.

**"Bush ran Arbusto into the ground, as he did every other company he was involved in, until finally one of his companies was bought by Harken Energy and they gave him a seat on their board."**

SOURCE: "Bush's name . . . was to help rescue him, just as it had attracted investors and helped revive his flagging fortunes throughout his years in the dusty plains city of Midland. A big Dallas-based firm, Harken Oil and Gas, was looking to buy up troubled oil companies. After finding Spectrum, Harken's executives saw a bonus in their target's CEO, despite his spotty track record. By the end of September 1986, the deal was done. Harken assumed

$3.1 million in debts and swapped $2.2 million of its stock for a company that was hemorrhaging money, though it had oil and gas reserves projected to produce $4 million in future net revenue. Harken, a firm that liked to attach itself to stars, had also acquired Bush, whom it used not as an operating manager but as a high-profile board member. . . . It was one of the biggest breaks of Bush's life. Still, the Harken deal completed a disappointing reprise of what was becoming a familiar pattern. As an oilman, Bush always worked hard, winning a reputation as a straight-shooter and a good boss who was witty, warm and immensely likable. Even the investors who lost money in his ventures remained admirers, and some of them are now raising money for his presidential campaign. But the story of Bush's career in oil, which began following his graduation from Harvard Business School in the summer of 1975 and ended when he sold out to Harken and headed for Washington, is mostly about his failure to succeed, despite the sterling connections his lineage and Ivy League education brought him." George Lardner Jr. and Lois Romano, "Bush Name Helps Fuel Oil Dealings," *Washington Post,* July 30, 1999.

**Bush was investigated by the SEC. "The James Baker law partner who helped Bush beat the rap from the SEC was a man by the name of Robert Jordan, who, when George W. became president, was appointed ambassador to Saudi Arabia."**

SOURCE: "A week before George W. Bush's 1990 sale of stock in Harken Energy Co., the firm's outside lawyers cautioned Bush and other directors against selling shares if they had significant negative information about the company's prospects. The sale came a few months before Harken reported significant losses, leading to an investigation by the Securities and Exchange Commission. The June 15, 1990, letter from the Haynes and Boone law firm wasn't sent to the SEC by Bush's attorney Robert W. Jordan until Aug. 22, 1991, according to a letter by Jordan. That was one day after SEC staff members investigating the stock sale concluded there was insufficient evidence to recommend an enforcement action against Bush for insider trading." Peter Behr, "Bush Sold Stock After Lawyers' Warning," *Washington Post,* November 1, 2002.

SOURCE: "President Bush has chosen as ambassador to Saudi Arabia a Dallas attorney who represented him against . . . allegations arising from his sale of stock in Harken Energy Co. 11 years ago." G. Robert Hillman, "Bush Taps Dallas Attorney to Be Ambassador to Saudi Arabia," *Dallas Morning News,* July 21, 2001.

## "After the Harken debacle, the friends of Bush's dad got him a seat on another board, of a company owned by the Carlyle Group."

SOURCE: "Fred Malek, a senior advisor to Carlyle, who also served as the director of the 1988 Republican Convention, suggested to Carlyle that the President's eldest son, George W. Bush, would 'be a positive addition to Caterair's board.' Mr. Malek was also a Caterair director and vice chairman of Northwest Airlines, a major Caterair customer. 'I thought George W. Bush could make a contribution to Caterair,' stated Malek. Malek further claimed, 'He would be on the board even if his father weren't President.'" Kenneth N. Gilpin, "Little-Known Carlyle Scores Big," *New York Times,* March 26, 1991.

SOURCE: Co-Founder of Carlyle Group, David Rubenstein, talking about setting up Caterair after Carlyle acquired it: "When we're putting together the board," Rubenstein said, "somebody came to me and said, 'Look, there is a guy who would like to be on the board. He's kind of down on his luck a bit. Needs a job. Needs some board positions. Could you put him on the board? Pay him a salary and he'll be a good board member and be a loyal vote for the management and so forth.' . . . We put him on the board and [he] spent three years. Came to all the meetings. . . . And after a while I kind of said to him, after about three years—'You know, I'm not sure this is really for you. Maybe you should do something else. Because I don't think you're adding much value to the board. You don't know that much about the company.'" The board member told him, Rubenstein said, "'Well I think I'm getting out of this business anyway. I don't really like it that much. So I'm probably going to resign from the board.' And I said, 'Thanks.' Didn't think I'd ever see him again. His name is George W. Bush," Rubenstein said. "He became president of the United States. So if you said to me, name 25 million people who would be president of the United States, he wouldn't be in that category. So you never know." Nicholas Horrock, "White House Watch: With Friends Like These," UPI, July 16, 2003.

# The Carlyle Group, the Saudi Connection, and the Profits to Be Made Post–9/11

"The Carlyle Group is a multinational conglomerate that invests in heavily government-regulated industries like telecommunications, health care, and, particularly, defense."

SOURCE: "The Carlyle Group is one of the world's largest private equity firms, with more than $18.3 billion under management. With 23 funds across five investment disciplines (management-led buyouts, real estate, leveraged finance, venture capital and turnaround), Carlyle combines global vision with local insight, relying on a top-flight team of nearly 300 investment professionals operating out of offices in 14 countries to uncover superior opportunities in North America, Europe, and Asia. Carlyle focuses on sectors in which it has demonstrated expertise: aerospace & defense, automotive & transportation, consumer, energy & power, healthcare, industrial, real estate, technology & business services, and telecommunications & media." Carlyle Group website, http://www.thecarlylegroup.com/eng/company/index.html.

**The bin Laden and Bush families were both connected to the Carlyle Group, as were many of the Bush family's friends and associates.**

SOURCE: In the early 1990s, George W. Bush served on the board of directors for Caterair, an airline catering company. Caterair was owned by the Carlyle Group. Kenneth N. Gilpin, "Little-Known Carlyle Scores Big," *New York Times,* March 26, 1991. "George W. Bush left the company in 1994, a year after his father's presidency ended." Ross Ramsey et al., "Campaign '94 Fisher's Staff Slips Up on Spanish," *Houston Chronicle,* September 17, 1994.

SOURCE: In the mid-1990s, George H. W. Bush joined up with the Carlyle Group. "Under the leadership of ex-officials like Baker and former Defense Secretary Frank C. Carlucci, Carlyle developed a specialty in buying defense companies and doubling or quadrupling their value. The ex-president not only became an investor in Carlyle, but a member of the company's Asia Advisory Board and a rainmaker who drummed up investors. Twelve rich Saudi families, including the Bin Ladens, were among them. In 2002, the *Washington Post* reported, 'Saudis close to Prince Sultan, the Saudi defense minister . . . were encouraged to put money into Carlyle as a favor to the elder Bush.' Bush retired from the company last October, and Baker, who lobbied U.S. allies last month to forgive Iraq's debt, remains a Carlyle senior counselor." Kevin Phillips, "The Barreling Bushes; Four Generations of the Dynasty Have Chased Profits Through Cozy Ties with Mideast Leaders, Spinning Webs of Conflicts of Interest," *Los Angeles Times,* January 11, 2004.

SOURCE: The bin Laden family first invested in Carlyle in

1994. Representing Carlyle's Asia Board, George H. W. Bush visited the bin Laden family's headquarters in Jeddah, Saudi Arabia. Kurt Eichenwald, "Bin Laden Family Liquidates Holdings with Carlyle Group," *New York Times*, October 26, 2001.

SOURCE: James Baker was a Carlyle Senior Counselor beginning in 1993. Carlyle Group website, http://www. thecarlylegroup.com/eng/team/l5-team391.html.

SOURCE: Bush's OMB chief, Richard Darman, was with Carlyle by 1994. Bob Cook, Mergers & Acquisitions Report, December 12, 1994.

SOURCE: George W. Bush was with Caterair—owned by Carlyle—until 1994, after Fred Malek, a senior adviser to Carlyle, who also served as the director of the 1988 Republican Convention, suggested to Carlyle that the President's eldest son would "be a positive addition to Caterair's board." Kenneth N. Gilpin, "Little-Known Carlyle Scores Big," *New York Times*, March 26, 1991.

"Carlyle Group was holding its annual investor conference on the morning of September 11 in the Ritz-Carlton Hotel in Washington, D.C. At that meeting were all of the Carlyle regulars, James Baker, likely John Major, definitely George H. W. Bush, though he left the morning of September 11. Shafiq bin Ladin, who is Osama bin Laden's half-brother, and was in town to look after his family's investments in the Carlyle Group. All of them, together in one room, watching as the, uh, the planes hit the towers."

SOURCE: On the morning of September 11, 2001, "in the plush setting of the Ritz-Carlton Hotel in Washington,

D.C., the Carlyle Group was holding its annual international investor conference. Frank Carlucci, James Baker III, David Rubenstein, William Conway, and Dan D'Aniellow were together, along with a host of former world leaders, former defense experts, wealthy Arabs from the Middle East, and major international investors as the terror played out on television. There with them, looking after the investments of his family, was Shafiq bin Laden, Osama bin Laden's estranged half-brother. George Bush Sr. was also at the conference, but Carlyle's spokesperson says the former president left before the terror attacks, and was on an airplane over the Midwest when flights across the country were grounded on the morning of September 11. In any circumstance, a confluence of such politically complex and globally connected people would have been curious, even newsworthy. But in the context of the terrorist attacks being waged against the United States by a group of Saudi nationals led by Osama bin Laden, the group assembled at the Ritz-Carlton that day was a disconcerting and freakish coincidence." Dan Briody, *The Iron Triangle* (John Wiley & Sons, Inc., 2003), pp. 139–140. See also, Melanie Warner, "What Do George Bush, Arthur Levitt, Jim Baker, Dick Darman, and John Major Have in Common? (They All Work for the Carlyle Group)," *Fortune*, March 18, 2002.

**"With all the weapons companies it owned, the Carlyle Group was in essence, the eleventh largest defense contractor in the United States."**

SOURCE: "By virtue of its holdings in companies like U.S. Marine Repair and United Defense Industries,

Carlyle is the equivalent of the eleventh-largest defense contractor in the nation. It has $16.2 billion under management and claims an average annual return of 35%." Phyllis Berman, "Lucky Twice," *Forbes*, December 8, 2003.

**"It owned United Defense, makers of the Bradley armored fighting vehicle. September 11 guaranteed that United Defense was going to have a very good year. Just six weeks after 9/11, Carlyle filed to take United Defense public and in December made a one-day profit of $237 million."**

SOURCE: "On a single day last month, Carlyle earned $237 million selling shares in United Defense Industries, the Army's fifth-largest contractor. The stock offering was well timed: Carlyle officials say they decided to take the company public only after the Sept. 11 attacks. . . . On Sept. 26, [2001], the Army signed a $665 million modified contract with United Defense through April 2003 to complete the Crusader's development phase. In October, the company listed the Crusader, and the attacks themselves, as selling points for its stock offering." Mark Fineman, "Arms Buildup Is a Boon to Firm Run by Big Guns," *Los Angeles Times*, January 10, 2002.

SOURCE: "Still, in its annual report for 2001, United announced that it had been awarded a three-year, $697 million contract to complete full upgrading of 389 Bradley units and had added a $655 million contract modification to complete the Crusader's 'definition and risk-reduction phase contract,' which would be worth $1.7 billion through 2003. Together, the Crusader and Bradley programs contributed 41 percent of United sales in 2001, the report said. With Crusader and the Bradley upgrade in hand, a decision was made to sell United stock to the public in late 2001." Walter Pincus, "Crusader a Boon to Carlyle Group Even if Pentagon Scraps Project," *Washington Post*, May 14, 2002.

**"[W]ith so much attention focused on the bin Laden family being important Carlyle investors, the bin Ladens eventually had to withdraw."**

SOURCE: "Following the attacks on September 11, the bin Laden family's investments in the Carlyle Group became an embarrassment to the Carlyle Group and the family was forced to liquidate their assets with the firm." Kurt Eichenwald, "Bin Laden Family Liquidates Holdings with Carlyle Group," *New York Times*, October 26, 2001.

**"Bush's dad, though, stayed on as senior adviser to Carlyle's Asia Board for another two years."**

SOURCE: "Former President Bush was at one time the Senior Advisor to the Carlyle Asia Advisory Board but retired from that position in October 2003. He holds no other positions at Carlyle." http://www.thecarlylegroup.com/eng/news/l4-presskit681.html#8.

SOURCE: "The former president is no longer a company adviser, but he still has investments there, Mr. Ullman (vice president for corporate communications) said." "Michael Moore Keeps Heat on at Premiere," *Dallas Morning News*, May 18, 2004.

## George H. W. Bush receives daily CIA briefings.

SOURCE: "One of the people who corresponded with [former ambassador Joseph] Wilson is George H. W. Bush, the only president to have been head of the C.I.A.—he still receives regular briefings from Langley." Vicky Ward, "Double Exposure," *Vanity Fair,* January 2004.

SOURCE: Former President Bush has made efforts to keep abreast of foreign affairs, partly by exercising his right to be briefed by CIA personnel about developments around the globe. "George Bush Sr. Vouches for Son's Support of Israel to the Saudis," *Ha'aretz,* July 16, 2001.

"[T]hey are benefiting from the confusion that arises when George H. W. Bush visits Saudi Arabia, on behalf of Carlyle, and meets with the royal family and meets with the bin Laden family. Is he representing the United States of America, or is he representing an investment firm in the United States of America or is he representing both?"

SOURCE: Few firms could have rivaled the Carlyle Group for its array of high-powered friends. The Washington-based venture capital house had been likened to a retirement home for Gulf War veterans, and the likes of George Bush Sr, James Baker, and John Major 'can take credit for its rapid rise.' " *The Observer* noted in a profile, "It used to be fashionable to deride Carlyle as a second-rate influence-peddler and dismiss its stable of retired politicians as superannuated 'access capitalists.' " Carlyle had sponsored visits by Bush Sr. to South Korea and China, and his clout with the Saudi government—perhaps Carlyle's most important customer—is also likely to be valued. Conal Walsh, "The Carlyle Controversy: With Friends in High Places: Former World Leaders Give Carlyle Group Unrivalled Prowess in Lobbying for Business," *The Observer*, September 15, 2002.

SOURCE: " 'It should be a deep cause for concern that a closely held company like Carlyle can simultaneously have directors and advisers that are doing business and making money and also advising the president of the United States,' says Peter Eisner, managing director of the Center for Public Integrity, a non-profit-making Washington think-tank. 'The problem comes when private business and public policy blend together. What hat is former president Bush wearing when he tells Crown Prince Abdullah not to worry about US policy in the Middle East? What hat does he use when he deals with South Korea, and causes policy changes there? Or when James Baker helps argue the presidential election in the younger Bush's favour? It's a kitchen-cabinet situation, and the informality involved is precisely a mark of Carlyle's success.' " Oliver Burkeman Julian Borger, "The Winners: The Ex-Presidents' Club," *The Guardian*, October 31, 2001.

SOURCE: "The Saudi family of Osama bin Laden is severing its financial ties with the Carlyle Group, a private investment firm known for its connections to influential Washington political figures. . . . In recent years, Frank C. Carlucci, the chairman of Carlyle and a former secretary of defense, has visited the family's headquarters in Jeddah, Saudi Arabia, as have former President George Bush and James A. Baker III, the former secretary of state. Mr. Bush works as an adviser to Carlyle, and Mr.

Baker is a partner in the firm." Kurt Eichenwald, "Bin Laden Family Liquidates Holdings with Carlyle Group," *New York Times,* October 26, 2001.

**"[A]nother group of people invest in you, your friends, and their related businesses $1.4 billion over a number of years."**

SOURCE: "In all, at least $1.46 billion had made its way from the Saudis to the House of Bush and its allied companies and institutions." Craig Unger, *House of Bush, House of Saud* (Scribner, 2004), p. 200. For a complete breakdown of the investments, see Unger's Appendix C, pp. 295–298. This number includes investments made and contracts awarded at the time Bush's friends were involved in the Carlyle Group:

SOURCE: James Baker was a Carlyle Senior Counselor beginning in 1993. Carlyle Group website, http://www.the carlylegroup.com/eng/team/l5-team391.html.

SOURCE: Bush's OMB chief, Richard Darman, was with Carlyle by 1994. Bob Cook, Mergers & Acquisitions Report, December 12, 1994.

SOURCE: George W. Bush was with Caterair—owned by Carlyle—until 1994, after Fred Malek, a senior adviser to Carlyle, who also served as the director of the 1988 Republican Convention, suggested to Carlyle that the President's eldest son would "be a positive addition to Caterair's board." Kenneth N. Gilpin, "Little-Known Carlyle Scores Big," *New York Times,* March 26, 1991.

SOURCE: Bush Sr. was first involved in Carlyle by the mid-1990s and no later than 1997. Kevin Phillips, "The Barreling Bushes; Four Generations of the Dynasty Have

Chased Profits Through Cozy Ties with Mideast Leaders, Spinning Webs of Conflicts of Interest," *Los Angeles Times,* January 11, 2004; Dan Briody, *The Iron Triangle* (John Wiley & Sons, Inc., 2003).

Additional backup for these numbers is as follows:

SOURCE: Saudi investments in the Carlyle Group worth $80 million. Craig Unger, "Saving the Saudis," *Vanity Fair,* October 2003. The number was reported to Unger by the head of Carlyle, David Rubenstein, in an interview.

SOURCE: In 1994, Carlyle-owned military contractor BDM was "awarded a contract to provide technical assistance and logistics support to the Royal Saudi Air Force." Worth: $46.2 million. PR Newswire, "BDM Federal Awarded $46 Million Contract to Support Royal Saudi Air Force," October 27, 1994.

SOURCE: During the 1990s, the Vinnell Corporation (a BDM subsidiary) held contracts to train the Saudi Arabian National Guard, worth $819 million. Robert Burns, "US Advises Saudi Military on Range Of Threats—Including Terrorism," Associated Press, November 13, 1995.

SOURCE: In 1995, BDM collected a contract to "augment Royal Saudi Air Force staff in developing, implementing, and maintaining logistics and engineering plans and programs." Worth: $32.5 million. "Defense Contracts," *Defense Daily,* June 23, 1995, as cited by Craig Unger.

SOURCE: In 1996, BDM was awarded a contract "to provide construction of 110 housing units at the MK-1 Compound, Khamis Mushayt, Saudi Arabia, for Technical Support Program personnel assisting the Royal Saudi Air Force. . . . This effort supports foreign military sales to Saudi

Arabia." Worth: $44,397,800. Department of Defense News Release, "BDM Federal, Incorporated," April 1, 1996.

SOURCE: During the late 1990s, Vinnell was awarded a contract "for the Saudi Arabian National Guard (SANG) Modernization Program. The three-year contract, awarded competitively, calls on Vinnell to continue to support SANG training operations and related activities." Worth: $163.3 million. PR Newswire, "Vinnell Selected for Award of $163.3 Million Contract for Saudi Arabian National Guard Modernization Program," May 3, 1995. Kashim Al-An, "Saudi Guard Gets Quiet Help from US Firm with Connections," Associated Press, March 22, 1997.

SOURCE: In 1997, BDM was awarded a contract "to provide for 400 contractor personnel to support the Royal Saudi Air Force in developing, implementing, and maintaining logistics, supply, computer, reconnaissance, intelligence and engineering plans and programs." Worth: $18,728,682 (note: this is a "face value increase to a firm fixed price contract"). "Defense Contracts," *Defense Daily*, February 4, 1997.

*Note:* Carlyle purchased BDM and its subsidiary Vinnell in 1992 and sold it to TRW in December 1997.

SOURCE: In November 2001, Dick Cheney's former company Halliburton was awarded "a contract to provide services for the Saudi Arabian Oil Company's (Saudi Aramco) Qatif Field development project in the eastern province of Saudi Arabia." Worth: $140 million. Halliburton press release, "Halliburton Awarded $140 Million Contract by Saudi Aramco," November 14, 2001.

SOURCE: The same month, a consortium of three companies led by Halliburton subsidiary KBR won a "contract for engineering, procurement, and construction of an ethylene plant for Jubail United Petrochemcial Company, a wholly owned company of Saudi Basic Industries Corporation." Worth: $40 million. Maggie Mulvihill et al., "Bush Advisers Cashed in on Saudi Gravy Train," *Boston Herald,* December 11, 2001.

SOURCE: Halliburton press release, "Halliburton KBR, Chiyoda, and Mitsubishi Win Saudi Arabian Ethylene Project," November 19, 2001. (*Note:* The $40 million figure cited for this contract in all likelihood is much too low. Three separate energy industry journals place the value of the contract at $350 million. While there are two other companies involved, all reports point out that Halliburton KBR led the consortium and thus, if the contract were $350 million, it is likely that their cut would be—as lead contractor—significantly more than $40 million.) See "News in Brief," *Petroleum Economist,* January 14, 2002; "KBR, Chiyoda, Mitsubishi Win Jubail Ethylene Contract," *Chemical Week,* December 5, 2001; "Projects Update: Petrochemicals," *Middle East Economic Digest,* March 7, 2000.

SOURCE: Soon after Harken bought out George W. Bush's company Spectrum 7 in 1986 and placed Bush on their board of directors, a Saudi sheik swooped in to save the troubled Harken. Abdullah Taha Bakhsh purchased a 17% stake in the company. Worth: $25 million. Thomas Petzinger Jr. et al., "Family Ties: How Oil Firm Linked to a Son of Bush Won Bahrain Drilling Pact; Harken Energy Had a Web of Mideast Connections; In the Background: BCCI; Entrée at the White House," *Wall Street Journal,* December 6, 1991.

SOURCE: In 1989, Saudi Arabia's King Fahd donated money to the Barbara Bush Foundation for Family Literacy. At the time, Ms. Bush was the First Lady of the United States. The King's contribution represented almost half the amount the organization was able to raise that year. Worth: $1 million. Thomas Ferraro, "Saudi King also Contributed to Barbara Bush's Foundation," United Press International, March 13, 1990.

SOURCE: Following George H. W. Bush's departure from office, Saudi Ambassador to the United States, Prince Bandar, donated money to the Bush Sr. Presidential Library fund. Worth: at least $1 million. Dave Montgomery, "Hail to a Former Chief," *Fort Worth Star-Telegram,* November 7, 1997.

SOURCE: Both George H. W. Bush and George W. Bush attended the elite Phillips Academy–Andover in Massachusetts. In the summer of 2002 the Academy announced it had established a scholarship in Bush Sr.'s name. Saudi Prince Alwaleed bin Talal bin Adul Aziz Alsaud—the same prince who bailed out EuroDisney in the mid-nineties—was among the donors to the scholarship. Worth $500,000. Phillips Academy–Andover press release, "A Statement from Phillips Academy–Andover Regarding the Bush Scholars Program," December 31, 2002.

SOURCE: Among the many presents George W. Bush has received from foreign leaders and dignitaries during his term as President, perhaps none is grander than the one Prince Bandar bestowed upon him. Bandar gave the current president a "C. M. Russell oil canvas painting of a native American buffalo hunt. . . ." Worth: $1 million.

Siobhan McDonough, "Gifts to President Are Gratefully Received, Quickly Carted into Storage," Associated Press, July 14, 2003.

## Amnesty International condemns Saudi Arabia as a human rights violator.

SOURCE: "Saudi Arabia systematically violates international human rights standards even after agreeing to be bound by them. For example, in September 1997 Saudi Arabia acceded to the Convention against Torture. Yet, torture is widespread in Saudi Arabia's criminal justice system. (Saudi Arabia acceded to the Convention against Torture and the Convention against Discrimination on Sept. 23, 1997.)" Amnesty International, "Saudi Arabia: Open for Business," February 8, 2000.http://web.amnesty.org/library/Index/engMDE230822000?OpenDocument&of=COUNTRIES% 5CSAUDI+ARABIA.

SOURCE: "Sharon Burke, Amnesty International USA's advocacy director for the Middle East and North Africa, said her organization confirmed with the Saudi Ministry of the Interior that three men were beheaded for sodomy." *Washington Blade,* January 4, 2002, http://www.sodomylaws.org/world/saudi_arabia/saudinews15.htm.

## "Bush tried to stop Congress from setting up its own 9/11 investigation. . . . When he couldn't stop Congress, he then tried to stop an independent 9/11 commission from being formed."

SOURCE: The original effort by the White House was to limit the scope of the 9/11 investigation to only two congressional committees. "President Bush asked House and

Senate leaders yesterday to allow only two congressional committees to investigate the government's response to the events of Sept. 11, officials said." Mike Allen, "Bush Seeks to Restrict Hill Probes of Sept. 11; Intelligence Panels' Secrecy Is Favored," *Washington Post*, January 30, 2002.

SOURCE: "'I, of course, want the Congress to take a look at what took place prior to Sept. 11. But since it deals with such sensitive information, in my judgment, it's best for the ongoing war against terror that the investigation be done in the intelligence committees,' President Bush said." David Rosenbaum, "Bush Bucks Tradition on Investigation," *New York Times*, May 26, 2002.

SOURCE: "Angry lawmakers [McCain, Pelosi, Lieberman] accused White House Friday of secretly trying to derail creation of an independent commission to investigate the Sept. 11 terrorist attacks while professing to support the idea." Helen Dewar, "Lawmakers Accuse Bush of 9/11 Deceit," *Los Angeles Times*, October 13, 2002.

## The White House censored 28 pages of the Congressional 9/11 report.

SOURCE: "Top U.S. officials believe the Saudi Arabian government not only thwarted their efforts to prevent the rise of al-Qaida and stop terrorist attacks, but also may have given the Saudi-born Sept. 11 hijackers financial and logistical support, according to a congressional report released Thursday. Those suspicions prompted several lawmakers to demand that the Bush administration aggressively investigate Saudi Arabia's actions before and after Sept. 11, 2001—in part by making public large sections of the report that pertain to Riyadh but remain classified. The passages, including an entire 28-page section, discuss in detail whether one of America's most reluctant allies in the war on terrorism was somehow implicated in the attacks, according to U.S. officials familiar with the full report." Josh Meyer, "Saudi Ties to Sept. 11 Hinted at in Report," *Houston Chronicle*, July 25, 2003.

**"[M]ore than 500 relatives of 9/11 victims filed suit against Saudi royals and others. The lawyers the Saudi Defense Minister hired to fight the 9/11 families? The law firm of Bush family confidant James A. Baker."**

SOURCE: "James Baker, whom Bush recently sent abroad seeking help to reduce Iraq's debt, is still a senior counselor for the Carlyle Group, and Baker's Houston-based law firm, Baker Botts, is representing the Saudi defense minister in Motley's [plaintiff's counsel in class-action suit in connection with September 11 attacks] case." "A Nation Unto Itself," *New York Times*, March 14, 2004.

**Saudis have $860 billion invested in America.**

SOURCE: "Over the next twenty-five years, roughly eighty-five thousand 'high-net-worth' Saudis invested a staggering $860 billion in American companies—an average of more than $10 million a person and a sum that is roughly equivalent to the gross domestic product of Spain." Craig Unger, *House of Bush, House of Saud* (Scribner, 2004).

SOURCE: "Allan Gerson, an attorney who represents

about 3,600 family members of victims of the September 11 terrorist attacks . . . said he is not suing the Saudi government, but he is pursuing 'Saudi interests' in the United States he estimated totaled about $860 billion." "$113 Million in Terrorism Funds Frozen," CNN, November 20, 2002.

**In terms of investments on Wall Street, $860 billion is "roughly six or seven percent of America."**

SOURCE: "With a total market capitalization exceeding $12 trillion, the NYSE Composite represents approximately 82 percent of the total U.S. market cap" ($860 billion is about 7 percent of $12 trillion). New York Stock Exchange News Release, "NYSE to Reintroduce Composite Index," January 2, 2003.

**Citigroup, AOL TimeWarner have big Saudi investors.**

SOURCE: "His name is Alwaleed bin Talal. His grandfather was Saudi Arabia's founding monarch. With huge stakes in companies ranging from Citigroup Inc. to the Four Seasons luxury hotel chain, he is one of the richest men on the planet. . . . Last year, *Forbes* magazine ranked Alwaleed the fifth-richest man in the world, with a net worth of nearly $18 billion. His Kingdom Holding Co. spans four continents. Over the years, he has acquired major stakes in companies such as Apple Computer Inc., AOL Time Warner Inc., News Corp., and Saks Inc., parent of retailer Saks Fifth Avenue." Richard Verrier, "Disney's Animated Investor; an Ostentatious Saudi Billionaire Prince Who Helped Bail Out the Company's

Paris Resort in the Mid-'90s Is Being Courted to Do So Again," *Los Angeles Times*, January 26, 2004.

SOURCE: "Carlyle's first major transaction with the Saudis took place in 1991 when Fred Malek steered Prince Al-Waleed bin Talal, a flamboyant 35-year-old Saudi multibillionaire, to the firm for a deal that would enable him to become the largest individual shareholder in Citicorp." Craig Unger, *House of Bush, House of Saud* (Scribner, 2004).

**"I read where, like, the Saudis have a trillion dollars in our banks, their money."**

SOURCE: "Others have said the investment is even more, as much as a trillion dollars on deposit in U.S. banks—an agreement worked out in the early 1980s by the Reagan administration, in yet another effort to get the Saudis to offset the US budget deficit. The Saudis hold another trillion dollars or so in the US stock market." Robert Baer, *Sleeping with the Devil* (Crown Publishers, 2003), p. 60.

**Bandar is one of the best protected ambassadors in the U.S. with a six-man security detail provided by the State Department.**

SOURCE: "The dean of the diplomatic corps by virtue of his long assignment in Washington, Bandar is the only ambassador who has his own State Department security detail—granted to him because of 'threats' and his status as a prince, according to a State Department spokesman." Robert G. Kaiser et al., "Saudi Leader's Anger Revealed Shaky Ties," *Washington Post*, February 10, 2002.

SOURCE: "Prince Bandar is often considered the most politically savvy of all the foreign ambassadors living in Washington. That may or may not be true—but he certainly is the best-protected. According to a Diplomatic Security official, Prince Bandar has a security detail that includes full-time participation of six highly trained and skilled DS officers. (DS officers are federal government employees charged with securing American diplomatic missions.)" Joel Mowbray, *Dangerous Diplomacy: How the State Department Threatens American Security* (Regnery, 2003).

**"Prince Bandar was so close to the Bushes, they considered him a member of the family. And they even had a nickname for him, 'Bandar Bush.' "**

SOURCE: "When President [George H. W.] Bush arrived in Riyadh, he took Bandar aside and embraced him. 'You are good people,' the president said. Bandar claims that Bush had tears in his eyes. Visiting the Bush summer home in Kennebunkport, Maine, the Saudi ambassador was affectionately dubbed 'Bandar Bush.' Bandar returned the favor, inviting Bush to go pheasant hunting at his English estate. (Since leaving the White House, Bush has also profited by acting as a kind of glorified door-opener for the Carlyle Group, an investment company that handles considerable Saudi wealth.)" Evan Thomas et al., "The Saudi Game," *Newsweek*, November 19, 2001.

SOURCE: "The Saudi ambassador attended the unveiling of former President George H.W. Bush's official portrait when he returned to the White House in 1995. He was among the guests at a surprise 75th birthday party in 2000 for former first lady Barbara Bush, and the former president has vacationed at Bandar's home in Aspen, Colo. Bandar has been a guest at the Bush ranch in Crawford, Texas. Just last year he presented the first family with a C. M. Russell painting, a gift worth $1 million that will be stored in the National Archives, along with other presents from well-wishers destined for a [George W.] Bush presidential library." Mike Glover, "Kerry Criticizes Bush on Saudi Meeting," Associated Press, April 23, 2004.

**"Two nights after September 11, George Bush invited Bandar Bush over to the White House for a private dinner and a talk."**

SOURCE: Two days after the attacks, the President asked Bandar to come to the White House. Bush embraced him and escorted him to the Truman balcony. Bandar had a drink and the two men smoked cigars. Elsa Walsh, "The Prince," *The New Yorker,* March 24, 2003.

**Bandar's government blocked American investigators from talking to the relatives of the fifteen hijackers.**

SOURCE: "The report strongly criticized top Saudi officials for their 'lack of cooperation' before and after the Sept. 11 attacks, even when it became known that 15 of the 19 hijackers were Saudis. . . . One top U.S. official told the joint inquiry staff that the Saudis since 1996 would not cooperate on matters relating to Osama bin Laden. Robert Baer, a former CIA officer, said the Saudis blocked FBI agents from talking to relatives of the 15 hijackers and following other leads in the kingdom." Frank Davies et al., "Bush rejects call to give more 9/11 data," *Philadelphia Inquirer,* July 30, 2003.

## Saudi Arabia was reluctant to freeze the hijackers' assets.

SOURCE: Riyadh has not yet fully joined the international effort to block bank accounts thought to be financing terrorist operations, U.S. officials say. But the Bush administration, fearful of offending the Saudis, has not yet raised a public complaint." Elaine Sciolino et al., "U.S. Is Reluctant to Upset Flawed, Fragile Saudi Ties," *New York Times,* October 25, 2001.

## "In 1997, while George W. Bush was governor of Texas, a delegation of Taliban leaders from Afghanistan flew to Houston to meet with Unocal executives to discuss the building of a pipeline through Afghanistan."

SOURCE: "A senior delegation from the Taleban movement in Afghanistan is in the United States for talks with an international energy company that wants to construct a gas pipeline from Turkmenistan across Afghanistan to Pakistan. A spokesman for the company, Unocal, said the Taleban were expected to spend several days at the company's headquarters in Sugarland, Texas." "Taleban in Texas for Talks on Gas Pipeline," BBC News, December 4, 1997. (Sugarland is twenty-two miles outside Houston.)

SOURCE: "The Taliban ministers and their advisers stayed in a five-star hotel and were chauffeured in a company minibus. Their only requests were to visit Houston's zoo, the

NASA space centre and Omaha's Super Target discount store to buy stockings, toothpaste, combs and soap. The Taliban, which controls two-thirds of Afghanistan and is still fighting for the last third, was also given an insight into how the other half lives. The men, who are accustomed to life without heating, electricity or running water, were amazed by the luxurious homes of Texan oil barons. Invited to dinner at the palatial home of Martin Miller, a vice-president of Unocal, they marvelled at his swimming pool, views of the golf course and six bathrooms. After a meal of specially prepared halal meat, rice and Coca-Cola, the hardline fundamentalists—who have banned women from working and girls from going to school—asked Mr. Miller about his Christmas tree." Caroline Lees, "Oil Barons Court Taliban in Texas," *The Telegraph* (London), December 14, 1997.

"And who got a Caspian Sea drilling contract the same day Unocal signed the pipeline deal? A company headed by a man named Dick Cheney. Halliburton."

SOURCE: On October 27, 1997, both Unocal and Halliburton issued press releases about their energy work in Turkmenistan. "Halliburton Energy Services has been providing a variety of services in Turkmenistan for the past five years." Press release, "Halliburton Alliance Awarded Integrated Service Contract Offshore Caspian Sea in Turkmenistan," October 27, 1997. http://www.halliburton. com/news/archive/1997/hesnws_102797.jsp; "ASHGABAT, Turkmenistan, Oct. 27, 1997—Six international companies and the Government of Turkmenistan formed Central Asia Gas Pipeline, Ltd. (CentGas) in formal signing ceremonies

here Saturday." Press release, "Consortium Formed to Build Central Asia Gas Pipeline," October 27, 1997.

## Enron stood to benefit from the pipeline.

SOURCE: Dr. Zaher Wahab of Afghanistan, a professor in the U.S., speaking at International Human Rights Day event, "explained that Delta, Unocal as well as Russian, Pakistani and Japanese oil and gas companies have signed agreements with the Turkmenistan government, immediately north of Afghanistan, which has the fourth largest gas reserve in the world. Agreements also have been signed with the Taliban, allowing these oil and gas giants to pump Turkmenistan gas and oil through western Afghanistan to Pakistan, from which it then will be shipped all over the world. The energy consortium Enron plans to be one of the builders of the pipeline." Elaine Kelly, "Northwest Groups Discuss Afghan, Iranian and Turkish Rights Violations," Washington Report on Middle East Affairs, March 31, 1997.

## Kenneth Lay of Enron was Bush's number one campaign contributor.

SOURCE: "Mr. Lay, also a friend to former President George Bush, was the top campaign contributor to Mr. Bush's 2000 presidential election." Jerry Seper, "Colossal Collapse: Enron Bankruptcy Scandal Carves a Wide Swath," *Washington Times*, January 13, 2002. "Although Enron is George W. Bush's No. 1 career donor, the president also is heavily indebted to the professional firms that aided and abetted the greatest bankruptcy and shareholder meltdown in U.S. history." Texans for Public Justice, "Bush

Is Indebted to Enron's Professional Abettors, Too," January 17, 2002; http://www.tpj.org/page_view.jsp?pageid=255.

**"Then in 2001, just five and a half months before 9/11, the Bush administration welcomed a special Taliban envoy to tour the United States to help improve the image of the Taliban government."**

SOURCE: "A Taliban envoy appealed to the Bush administration Monday to overlook his group's support of extremist Osama bin Laden and the destruction of priceless centuries-old Buddhist sculptures and lift sanctions on Afghanistan to help alleviate a humanitarian crisis threatening the lives of a million people. Sayed Rahmatullah Hashemi delivered a letter from the Taliban for President Bush that called for better U.S.-Afghan relations and negotiations to solve the dispute over the Saudi-born Bin Laden." Robin Wright, "Taliban Asks US to Lift Its Economic Sanctions," *Los Angeles Times,* March 20, 2001.

SOURCE: "The Town Hall forum was Hashemi's final meeting in a weeklong visit to California, where he spoke at several universities, including USC, UCLA and UC Berkeley. Later Thursday, he left for New York for another stop on his public relations tour before going to Washington, where he is scheduled to deliver a letter from his party to the Bush administration." Teresa Watanabe, "Overture by Taliban Hits Resistance," *Los Angeles Times,* March 16, 2001.

**"[T]he Taliban were harboring the man who bombed the USS *Cole* and our African embassies."**

SOURCE: "Osama bin Laden has claimed credit for the attack on U.S. soldiers in Somalia in October 1993, which killed 18; for the attack on the U.S. Embassies in Kenya and Tanzania in August 1998, which killed 224 and injured nearly 5,000; and were linked to the attack on the U.S.S. *Cole* on 12 October 2000, in which 17 crew members were killed and 40 others injured. They have sought to acquire nuclear and chemical materials for use as terrorist weapons." "Britain's Bill of Particulars," *New York Times,* October 5, 2001.

SOURCE: "Osama bin Laden, in recent years, has been America's most wanted terrorism suspect, with a $5 million reward on his head for his alleged role in the August 1998 truck bombings of two American embassies in East Africa that killed more than 200 people, as well as a string of other terrorist attacks. . . . Most recently, the F.B.I. has named Mr. bin Laden as a prime suspect in the suicide bombing of the American destroyer *Cole,* which was attacked in Aden harbor, 350 miles by road southwest of here, on Oct. 12, with the loss of 17 sailors' lives." John F. Burns, "Where bin Laden Has Roots, His Mystique Grows," *New York Times,* December 31, 2000.

## Hamid Karzai was a former Unocal adviser.

SOURCE: "Cool and worldly, Karzai is a former employee of US oil company Unocal—one of two main oil companies that was bidding for the lucrative contract to build an oil pipeline from Uzbekistan through Afghanistan to seaports in Pakistan—and the son of a former Afghan parliament speaker." Ilene R. Prusher, Scott Baldauf, and Edward Girardet, "Afghan power brokers," *Christian Science Monitor,* June 10, 2002. http://www.csmonitor.com/2002/0610/p01s03e-wosc.html.

SOURCE: "Afghan President Hamid Karzai, a former Unocal adviser, signed a treaty with Pakistani leader Pervez Musharraf and the Turkmen dictator Saparmurat Niyazov to authorize construction of a $3.2 billion gas pipeline through the Heart-Kandahar corridor in Afghanistan." Lutz Kleveman, "Oil and the New 'Great Game,'" *The Nation*, February 16, 2004.

SOURCE: *Translated from French:* "He was a consultant for the American oil company Unocal, while they studied the construction of a pipeline in Afghanistan." Françoise Chipaux, "Hamid Karzaï, Une Large Connaissance Du Monde Occidental," *Le Monde*, December 6, 2001.

## "Bush also appointed as our envoy to Afghanistan Zalmay Khalilzad, who was also a former Unocal adviser."

SOURCE: "Mr. Khalilzad himself knows how compasses change. In the mid-1990s, he briefly defended the Taliban while working as a consultant for Unocal, the oil company that was then trying to build a pipeline through Afghanistan. He later became one of the Taliban's fiercest critics." Amy Waldman, "Afghan Returns Home as American Ambassador," *New York Times*, April 19, 2004.

## "Afghanistan signed an agreement . . . to build a pipeline through Afghanistan carrying natural gas from the Caspian Sea."

SOURCE: "The framework agreement defines legal mechanisms for setting up a consortium to build and operate the long-delayed US$3.2-billion natural gas pipeline, known as the Trans-Afghanistan Pipeline, which would carry gas from energy-rich Turkmenistan to Pakistan. It would be one of the first major investment projects in Afghanistan in decades." Baglia Bukharbayeva, "Pakistani, Turkmen, Afghan Leaders Sign US$3.2 Billion Pipeline Deal," Associated Press, December 27, 2002.

# Creating Fear as a Pretext to War—a War Built on Deceit

**"In 2000, [John Ashcroft] was running for reelection as Senator from Missouri against a man who died the month before the election. The voters preferred the dead guy."**

SOURCE: "Sen. John Ashcroft on Wednesday graciously conceded defeat in his re-election campaign against the late Gov. Mel Carnahan and urged fellow Republicans to call off any legal challenges." Eric Stern, "Ashcroft Rejects Challenge to Election; Senator Says He Hopes Carnahan's Victory Will Be 'of Comfort' to Widow," *St. Louis Post-Dispatch*, November 9, 2000.

**"During the summer before 9/11, Ashcroft told acting FBI director Thomas Pickard that he didn't want to hear anything more about terrorist threats."**

SOURCE: "Former interim FBI chief Thomas Pickard testified Tuesday that Atty. Gen. John Ashcroft didn't want to hear about terrorism when Pickard tried to brief him during the summer of 2001, as intelligence reports about terrorist threats were reaching a historic level." Cam Simpson, "Ashcroft Ignored Terrorism, Panel Told; Attorney General Denies Charges, Blames Clinton," *Chicago Tribune*, April 14, 2004.

See also film footage.

## "His own FBI knew that summer that there were al Qaeda members in the U.S., and that bin Laden was sending his agents to flight schools around the country."

SOURCE: "[T]he July 2001 'Phoenix' memo, written by an FBI agent in Arizona, warned about 'an inordinate number of individuals of investigative interest' taking flight training. It urged the agency to collect data on flight schools and foreign students, and to discuss the potential threat with other intelligence agencies. . . . [O]ne of the men mentioned in the memo was arrested in Pakistan in 2002 with a senior al Qaeda facilitator, Abu Zubayda." R. Jeffrey Smith, "A History of Missed Connections; U.S. Analysts Warned of Potential Attacks but Lacked Follow-Through," *Washington Post*, July 25, 2003.

SOURCE: Excerpt from "Phoenix Memo": "The purpose of this communication is to advise the Bureau and New York of the possibility of a coordinated effort by USAMA BIN LADEN (UBL) to send students to the United States to attend civil aviation universities and colleges. Phoenix has observed an inordinate number of individuals of investigative interest who are attending or who have attended civil aviation universities and colleges in the State of Arizona." Read the entire Phoenix Memo at: http://www.gpoaccess.gov/serialset/creports/911.html.

**"[T]he photo of the man in the newspaper was not the Aaron Stokes they had come to know [a member of Peace Fresno]. He was actually Deputy Aaron Kilner. And he had infiltrated their group."**

SOURCE: "Aaron Kilner, 27, who joined the force in June 1999 and had been assigned the last 18 months to the anti-terrorist team under the vice-intelligence unit, apparently was killed instantly when his blue Yamaha motorcycle slammed into the right front side of a 1999 Buick, Fresno police said." Louis Galvan, "Crash Kills Off-Duty Detective, Victim Joined Fresno County Force in 1999," *Fresno Bee,* August 31, 2003.

SOURCE: "It remains unclear why the Fresno County Sheriff's Department infiltrated the peace group there, but Pierce said his department's actions were legal. 'We can be anywhere we want to that's open to the public,' Pierce said in a telephone interview from his Fresno office." Sam Stanton and Emily Bazar, "More Scrutiny of Peace Groups, Public Safety Justifies Surveillance Since 9/11, Authorities Say," *Sacramento Bee,* November 9, 2003.

## Barry Reingold's story.

SOURCE: "Then there's San Franciscan Barry Reingold, who was awakened from his afternoon nap by a buzzing intercom on Oct. 23. He called down to the street to find out who it was. 'The FBI,' was the response. He buzzed

the two men up, but decided to meet them in the hall. 'I
was a little bit shaken up,' says Mr. Reingold. 'I mean, why
would the FBI be interested in me, a 60-year-old retired
phone company worker?' When they asked if he worked
out at a certain gym, he realized the reason behind the
visit. The gym is where he lifts weights—and expounds on
his political views." Kris Axtman, "Political Dissent Can
Bring Federal Agents to Door," *Christian Science
Monitor,* January 8, 2002. See also, Sam Stanton, Emily
Bazar, "Security Collides with Civil Rights, War on
Terrorism Has Unforeseen Results," *Modesto Bee,*
September 28, 2003.

## Congress did not read the Patriot Act before voting on it.

SOURCE: "Later that morning [of October 12], the
House voted 337–79 to pass the bill. The outraged dis-
senters complained that no one could possibly have had
the time to read the enormously complex 342-page law
that amended fifteen different federal statutes and that
had only been printed out hours before." Steven Brill,
*After: How America Confronted the September 12 Era*
(Simon & Schuster, 2003).

SOURCE: "Many lawmakers were outraged that a bipartisan bill, which had passed the Judiciary Committee by a
unanimous vote, was set aside for legislation negotiated at
the last minute by a very small group. Members rose to say
that almost no one had read the new bill, and pleaded for
more time and more deliberation. . . . Asked about complaints that lawmakers were being asked to vote on a bill

that they had not read, the chairman of the Rules Committee, Representative David Dreier, Republican of California, replied, 'It's not unprecedented.'" Robin Toner and Neil A. Lewis, "House Passes Terrorism Bill Much Like Senate's, but with 5-Year Limit," *New York Times*, October 13, 2001.

See also film footage of Congressmen Conyers and McDermott.

**"Transportation Security Agency say[s] it's okay to take four books of matches and two butane lighters in your pockets as you board an airplane."**

SOURCE: "Consistent with Department of Transportation regulations for hazardous materials, passengers also are permitted to carry no more than four books of matches (other than strike anywhere matches) and no more than two lighters for individual use, if the lighters are fueled with liquefied gas (BIC- or Colibri-type) or absorbed liquid (Zippo-type)." 49 CFR 1540; http://www.tsa.gov/interweb/asset library/68_FR_9902.pdf.

**"[T]hanks to the budget cuts, Trooper Kenyon had to come in on his day off to catch up on some paperwork."**

SOURCE: "Budget cuts that laid off 129 Oregon State Police officers earlier this year have left a single trooper to cover the 1,400-square-mile territory and 100 miles of state roads around this city on Oregon's central coast." "Layoffs Leave Oregon Trooper Alone in Big Coastal Territory," *Seattle Times*, October 6, 2003.

**"On March 19, 2003, George W. Bush and the United States military invaded . . . Iraq—a nation that had never attacked the United States. A nation that had never threatened to attack the United States. A nation that had never murdered a single American citizen."**

SOURCE: "Iraq has never threatened nor been implicated in any attack against U.S. territory and the CIA has reported no Iraqi-sponsored attacks against American interests since 1991." Stephen Zunes, "An Annotated Overview of the Foreign Policy Segments of President George W. Bush's State of the Union Address," *Foreign Policy in Focus,* January 29, 2003; segments of President George W. Bush's State of the Union Address, *Foreign Policy in Focus,* January 29, 2003.

SOURCE: "Iraq never threatened U.S. security. Bush officials cynically attacked a villainous country because they knew it was easier than finding the real 9/11 villain, who had no country. And now they're hoist on their own canard." Maureen Dowd, "We're Not Happy Campers," *New York Times,* September 11, 2003.

SOURCE: "Iraq never threatened the US, let alone Australia. The basic consideration was and remains the perception of America's wider strategic interest in the Middle East." Richard Woolcott, "Threadbare Basis to the Homespun Yarn That Led Us into Iraq," *Sydney Morning Herald,* November 26, 2003. (Woolcott was Australia's Secretary of the Department of Foreign Affairs and Trade during the first Gulf War.)

SOURCE: For definition of murder of civilians (as opposed to combatants), see Article 3 of the Geneva

Convention. ("For persons taking no active part in the hostilities, the following acts are and shall remain prohibited at any time [a] Violence to life and person, in particular murder of all kinds.")

**The Coalition of the Willing included Palau, Costa Rica, Iceland, Romania, The Netherlands, and Afghanistan.**

SOURCE: White House list of Coalition members, March 20, 2003: http://www.whitehouse.gov/news/releases/2003/03/print/20030320-11.html.

**Morocco, according to one report, offered to send two thousand monkeys to help detonate land mines.**

SOURCE: "The administration has even turned to the animal kingdom for help in the war. First came the dolphins, those really smart mammals recruited to help clear mines at the Iraqi port of Umm Qasr. Then came word that Morocco was offering 2,000 monkeys to help detonate land mines." Al Kamen, "They Got the 'Slov' Part Right," *Washington Post*, March 28, 2003.

**"The government would not allow any cameras to show the coffins coming home."**

SOURCE: "For the past 13 years, the Pentagon has barred reporters from witnessing the transport of soldiers' flag-draped coffins to Dover Air Force Base in Delaware." Amanda Ripley, "An Image of Grief Returns," *Time*, May 3, 2004.

**"At the end of January of '04, the unemployment rate in Flint was actually 17 percent."**

SOURCE: Flint City, January 2004, Unemployment Rate, 17.0 percent. Office of Labor Market Information, Michigan State Government. http://www.michlmi.org/LMI/lmadata/laus/lausdocs/049lf04.htm.

## Bush "proposed cutting combat soldiers' pay by 33 percent and assistance to their families by 60 percent."

SOURCE: The Bush administration announced that it would roll-back "modest" increases of benefits to troops. The *Army Times* noted, "the administration announced that on Oct. 1 it wants to roll back recent modest increases in monthly imminent-danger from $225 to $150 (a cut of 33%) and family-separation allowances from $250 to $100 (a cut of 60%) for troops getting shot at in combat zones." http://www.armytimes.com/story.php?f=1-292259-1989240.php.

SOURCE: "Thanks to a law passed this year, troops in Iraq, Afghanistan and other high-risk areas now receive $225 a month in supplemental pay. That's an increase of $75 from the previous amount for combat pay. Under that same law, soldiers who have been forced to leave behind spouses and children receive $250 a month in additional separation pay to help cover child care and other additional expenses caused by assignment overseas. That's an increase of $150 over the previous supplement. . . . In its 2004 budget request, the Pentagon asked Congress to cut both combat pay and separation pay back to the previous levels." "Our Opinions: Proposal to Reduce Pay No Way to Salute Military," *Atlanta Journal-Constitution,* August 15, 2003.

"He opposed a \$1.3 billion increase . . . in veterans' health care, and closing seven veterans' hospitals, and he tried to double the prescription drug costs for veterans and opposed full benefits for part-time reservists."

SOURCE: "On Nov. 12, the Office of Management & Budget opposed restoring \$1.3 billion in funding for Veterans Administration hospitals that the House Appropriations Committee had cut. 'It's as if they're not even aware [that] there's a war on terror going on,' says Steve Thomas, an American Legion spokesman and Navy vet who notes casualties in Iraq could make demand for VA services soar." Stan Crock in Washington, with William C. Symonds in Boston, "Will the Troops Salute Bush in '04?," *Business Week*, December 8, 2003.

SOURCE: "The White House had expressed its 'strong opposition' to the Senate's effort to expand military health benefits to reservists and National Guard members, and boost veterans' health care spending by \$1.3 billion." Jonathan Weisman, "Bush Aides Threaten Veto of Iraqi Aid Measure," *Washington Post*, October 22, 2003.

SOURCE: In early 2003, the Bush administration announced that it was closing "seven of its 163 veteran's hospitals in an effort to 'restructure' the Department of Veterans Affairs." Suzanne Gamboa, "VA Proposes Overhaul, 13 Facilities Would Close or See Major Changes," Associated Press, August 4, 2003.

SOURCE: In 2003, the Bush administration proposed increasing prescription drug costs for veterans, a proposal that would have doubled the cost of prescription drugs.

"The Bush plan would have included a new $250 enroll-ment fee and a co-pay increase from $7 to $15 for veterans earning over $24,000." The House amended the proposal to reject the Bush administration's fee increases and to recoup the $264 million in costs by reducing administra-tive funding for the VA. "Panel Rejects Extra Funds for AmeriCorps," *Washington Post,* July 22, 2003.

SOURCE: "The Bush administration is flatly opposed to giving the Guard and Reserve access to the Pentagon's health system." Opinion, *Daily News Leader* (Staunton, Virginia), October 25, 2003.

SOURCE: "U.S. Sen. Lindsey Graham (R-S.C.), has helped push a bill through the Senate to improve the health care benefits of Guard and Reserve members. This bill has had broad bipartisan support since it was introduced in May. Last week Graham had his health care plan attached as an amendment to the $87 billion supplemental appropriations bill that President Bush is seeking to pay for ongoing operations in Iraq and Afghanistan. The House should take up the amendment next week. Strangely, the Bush administration has opposed this new benefit for Guard and Reserve mem-bers, arguing that it would be too expensive." Staff, "Helping Our Guard and Reserve," *Greenville News,* October 16, 2003.

### Nearly 5,000 wounded in the . . . war.

SOURCE: "A year ago at this time, more than 160 American soldiers had been killed in Iraq. The total since has risen to more than 800, and last week the Pentagon reported that the number wounded in action is approaching 4,700." Pete Yost, "Bush Hails U.S. War Dead and Veterans," Associated Press, June 1, 2004.

**"[O]ut of the 535 members of Congress, only one had an enlisted son in Iraq."**

SOURCE: "Only four of the 535 members of Congress have children in the military; only one, Sen. Tim Johnson (D-S.D.), has a child who fought in Iraq." Kevin Horrigan, "Hired Guns," *St. Louis Post-Dispatch,* May 11, 2003.

# PART III

---

# What the Public Thought of *Fahrenheit 9/11*

FROM: Susan
SENT: Wednesday, July 07, 2004 6:36 AM
TO: mike@michaelmoore.com
SUBJECT: THANK YOU

Dear Mr. Moore,

As the single mom of three teenage boys (13, 17, 19), I thank you from the bottom of my heart. I sat in the theater with my oldest two, fully prepared to be given the same old rhetoric about the evils of the Bush administration.

Instead, I was educated, and, as a result, I cried.

I cried for our men and women who have died unnecessarily in this illegal war. I cried for my own 17-year-old, who has decided to join the Navy. I cried for our country and for those who live each day in poverty, seemingly without hope.

And then, I was inspired.

I've made the decision to become active in my church—a small place in the middle of a really poor section of town . . . a place that reaches out to the low income, poorly educated of the neighborhood and offers hope.

That's what being an American is about—reaching out to the afflicted of the world and offering hope.

So, again, I thank you . . . my children thank you.

Susan
Rochester, NY

FROM: Jennifer Layton
SENT: Saturday, July 24, 2004 4:29 PM
TO: mike@michaelmoore.com
SUBJECT: I'm registered!

Hello, Mr. Moore. I recently moved to a new home, and my new voter registration card arrived a couple of weeks ago. When I got my last card, I just signed it and put it in my purse, not really thinking much about it until it was time to show it on Election Day. But when I got this card, I don't know how to describe how I felt. I had seen your movie. Even before I saw it, I was angry about George W. Bush stealing the last election and worried that he might pull through this next one. But I have a voter card. And my voting place is the elementary school right across the street. My new voter card, as melodramatic as it sounds, gives me hope and just a little bit of power.

On Election Day, I don't care if there's fifty feet of snow outside and I've broken both legs and the Terror Alert is raised to Panic-Stricken Pink—I'm dragging my ass across the street to that school with my new voter registration card, and I'm going to vote.

Thank you for helping me realize just how important my voter registration card is. See you at the polls.

Jennifer Layton

FROM: Adam Shoup
SENT: Thursday, July 29, 2004 11:24 AM
TO: mike@michaelmoore.com
SUBJECT: Thanks . . . for making me a voter!

Mr. Moore,

I know you're a busy man, but I wanted to personally thank you for making me more aware of what's going on in our government. If I want to make a difference I need to vote. Thanks to your movie *Fahrenheit 9/11*, I will now be in the voter's box in this year's coming election.

Thanks,

Adam Shoup

From: Diamond, Elizabeth A.
SENT: Thursday, July 01, 2004 4:09 PM
TO: mike@michaelmoore.com
SUBJECT: Thank You

Thank you so much for this movie. I have already registered to vote. I am 27 and this is the first year that I am voting . . . I know, I know!!! I have seen what truly happens if you don't think your vote makes a difference. I have been stalking my co-workers not only to see *Fahrenheit 9/11*, but also to register to vote. My cousin was on the USS *Abraham Lincoln* when Bush was there. I was saddened to see the "Mission Accomplished" banner there. Especially when these men and women were to come home many months before that. My cousin has since been shipped out again. I just wanted to take the time to thank you for making people aware. If you are ever in the Connecticut area please let us know. My husband and I would love to meet you. You really made him think about Bush. He wanted to vote for him, but I wouldn't let him since it would cancel my vote—the ongoing battle at our house.

Thank you again,


Liz Diamond

FROM: Damian Geiss
SENT: Monday, July 05, 2004 6:06 PM
TO: mike@michaelmoore.com
SUBJECT: First Vote in My Life :)

Hi Mr. Moore,

I am certain this email will be lost amidst the thousands, but I had to say thank you—if only for me to know I tried to tell you thank you, Mr. Moore.

I am 42 years old, a federal employee, and a former military serviceman, and have *never* voted in my life. However, your courage to practice free speech and to demonstrate genuine critical reasoning, has made me *register to vote for the first time in my life.*

Thank you and may we meet one day and shake hands, and I can buy you a cup of coffee. I can't wait for November!

Peace and Goodwill, Mr. Moore,

Your Friend in the Masses,


Damian Geiss

FROM: Janell M. Schuller
SENT: Thursday, July 01, 2004 1:37 AM
TO: mike@michaelmoore.com
SUBJECT: Thank you for your bravery

Mr. Moore,

I know that you are inundated with emails, and you probably won't even see this, but I feel compelled to write anyway.

I just saw *Fahrenheit 9/11* tonight with my husband and I must say that I am still numb. I feel so naive . . . almost like I have been living in a bubble! Thank God my husband dragged me out to that movie theater!!

I am a stay-at-home mom of two little boys, 4 [years] and 11 months old. We're pretty much your average middle-class family living in a Seattle suburb.

I am ashamed to say that I voted for George Bush. I'm not exactly sure why, now that I think about it, but I did. I won't make the same mistake twice. My husband reads the alternative news websites and fills me in on what is really going on in America and how the government and media have duped the American people, yet I kept my blinders on.

Ever since 9/11, I have regretted voting for G.W.B. I do not agree with the Iraq war and the mess that G.W.B. has gotten us into. I support our soldiers and want them to come home safely but the war hasn't actually touched MY family. I haven't lost a family member or friend to the war or the events of 9/11. Thus, I have carried on with my life as usual. I watch the news and read the paper and feel for those who have experienced loss, but still, I've been unable to relate.

Your documentary brought it all front and center for me. It was the best $8.50 I have EVER spent. I cried so hard and I can't get it out of my head. When I saw that little Iraqi boy lying on that stretcher, I imagined my son. I don't think that I'll ever forget that image.

Your film awakened something in me. It made me want to challenge our nation's leaders and stand up and be counted. You have opened my eyes, and for that I want to thank you. I don't want my children to grow up in a world of corruption and lies. I have to try to make a difference for their futures. I am going to get more involved and encourage people to vote and take an active role in changing this country for the better. There are more of us little people, and if we band together, that's got to count for something. I have encouraged my Bush-supporting parents to see your film. They NEED to watch it. I think that they'll feel differently after they have. One can only hope!!

So, Mr. Moore, thank you for your bravery and forthrightness. I do believe that you and your film have had a profound impact on many Americans. I know that I will no longer turn the other cheek and keep my mouth shut. You're a hero in my book!!

Sincerely,

Janell Schuller
Auburn, WA

FROM: Dave
SENT: Friday, July 02, 2004 11:40 AM
TO: mike@michaelmoore.com
SUBJECT: great

Saw your movie yesterday. Wow, was I blown away. I
voted for Bush in 2000 and, boy, was I wrong. Never
again!!! Thanks again for making a great movie. . . .

Dave Kidd


FROM: Matthew Heffelfinger
SENT: Saturday, June 26, 2004 11:09 AM
TO: mike@michaelmoore.com
SUBJECT: Las Vegas Premiere

What a night in Vegas!

Standing room only, oversold theaters, lines so long
it felt like the 1977 premiere of *Star Wars*. But wait,
there is more: local TV news crews, so many applauses,
standing ovations, and after the movie ended, people
asking others to register to vote. What a powerful film,
when people actually are so moved to register to vote
on the spot.

Heff in Las Vegas, Nevada

FROM: Faye
SENT: Wednesday, July 07, 2004 1:23 AM
TO: mike@michaelmoore.com
SUBJECT: I will vote for the first time!

I am a 37-year-old African American female and I have never voted in any election in my life. Your movie has encouraged me to register to vote. (I don't know how to go about it, but I will certainly find out!)

Thank you for your movies. I have been a fan of your work since *Roger & Me*. *Fahrenheit 9/11* is an excellent composition of facts and I applaud you for your gift to the American public.

I agree that the "Liberals have failed us, the working people of this country." I can only pray that the Democrat who replaces Bush does a better job for America than the Democrats have done in Congress and the Senate. Either way, Bush and his posse are persona non grata.

It would be interesting if Lila Lipscomb and other military families filed a wrongful death lawsuit against Bush and his administration on behalf of the soldiers who gave their lives in Iraq in order for Bush and "his base" to profit.

I'm sure that you are aware that it would be a great idea to release *Fahrenheit 9/11* on DVD in late October to ensure its effect on the upcoming election.

Please keep up the good work! Yours is a necessary voice in American society.

Faye (soon to be a newly registered voter)
Chicago, IL

FROM: Terry Endres
SENT: Tuesday, July 06, 2004 7:39 PM
TO: mike@michaelmoore.com
SUBJECT: none

Mr. Moore,

My name is Terry Endres from Seattle, WA. I am 29 years old and have never voted in my life. I am ex-military and have always just honored my country. After watching your movie, not only will I vote for anyone or anything going against any Bush, but I want more answers to a lot of the things I now have questions about. Thank you for opening my eyes to what I was taught to ignore by the very people creating the problems. I think the world needs to know what is going on in our "ELECTED" government officials' lives and jobs. I am sickened. If there is anything I can do to help please let me know.

Terry Endres

FROM: Cassandra Smith
SENT: Thursday, July 01, 2004 11:28 AM
TO: mike@michaelmoore.com
SUBJECT: Just saw your movie

Hi Mike,

I just saw your movie yesterday, and I wanted to thank you personally. I laughed, I cried, and I was very angry. More importantly I took my two kids, ages 20 and 18, to see it and now there are two more registered voters in this country.

I just wanted to let you know that what you are doing is very important and that you have made a difference in this corner of the world.

Keep up the good fight!

Cassandra Smith

FROM: Kimberly Green
SENT: Saturday, June 26, 2004 10:34 AM
TO: mike@michaelmoore.com
SUBJECT: I have seen the light!! (in Texas)

Dear Mr. Moore,

I have to admit that I have been a Republican, voted
for Bush for Governor of Texas, worked on his presidential campaign in 2000, and am a registered volun-
teer for his re-election campaign. I heard your remarks
at the Oscars and thought, "I'll never see one of his
movies! What a jerk." Well, I am not so closed-minded
that I can't admit when I have been wrong. I have
recently been exposed to several stories about Bush,
his family, friends, and shady connections over the last
couple of months (many facts that you addressed in
your movie) and have started questioning what is the
real truth. My opinion was slowly starting to change,
but, after seeing your movie at 11:30 A.M. on opening
day in Frisco, Texas, I am officially a changed woman!
I feel like it all came together and the lightbulb came
on! You tied in the missing pieces of the puzzle for me.
I walked out of the theater angry that I was so blind
for so long and that I actually helped Bush get to
where he is today! I will be working on a campaign this
year . . . to get Bush OUT of office. I have already
begun calling people, posting messages, etc., trying to
get people to go see your movie and have their eyes
opened as well.

Thank you for taking the time . . . and the risk to

put the truth out there for the public to see. I hope many more people will feel the way I do now.

Keep up the good work!!

Kim,
Plano, TX

From: Robyn Larsen
Sent: Thursday, July 22, 2004 3:18 PM
To: mike@michaelmoore.com
Subject: my hat's off to you

Dear Michael,

Before I begin, I want to say that I realize how swamped you must be with all the activity generated from *Fahrenheit 9/11,* and I do not need or expect a reply. I simply wanted to take a moment to thank you and offer you a word of encouragement in your future projects.

I am the kind of person who has been guilty of talking the talk and not walking the walk when it comes to politics. I savor a healthy, impassioned political discussion with my friends, and I consider it crucial to read the news from a variety of sources outside the mainstream mass media, in order to feel more informed and less duped. However, I have been guilty of sporadic voting in the past, and after seeing your recent film, I doubt I will ever allow myself to neglect my civic duty to vote ever again. I am eagerly awaiting the chance to vote in November now.

After seeing the film for the first time (I just saw it again), my friends and I went to a local bar to chat about it together. And we did—for hours. This film has generated immense quantities of discussion EVERY-WHERE, and we all agreed that night that the most powerful objective the film may produce is nationwide discussion. We desperately need to question the war in Iraq, as well as the glossed over version of information we are bombarded with on the evening news. We need you, Michael, because you help balance the outspoken nature of the far right wing politico. You have voiced opinions that I have also formed on my own, and in doing so, I feel more represented in this country at large.

Thank you for taking the painstaking steps to have your facts checked and rechecked. Thank you for showing the actual cost of war in terms of blood, lost limbs, lost homes.

Thank you for forcing us to look the weeping Iraqi mothers in the eye.

Thank you for bringing up the mockery of the 2000 election again—may we never forget.

Most of all, thank you for asking questions and truly listening to the answers you hear. By listening to someone like Lila Lipscomb you have illustrated where your heart is—with the people, for the people.

I'll be looking forward to your next project.

Sincerely,

**Robyn Larsen**

FROM: Eric Sparks
SENT: Wednesday, July 28, 2004 5:04 PM
TO: mike@michaelmoore.com
SUBJECT: Never Voted till now!

Michael Moore,

I am a 26-year-old white male and I have never voted in a presidential election before. You have encouraged one more person to make that leap and vote. I don't care what it takes, I will make it to that booth and vote against Bush. I would like to thank you for everything you have done—you are a true rebel.

Eric Sparks

FROM: Tom Williamson
SENT: Friday, July 02, 2004 10:27 AM
TO: mike@michaelmoore.com
SUBJECT: You reached at least one

Hello,

Saw *Fahrenheit 9/11* last night.
   Thank you.
   I registered to vote today.

Tom Williamson

FROM: Kirk Riutta
SENT: Saturday, June 26, 2004 11:34 AM
TO: mike@michaelmoore.com
SUBJECT: Fahrenheit in the Heartland

Living in Indiana, I have to admit I was a bit nervous about what kind of crowd would be drawn to see *Fahrenheit 9/11*. When I got to the Kerasotes Showplace 16 on the Southside of Indianapolis, I was dumbfounded to find the movie ended up selling out, as well as the next show and the next. Where were these people, standing in long lines, coming from? The audience was initially very reserved, but after a few spontaneous hoots and cheers it became a non-stop two hours of cheering, clapping, and hooting, and at the end, several people shouted "VOTE!" Honestly, if the movie can sell out here in Conservative USA, maybe there really is hope come Election Day. The oddest thing about the movie, it made me feel for the first time in my life some sense of patriotic solidarity with my fellow Hoosiers. My hope is that people everywhere of every political persuasion do go see the movie and think and discuss the direction of our country.

Kirk Riutta
Shelbyville, IN

From: Colleen Russell
Sent: Tuesday, June 29, 2004 7:45 PM
To: mike@michaelmoore.com
Subject: disturbing reaction to "Fahrenheit 9/11"

I am a Republican and from a long history of family members who are hard-core Republicans. I saw your movie today alone and I cried the whole time. I have not been moved by a movie ever and I am ashamed as an American that I know so little about who is in power in our country. I wish I could be a part of your team in exposing the truth about our nation. I am a Registered Nurse but wish I had film experience. Thank you for having the balls and education to make a difference. I am now afraid to live in this country and wish I could move to Canada.

Colleen Russell

FROM: Lourdes Luis
SENT: Friday, July 02, 2004 9:23 PM
TO: mike@michaelmoore.com
SUBJECT: First Time Voter

Hi Mike!

Just wanted to let you know that I saw you on Charlie
Rose last night and heard you mention that you hope
*Fahrenheit 9/11* will get non-voters to register to vote.
Well I'm one of those non-voters, but I had been
thinking about voting this year because I couldn't
stand that clown anymore. I've never been a political
person, but after seeing what he's done and is trying to
do to this country, and after seeing *Fahrenheit 9/11*, I
will be voting for the first time ever! This time it's personal! I feel that my vote will be very important and
will hopefully make a difference!

Thanks for the great documentaries!

Lourdes
Miami, FL

FROM: Lois
SENT: Tuesday, July 27, 2004 9:37 PM
TO: mike@michaelmoore.com
SUBJECT: the movie—an 84-year-old Republican's
response

Hello:

I took an 84-year-old, lifelong Republican to see the
movie. She was already leaning against voting for
Bush—she hates his fundamentalism, among other
things. She LOVED your movie, and now plans to take
others to see it.

   BRAVO!

Lois

FROM: Thomas O'Keefe
SENT: Sunday, July 11, 2004 1:18 AM
TO: mike@michaelmoore.com
SUBJECT: thank you

Mike,

Just had a chance to see your film this evening. I don't always agree with all your interpretations, but what a powerful piece of documentary film. I sincerely appreciate the fact that you've put a human face on events that have transpired over the past few years. Thank you for your dedication to those who have lost their lives; that meant a lot to me. On September 11th I lost a friend; he was working on one of the top floors of the World Trade Center . . .

Best,

Tom
Seattle, WA

FROM: John Carr
SENT: Sunday, July 04, 2004 1:48 PM
TO: mike@michaelmoore.com
SUBJECT: My effort to get "Fahrenheit 9/11" tickets to anybody who wants them.

This is my small part to get the message out. I have sent it to everybody I know, feel free to forward it on:

Hello friends, family, and friends and family of friends and family.

I apologize for sending this mass e-mail, however, this is an important matter, and I am hoping to spread this message as far as possible.

Two nights ago my wife and I saw Michael Moore's new movie *Fahrenheit 9/11*. I will spare you the hype—which is amply available elsewhere—but I will say that it raised some very important questions about our political process and the direction that this country is headed.

I believe that getting people engaged with AND DISCUSSING the issues surrounding our economy, the Iraq war, terrorism, and the media is essential to the functioning of our democracy.

I also believe that, regardless of how you come down on the current administration and/or Michael Moore, *Fahrenheit 9/11* is a good starting point for this discussion.

Towards that end I am making the following request and the following offer.

1. I would ask every recipient of this e-mail to go see *Fahrenheit 9/11* in the theaters, and to for-

ward on this e-mail to at least 10 people you know, regardless of their political views.

2. I HAVE SET ASIDE $200.00 OF MY OWN MONEY TO BUY TICKETS TO SEE *FAHRENHEIT 9/11* FOR ANY RECIPIENT OF THIS E-MAIL who does not have the money to buy their own ticket, or would not otherwise pay their own money to see it. As a graduate student who is making little more than minimum wage as a teaching assistant, and who is not employed this summer, I do not have a lot of money. That said, I think that this is important enough that I will put my money where my mouth is to try to get some discussion started. PLEASE FORWARD THIS E-MAIL to anybody you think may want a ticket.

In return for buying you a ticket to *Fahrenheit 9/11*, all that I ask is that you send me a brief e-mail after you see it to let me know what you thought, and telling me who you have discussed it with or are going to discuss it with. (You can leave out people's names, for the sake of privacy. Something like "my neighbor Jim" is fine with me.)

I will buy tickets through Fandango for anybody who asks for them until I have used up the $200.00 I have set aside for this. Just send me an e-mail with the theater and show time where you would like to see *Fahrenheit 9/11*.

If you have seen the movie already and you agree with me that it is a good starting point for discussion, I can only encourage you to do the same thing I am doing. Offer to take a friend or acquaintance to see the movie and discuss it afterwards. I hope that I will get a lot of requests, that I will spend down this modest amount quickly, and that others will pick up where I leave off.

Democracy is meaningless unless we are all prepared to take the 3 following steps: (1) discuss the issues with each other, (2) register to vote, and (3) vote.

Thank you for your time reading this message.

John Newman Carr
Seattle, WA

FROM: Andrew J. Marsico
SENT: Friday, July 02, 2004 9:20 AM
TO: mike@michaelmoore.com
SUBJECT: "Fahrenheit 9/11"

Michael,

I just wanted to thank you for the masterpiece that you created. My cousin and I just saw the movie. We live in New York City and while waiting for the movie to begin it felt like I was at a family reunion. Everyone was talking to one another and having a good time, almost sensing that maybe the end of this four-year nightmare is near. I knew it would get this kind of reaction in New York. I hope that it does in parts of the country that are conservative.

I lost many friends, and business associates on September 11, and the months after that horrible day were surreal in the city. It was our generation's "day that will live in infamy."

In the movie when you showed the footage of the people in New York on 9/11 and also the blank screen with the audio I got chills and I cried. You could hear a pin drop in the theater. I think everyone in the theater was crying. It was very powerful. As New Yorkers we lost a part of our soul that day and we still are not done healing. Those towers and many of the people in the towers were such a big part of my life and now they are gone.

Thank you for what you have done. You are a true hero. This is truly an Evil Regime of evil-doers!

Mike, I am very concerned about what is going on in this country. How can it be possible that this presidential race can still be this close. There are too many idiots in this country that are too lazy to read and educate themselves as to what's going on with this government and in the world because it might interfere with *The Bachelor, Survivor* (which I admit I do watch), and *American Idol*. When they do want an update on news they will turn to FOX News while they are waving their flags at the TV sets and cheering on Hannity and Colmes (Al Franken is hysterical), Bill O'Reilly, and listening to Rush Limbaugh on the radio.

Sorry for being so long-winded and I know you have millions of e-mails and letters that you must get on a daily basis, but I just wanted to thank you for making a movie like this at a time like this. This is patriotism, this is freedom of speech, this is the truth! I am doing everything that I can in my little part of the world to make sure that Bush does not get another four years.

Thank you,

Andrew J. Marsico

FROM: Marge McCarthy
SENT: Thursday, July 01, 2004 6:39 PM
TO: mike@michaelmoore.com
SUBJECT: "Mom, your Democrats are home!" is
proudly declared by one less Republican after
viewing "F9/11"

I went to *F9/11* by myself. My husband is a registered
Republican, and he would have gone, but I wanted to
experience this without his influence. I asked him to take
our 19-year-old, know-it-all, son to dinner and to see
*F9/11*. They went and walked in the door after proclaim-
ing, "Mom, your Democrats are home!"

Now I am not one to vote party lines, especially
since there are few choices in my neck of the woods,
but this movie changed my family dynamics. My son,
who has been very rebellious lately, came to me, crying
tears and said, "Thanks for making us go, Mom." I
didn't MAKE them go, but I strongly encouraged and
the whole thing was good. My husband is no longer
considering himself a Republican and my son is hanging around the house and being nice to us. (Maybe
actually seeing what he could be faced with if the draft
is reinstated is a little eye opening.)

Lastly, my best friend's daughter is the granddaugh-
ter of a man who not only ran for governor in Colorado
in the 80s, but he is also single-handedly funding the
largest campaign to create a voucher system for our
public schools. This beautiful, but naive, 16-year-old
young lady told me that she wanted to see *F9/11* and
was going to ask her father or grandfather to take her

to see it this week. I need not say that she hasn't seen the movie, but her mother (divorced) will take her.

Thanks to you and everyone that is involved in the creation of the powerful *F9/11*. Thanks to Lila for sharing and allowing all of us to share her pain.

Marge McCarthy
Colorado Springs, CO

FROM: Michael H.
SENT: Thursday, July 22, 2004 12:07 AM
TO: mike@michaelmoore.com
SUBJECT: Changed Person

Dear Mr. Moore,

I am a 24-year-old student from Tulsa, OK. I have been a registered Republican since I was old enough to vote. I have always been rather "middle-of-the-road" but always put on a conservative front as to avoid any criticism from my family and friends who, for the most part, are extremely conservative. Knowing that I would have very little chance of persuading any of my friends to join me in watching *Fahrenheit 9/11*, I went alone between classes this afternoon. By this time you may be asking yourself, "What is the point of this letter?" Well here it is: I would like to thank you. Your film opened my eyes to many things. America is a great country, but we are not the only people in the world. Americans have a tendency to put the flag before people. As great as any country is, it still stands at no higher worth than that of a single human life.

I am not an overly sentimental person. I can think of no more than five times in my adult life when I actually cried. One of those five was on 9-11-01. Another was this afternoon. Hearing Mrs. Lipscomb speak at the end of the film about her son and nearly collapse on the sidewalks of D.C. from the grief brought the war home to me. Images on TV don't do that. On TV, the war is a place getting leveled by bombs. In life, it's something much more: people. Your film opened my eyes in a way that I did not think possible. In the last 12 hours since I saw it, I have "outed" my liberalism to my mom and proudly exclaimed that I viewed a film that changed me more than I thought possible. I am seriously considering volunteering my time to the local Democratic Party, much like the soldier in your film. In the last 12 hours, I have become a valiant supporter of yours, when just yesterday, I was a critic. Critics will always be there to speak against you and your film, but that's OK. Why is it OK? Because this is America, the place that you obviously love enough to question your leaders. There's nothing anti-American about that. Thank you for your time and I hope this letter finds you well.

Michael H.
Tulsa, OK

FROM: Stefanie Mathew
SENT: Friday, July 23, 2004 9:25 PM
TO: mike@michaelmoore.com
SUBJECT: thank you

Hi,

I just wanted to add my voice to the thousands that are thanking you for making *Fahrenheit 9/11*. I've long been a part of the choir, but I am amazed that—after 56 years as a die-hard Republican—it was your movie that has finally made my father decide to vote Democrat. He's been unhappy with the war and unhappy with Bush as a man for a while, but seeing the stories that you were able to tell pushed him over the line. I never thought I would see it happen, but my Dad's decision has given me hope that there is still a core of decent, honest Americans who, no matter what their particular political beliefs, still know the difference between what's right and what's unacceptable and will vote their conscience in November. Thank you.

Stefanie Mathew
Washington, DC

FROM: Pam & Rick Bennett
SENT: Sunday, July 25, 2004 12:08 PM
TO: mike@michaelmoore.com
SUBJECT: another man sees the light . . . thank you

Michael:

I want to tell you about taking my father to see your
movie today. Over the past two years my father has
been a Bush supporter in every way. At one point he
even stopped talking to me for a couple of months
because I was so vocal in my opposition about going to
war in Iraq. He has truly believed that Bush is a man
of God. Today, I took my parents to lunch and then
told them I was taking them to a movie. The movie
was *Fahrenheit 9/11*. I was afraid my father would be
mad or would walk out. But he took in every word, and
upon leaving commented that it was "a real eye
opener." A bit later he said that he was going to write a
letter to the editor of his hometown newspaper to say
that all Christians should see this movie. If you knew
my father, you'd know that this is testimony to the
power of the film. Thank you so much for making it.
Not only have you made one man see the truth, you
have also made him understand his daughter's ranting
over the past couple of years. I truly fear for our country. Please keep up the good work. . . .

Long may you run . . .

Pam Bennett
Lewis Center, OH

FROM: Miss Taylor Parson
SENT: Friday, July 23, 2004 5:38 PM
TO: mike@michaelmoore.com
SUBJECT: A moment in history . . .

Michael,

I am a 25-year-old student, attending the University of North Carolina at Wilmington, North Carolina. My father, a strict Republican businessman, but one of the most rational, honest, and open-minded people I have ever known, lives in Kinston, North Carolina, and went to see *Fahrenheit 9/11* on Tuesday, July 20th.

After hearing about the film from the media, myself, and my siblings, he decided to go and view it. He felt it was only fair to see a different side.

As I mentioned above, he is considerably open-minded, and has neither a Bill O'Reilly nor a Rush Limbaugh personality. He has investigated the allegations against Bush, and is well aware of Bush's untidy career as the "president." He is not a Republican in denial, needless to say. But I was surprised at his wishing to see your film. I went with my father to see this film, my fourth time seeing it. After the film, my father turned to me and said, "I guess I need to change my registration to Independent so I can vote for John Kerry."

My father, who is 58 years old, has NEVER voted for a Democrat in his life. This will be the FIRST TIME. He stated that the facts you presented were indeed true, and believe me when I tell you, my father is not naive nor is he stupid. He is a brilliant man with an IQ twice Bush's, and if he says you are telling the truth, then it's true. Period.

Because of his own independent research into George W(ar) Bush's own discredible record, and the confirmation of your incredible film, my father desires a swift change, and will be voting for Kerry on November 2nd.

My father has now insisted on reading and watching all of your excellent work, which I informed him of chronologically and with much enthusiasm. And if he says he is going to watch all of your films and read every book, I believe him. He, unlike our cowboy, has credibility, honor, strength, and is very literate.

So on behalf of myself and my father, thank you Michael for validating everything we've already known, and for enlightening us on the things we didn't. My father says you are an important and legitimate American. And, remember, he's always right.

Miss Taylor Parson

FROM: Angela
SENT: Wednesday, June 30, 2004 9:27 AM
To: mike@michaelmoore.com
SUBJECT: thank you so much

Dear Mike,

Thank you so much for making *Fahrenheit 9/11*. I cannot begin to express how thankful I am that you made this film.

I was living in New York City on September 11, 2001, working in lower Manhattan, and I saw the second plane hit the World Trade Center a little after 9 AM from the street. I can honestly say that I remember every minute of that day. From running to my office to hiding under my desk to feeling the city quake with the falling towers.

I will always remember the sound of the plane hitting the building—it is a sound that is burned into my memory. Watching your movie—and hearing the sounds of the attack with just a black screen—made my heart race. It was the first time I had heard the sounds since that day. Thank you for being respectful and not showing the burning towers and people jumping from the buildings. The NYC news channels showed that footage every day.

The months that followed were very frightening, with elevated terror–level "warnings" and daily threats. But the most difficult thing for me was passing a woman on the street outside my building every day for months. Her daughter worked in the World Trade Center and had not been seen since 9/11. But her mother stood outside my building every day for months, asking if I had seen her daughter, handing out flyers of her photo to passersby. The girl was my neighbor, and she was exactly my age. She, too, had just graduated from college and had begun her career in New York City. It broke my heart to see her mom every day, and having to tell her that no, I had not seen Sarah. I remember how I cried when Sarah's mom stopped showing up in the morning, sometime around Christmas.

My cousin was sent to Iraq shortly after 9/11. I remember thinking at the time, "Why Iraq? Why not Afghanistan?" It seemed so strange to me. When Bush waged war on Iraq I realized that we were all manipulated by the Administration—that these "terror level" warnings were elevated every time we started to feel safe again.

You have probably heard thousands of stories of people living in NYC on September 11th. Although I am originally from a small coastal town in Maine, I will forever be a New Yorker at heart because of this experience. I remember wearing my American flag pin with pride, in honor of our fallen heroes. I stopped wearing the pin after we invaded Iraq, after I realized that we had been manipulated by an administration we so desperately wanted to believe.

Mike, thank you for making your film. You have made me a proud American again. I think I'll take my flag pin out of my jewelry box.

Sincerely,

Angela

FROM: Susan Brown
SENT: Friday, July 02, 2004 10:58 AM
TO: mike@michaelmoore.com
SUBJECT: you don't have to answer this, as I know you're busy, but

thought you would be happy to read it. My mother, who is the most apolitical person ever and who has always voted Republican because her father did and her husband does, saw *Fahrenheit 9/11* two days ago. (Mom is 71.) She called the next day to ask how to get unregistered as a Republican and re-registered as a decline-to-state. She called me because I am a flaming liberal and work the polls every election as poll worker, and she didn't want to tell my dad that she was doing this.

She wasn't sure about doing it prior to the election, but I told her it was important that she do it now so the party could see that the movie is having an effect (my hope is many more people take the same step).

So, I mailed Mom a voter registration card yesterday.

On behalf of my liberal siblings and I,

Thank you! You got Mom interested in politics!!!

Susan Brown
Davis, CA

FROM: A. Keith Rutherford
Sent: Thursday, June 17, 2004 4:21 PM
TO: mike@michaelmoore.com
SUBJECT: 9/11

Dear Mr. Moore:

I just saw your movie today and to tell you the truth I am stunned!!! I voted for Bush and I am ashamed of that!!! I wish he had been a different kind of President. Thanks so much for opening my eyes. . . .

A. Keith Rutherford
Los Angeles, CA

FROM: Charlene Wall
SENT: Friday, July 02, 2004 2:03 PM
TO: mike@michaelmoore.com
SUBJECT: Mr. Moore I went to see your film

Hello Mike,

My name is Charlene Wall and I am a registered Republican engaged to a Democrat. I am an open-minded Republican and my home is full of lively debate. I believe in being honest and I honor truth. Your film *Fahrenheit 9/11* was moving and well done. It haunted my thoughts for days. I had decided on my own that President George W. Bush had lied to me and that I was not going to support his re-election campaign. Upon seeing the film, I picked up a John Kerry for President bumper sticker and placed it on my car. I feel like a schmuck for voting for and supporting GWB and I am encouraging all my friends and co-workers to become informed. In fact, I have made an offer to my Republican friends that I would pay their way to see *Fahrenheit 9/11,* but so far, no one has had the courage to take me up on my offer. Instead, they give me rhetoric and fear statements and condemn you as a person. I admire you for standing up for your beliefs and then doing something about it. You are one gutsy man.

If you are ever in town (Camarillo, California, Ventura County), Todd and I would love to take you to dinner.

Warm regards,

Charlene

# A Few Last Words on
## *Fahrenheit 9/11*

"I think every American ought to see it."

　　—PRESIDENT BILL CLINTON, *Rolling Stone,* 7/13/04

"It'll be a good bonding experience no matter what your political belief. It's a good thing as an American to go see."

　　　　—NASCAR CHAMP DALE EARNHARDT JR.
　　　　(who took his crew to see *Fahrenheit 9/11*
　　　　the night before), FOX TV, 6/27/04

" 'I think this is one of the most important films ever made. It has the potential of actually affecting the election, and if it does, it will change the world. There are very few films or works of art that have a profound effect on world affairs,' he said, mentioning *Uncle Tom's Cabin* and *I Am a Fugitive from a Chain Gang.* 'But this actually has a chance to change the world.' "

　　—ROB REINER, *Hollywood Reporter,* 6/10/04

"Seeing *Fahrenheit 9/11* made me think deeply about love of country, how it molds us, drives and emboldens us and how it can sometimes make us so angry we want to shout out to the world: 'No, this is wrong.' Many things have been said about the movie, and of course about its director, Michael Moore. But I don't think

I've heard anyone comment on Moore's love for America. It seemed evident to me that the film was born from that love."

—PATTI DAVIS, daughter of Ronald Reagan,
*Newsweek,* 7/20/04

"I don't think I ever cried so hard at a movie in my life. I urge each and every one of you to see it."

—MADONNA, New York *Daily News,* 6/18/04

"In the end, if we manage to get out of this without either World War III happening or whatever other scenarios this administration has for us, it'll be because people kept doing things like making statements, signing petitions. It'll be because the Michael Moores out there didn't quit."

—JOAN BAEZ, *San Diego Union-Tribune,* 6/17/04

"For a documentary to win over every other film in the Cannes Film Festival is unheard of, so he's quite a genius."

—TONY BENNETT, *Fahrenheit 9/11* premiere at
Ziegfeld Theater, New York City, 6/14/04

"Ms. Blige, who has never voted, said that after watching Michael Moore's documentary *Fahrenheit 9/11,* she was eager to head to the polls in November.

"'I have to vote this year,' she said. 'After seeing that movie, I can't do anything else.'"

—MARY J. BLIGE, *The New York Times,* 7/6/04

"I was convinced that it should be viewed and reflected upon by as many Americans as possible . . . especially young people who, in a few years, might be part of our military forces. I'm committed personally to the proposition, as more than just a lawyer, that everybody should see this film."

—MARIO CUOMO, after watching *Fahrenheit 9/11* for the third time, *Chicago Sun-Times*, 6/17/04

"With the Michael Moore movie, certain conservative talk show hosts call him un-American. Him and anybody else who says anything about the war. . . . To question your country's policy, especially in a war that kills people, is definitely not un-American. It's probably the most patriotic thing you can do."

—JOHN FOGERTY, Scripps Howard News Service, 7/14/04

"I was moved by it—especially the story of the woman who lost her son in the war. I went with a bunch of friends, and we all cried. I couldn't really talk after the film for about thirty minutes afterward."

—EMILY SALIERS of Indigo Girls, *The Denver Post*, 7/23/04

"The truth is it's so ironic. The best information we may get about this election may come from a combination of *The Control Room*, *Fahrenheit 9/11*, John Sayles, the nightly news from Jon Stewart."

—SEYMOUR HERSH, ACLU Membership Conference, San Francisco, 7/7/04

"I think a lot of people are going to be talking about this film. And I think a lot more people who are on the fence about who to vote for, after they see the film, they'll be solidified in their vote."

—LEONARDO DiCAPRIO,
*The New York Observer*, 6/21/04

[N]ot only urged folk to represent for the franchise but to take time to catch Michael Moore's *Fahrenheit 9/11*.

—BIG BOI of OutKast,
Fourth Annual BET Awards, 7/15/04

"I want Michael Moore to have my seven bucks for that movie."

—TOM HANKS, *USA Today*, 6/15/04

"I've been dedicating 'Desperado' every night to Michael Moore, trying to get people to go see *Fahrenheit 9/11*."

—LINDA RONSTADT,
*Las Vegas Review-Journal*, 7/16/04

"A lot of us look to Michael Moore to uncover the real truth."

—CAMRYN MANHEIM, *USA Today*, 6/10/04

"Last night I got the chance to see Michael Moore's new film *Fahrenheit 9/11*. It was utterly compelling and incredibly thought provoking. I'd highly recommend seeing it."

—ANNIE LENNOX, www.alennox.net, 7/9/04

"I think it's important that there's something that's provocative out there for younger people. I'm thirty, so for anybody who doesn't think about what's important to the country, at least there's something provocative that they can go see, make up their own mind."

—CARSON DALY, *Fahrenheit 9/11* premiere
at Ziegfeld Theater, New York City, 6/14/04

"I think we're going through the most dangerous time since I've been on the planet, and every time I perform these days, I'm protesting about this insane cycle of violence our government seems bent on. They're doing nothing to stop it, and the country is so bitterly divided right now. It's worse than during the Vietnam years.

"When Linda Ronstadt's innocuous remark about Michael Moore's film can cause such an uproar, you know it's time to take a stand. I think *Fahrenheit 9/11* should be required viewing in every school and college."

—KRIS KRISTOFFERSON, *The Toronto Star*, 8/26/04

"I think the reason *Fahrenheit 9/11* is so important is because it tells the truth about issues where the truth has been suppressed for the last three years."

—MOBY, CNBC, *Topic [A] With Tina Brown*, 6/20/04

"[It] should be required for everyone in America to see as part of their education in high schools."

—LEELEE SOBIESKI, actress, *USA Today*, 6/10/04

"When an Italian journalist complained that the film had 'only one point of view,' Ms. Swinton replied, 'We've heard what Bush has to say. We live with it. It's not a fair fight. This film helps to redress the balance.'"

—TILDA SWINTON, actress,
*Chicago Sun-Times*, 5/24/04

"We want you to know that the politics of your film had nothing to do with this award. . . . We're giving [it to] you, because you made a great movie."

—QUENTIN TARANTINO,
*Chicago Tribune*, 5/30/04

"A film can be funny and that's all it has to be. It can make me cry. It can make me laugh. It can disturb me. It can elate me. This film did all of those."

—QUENTIN TARANTINO, Cannes 2004 jury president,
*The Globe and Mail* (Toronto), 5/25/04

# PART IV

## Essays
## and Critiques of
## *Fahrenheit 9/11*

# "Moore's Message Delivered, Big-Time"

*New York Daily News*

DENIS HAMILL, June 29, 2004

You could have heard a tear fall.

As an American mother named Lila Lipscomb drowned in anguish over the death of her son in Iraq, the packed Loews Bay Terrace theater in Queens was so silent at the 11 AM show of *Fahrenheit 9/11* on Friday that all you could hear was the rustle of tissues. I sat in the back of the theater, with an unemployed construction worker from Brooklyn, and as the movie played, I watched men and women, young and old, wiping their eyes in silhouette.

They were the tears of the nation this weekend as *Fahrenheit 9/11* blazed from sea to shining sea as the No. 1 movie in America.

This was a brand-new moviegoing experience.

Since I started going to the movies at age 4 at the RKO Prospect in Brooklyn, I don't think I've ever sat with an audience so personally involved with the story being told on screen. This was not, after all, some exploding-fireball blockbuster.

No, the exploding fireballs in this film are real. The dead people in this film are real. The dialogue is real. Real soldiers, real victims, real mothers, real dead kids. The bad guys, as portrayed by filmmaker Michael Moore, are all too real.

The only thing fake is this administration's reasons for going to war, exploiting the nearly 3,000 deaths of Sept. 11 so that a rich kid who went AWOL from the National Guard during the Vietnam War could send American troops to die in Iraq and call himself a "war prez'dint."

And the reason the people in the audience, the American people, get so involved in this movie is because we are all extras in the story.

The film—as sidesplitting as it is heartbreaking—is a soaring display of American patriotism, one that defies classification because it is a personal statement, the way Thomas Paine's *Common Sense* was something brand new in its bloody day. As Paine wrote, "Government, even in its best state, is a necessary evil; in its worst state, an intolerable one."

Moore doesn't tolerate Bush's government. Sometimes we need a smart, funny, common Joe to make some common sense out of what's happening in his country. If there had been cameras around back in the day, Tom Paine might have made a documentary instead of writing a pamphlet urging independence from England.

*Fahrenheit 9/11* oozes with patriotism because it is a loud celebration of our great Bill of Rights, telling our commander in chief that we think his war stinks in an election year.

Look, the Bush campaign spent $85 million in three months trying to convince the electorate that John Kerry is a flip-flopping left-wing threat to national security. Moore spent $6 million to make his documentary showing that Bush is an arrogant, self-serving, dangerous buffoon who is a threat to national security.

*Fahrenheit 9/11* is also a corrective to the daily drumbeat of right-wing talk radio, which slants the news to fit a radical agenda. Yet the Rush Limbaughs and Sean Hannitys scorn Michael Moore for daring to express his point of view with pictures. But Americans don't like hypocrites. And so they are forking over $10 a head to say so, in places like Queens and Brooklyn and small working-class towns and neighborhoods across the fruited plain from which come the kids who do the dying in America's good and bad wars.

*Fahrenheit 9/11* also has been picked apart by the legitimate press. But this is because Moore spanks the American news media for being swept up in the myopic post-9/11 patriotic hysteria, allowing themselves to be "embedded" by the administration and spoon-fed jingoistic Iraqi war news.

*Fahrenheit 9/11* is also a testament to American capitalism, because nowhere else on the planet could a working-class guy from a place like Flint, Mich., grow up to skewer the President of the United States with his own words and actions and turn it into the biggest-grossing documentary in history, taking in $21.8 million in its opening weekend.

This is a great American Horatio Alger story, one that every American should applaud.

Which is exactly what the audience in Queens did last week after George W. Bush mangled his final sentence and the end credits rolled. I was as emotionally moved by the applause as I was by the film, because that was the powerful sound of "Joe Public," as Bush refers to We the People.

Out here in the opinionated boroughs, I expected some boos. I didn't hear one. Instead, I left with a deeply moved crowd, passing a long line for the next show.

Back in Brooklyn, the unemployed construction worker bought a bootleg copy of *Fahrenheit 9/11,* shot with a camcorder in a movie house.

He called to say, "Even the audience in the bootleg film applauds at the end."

## "Thank You, Michael Moore"

*t r u t h o u t | Perspective*

WILLIAM RIVERS PITT, June 25, 2004

*"The light at the end of the tunnel could be the bulb in a film projector."*

—JEANETTE CASTILLO

Screens in Bartlett, Chattanooga, Jackson, Knoxville, and Memphis, Tennessee, will be showing it. Screens in Layton and West Jordan, Utah, will be showing it. If you find yourself in Leawood, Merriam, Shawnee, or Wichita, Kansas, you can see it. The same goes for Centerville, Fairfax, and Abington, Virginia. If you happen to be in Akron, Bexley, Dublin, or Elyria, Ohio, you're all set. Hoover, Montgomery, and Mobile, Alabama, will not be left out.

Laramie, Wyoming? It's there. Bozeman, Montana? Indeed. Should you call home Grand Island, Lincoln, or Omaha, Nebraska, you have not been forgotten. The largest mall in the country, the Mall of America in Bloomington, Minnesota, will have it in its theater. If you are a soldier at Camp Lejune or Fort Bragg, about to be shipped to Iraq, you can see it in nearby Fayetteville, North Carolina.

These towns, large and small, along with towns large and small from sea to shining sea and straight through the American heartland, will begin screening Michael Moore's documentary, *Fahrenheit 9/11*, beginning at 12:01 AM Friday morning, the 25th of June, 2004. For the majority of people who will see this movie, in those towns large and small, the experience will be nothing short of a mind-bomb.

The Who once sang about how the hypnotized never lie, but as we have seen, people hypnotized by television and deliberately enforced fear can certainly support a war, and a President, which are fundamentally at odds with basic American decency. In fact, people hypnotized by television and deliberately enforced fear will feed themselves into the meat grinder with "God Bless America" on their lips.

Michael Moore's film will snap that hypnosis, but

good. Those Americans who believed what their President told them because they saw it on the TV will, after less than two hours in their local theater, look at both their television and their President with doubt and loathing when they walk from the darkness into the bright light of day. There are millions of Americans who believed what they were told—about 9/11, about Iraq, about George W. Bush himself—who will come into that bright light with the realization that they have been lied to.

Speaking personally, none of the data in this film surprised me. Having spent every day of the last three years working to expose as many Americans as possible to the truth of the man they call President, Mr. Moore was unlikely to explode any shells across my bow. The connections between Bush, the Saudis, the Carlyle Group, and the 9/11 attacks were there. The connections between Cheney and Halliburton were there. The connections between Enron, Unocal, natural gas pipelines, the war in Afghanistan, and a little-known country called Turkmenistan were there. I enjoyed the fact that Moore showed off unredacted copies of Bush's military service record, allowing us to see the parts of those documents which had been blacked out. I found no fact, no assertion in this film to question or doubt. I have done my homework, and as was made painfully clear, Michael Moore did his.

Most Americans don't know about this stuff, and seeing it fully documented and meticulously researched on the big screen will be, to say the least, revelatory. Yes, Virginia, there are billions of dollars to be made off this Iraq war for Bush's friends. The second door on the left is the recruiting office. Sign on the line that is dotted, and be the first kid on your block to die for the benefit of Carlyle's stock options. Be sure to save your pennies beforehand, however, because the Army will dock your pay for the days you are dead. It's policy, you see.

Mr. Moore put two daggers into me with this film, the first of which had to do with American soldiers. Trooper after trooper spoke frankly for Moore's camera, condemning both the war and the people who thrust them into it. Several scenes graphically explained what happens to a soldier's body when it is caught in an explosion. The result is ruinous, and the cries of the wounded and the dying will ring in my ears forever.

The most wrenching scenes in the film center around a woman named Lila, who loves her country, loves her flag, and above all loves her children whom she actively persuaded to join the armed services. We learn that Lila has a son in Iraq, and because of that, she despises those protesting the invasion. We find out later that her son was killed in Karbala on April 2nd, when his Black Hawk helicopter was shot down. We watch her read her son's last letter home, in which he rages against Bush and the war. We last see Lila standing at the gates of the White House, tears boiling from her eyes, as she discovers her true enemy, the one who took her baby from her.

The other dagger Moore put into me came during his montage of the media coverage of the war. Journalist after journalist is shown rhapsodizing Bush, his administration, and the war. Each and every one of them carried forth that which we now know to be bald-faced lies: that Iraq had WMDs, that Iraq was a threat, that we had to go, and that everything is fine. It was a slideshow of the nonsense Americans have been spoon-fed for far too long.

If you doubt this, Sidney Blumenthal's aggressive and effective actual journalism, as found in his most recent report titled "Reality Is Unraveling for Bush," should help you along. "Most of the media was on the bandwagon or intimidated," writes Blumenthal. "Cheney himself called the president of the corporation that owned one of the networks to complain about an errant commentator. Political aides directed by Karl Rove ceaselessly called editors and producers with veiled threats about access that was not granted in any case. The press would not bite the hand that would not feed it."

With a single stroke, Michael Moore has undone three years of poor, slanted, biased, factually bereft, compromised television journalism. This, in the end, is the final greatness of *Fahrenheit 9/11*. Not only will Americans get a sense of the depth of the deception they have endured, but "journalists" all across the country will be forced to endure the humiliation they so richly deserve.

I was privileged to see this film in the company of three groups—Military Families Speak Out, September 11 Families for Peaceful Tomorrows, and Veterans for Peace—which have stood against this disastrous war from day one. Many in the theater had family in Iraq, or had lost family in Iraq, or had lost family on 9/11 and seen their beloved dead used as an excuse for unwarranted war, and there was not a dry eye in the house.

*Fahrenheit 9/11* is not a victory for anyone. We the People should have known better, We the People should have been given the facts before sending 851 of our children to die. We the People have been betrayed, by our leaders and by a media that profited, and profits still, from the daily sale of lies. This film drove that horrid fact home with a mallet, and it hurt.

I was reminded, as I filed out with this company of heroes, of a portion of Shakespeare's rendition of Henry's speech before Agincourt:

He that outlives this day and comes safe home,
Will stand a tip-toe when this day is named,
And rouse him at the name of Crispian.
He that shall live this day, and see old age,
Will yearly on the vigil feast his neighbours,
And say, "To-morrow is Saint Crispian":
Then will he strip his sleeve and show his scars,
And say, "These wounds I had on Crispin's day."

Many of us were not hypnotized. Millions of us took to the streets in this country and around the world, to try and stop this madness before it was unleashed. The people in that theater with me had done this, had never stopped doing this, though their President and their media named them traitor. They were right. They were right. They were right.

Michael Moore has unleashed a wolf within Mr. Bush's fences. There is no getting around it. Perhaps, now that it is far too late, we as a nation will wake up.

On the day of that awakening, those of us who never stopped standing, never stopped marching, learned to live without sleep, learned to live in a nation that scorned truth for televised fantasy, those patriots I was with tonight in that theater can pause for breath. We can sit upon the grass on a bright day, strip our sleeves, and show our scars.

William Rivers Pitt is the managing editor of Truthout.org and the author of *The Greatest Sedition Is Silence*.

# *"Fahrenheit 9/11:* Connecting with a Hard Left"

### *Fahrenheit 9/11* Slices and Dices Bush's Presidency into 1,000 Satirical Pieces

*The Washington Post*

DESSON THOMSON, May 18, 2004

CANNES, France—*Fahrenheit 9/11*, Michael Moore's most powerful film since *Roger & Me*, slices and dices President Bush's presidency into a thousand satirical pieces. It's a wonder the chief executive—at least, the one portrayed in this movie—doesn't scatter to the four winds like Texas dust.

Judging by the spirited pandemonium that has

greeted this documentary at the Cannes Film Festival, *Fahrenheit 9/11* not only is the film to beat in the competition for the Golden Palm, it also has the makings of a cultural juggernaut—a film for these troubling times.

With an ironic narrative that takes us from the Florida debacle that decided the 2000 presidential election to the current conflict in Iraq, Moore has almost endless fun at the president's expense. And he frequently uses the president as his own tragicomic scourge—in other words, hanging him with his own words and facial expressions.

In one of the film's most dramatic moments, we watch the president attending an elementary school class on that ill-fated morning of Sept. 11. An aide whispers to him news of the plane crash into the North Tower of the World Trade Center. The look on Bush's face is stunned, as any person's would be. A clock ticks away. The president looks as though he'll never get up from that seat. The minutes tick by.

"Was he wondering if he should have shown up to work more often?" Moore says in voice-over, this comment connecting with glimpses earlier in the movie of Bush's frequent stays in Texas to clear brush and play golf. The president stares at the children's book he's holding. It's called *My Pet Goat*.

But there's more to *Fahrenheit 9/11* than partisan ridicule. Just before that scene, we have confronted the unspeakable: when those two planes hit the twin towers in Manhattan. Moore shows only a black screen. We hear the buzzing of the aircraft. We know what's coming. We hear the impact and, a second later, the agonized cries and gasps of the witnesses.

Then comes the second crash. Only then does Moore cut to the faces of those watching. A tearful woman cries out to God to save the souls of those leaping from the windows. Another, devastated, sits down on the sidewalk. We don't see the jumpers. But we feel we do.

What's remarkable here isn't Moore's political animosity or ticklish wit. It's the well-argued, heartfelt power of his persuasion. Even though there are many things here that we have already learned, Moore puts it all together. It's a look back that feels like a new gaze forward. The movie points to social and financial connections between the Bush family and wealthy Saudis, including the royal family, Prince Bandar (the Saudi ambassador to Washington), and the bin Laden family.

It shows startling footage taken by camera crews who were embedded with the American forces in Iraq. And it spends time with such people as Lila Lipscomb, a Michigan mother who changes from patriotic support for the Bush administration to heartbroken despair after she loses a son to the war.

There are so many powerful moments to point to, all for different reasons: the visceral terror of a household in Baghdad, as young American soldiers break in to arrest someone; the candid testimony of American soldiers who express their disgust at the situation there; interviews in Michigan with impoverished African-Americans, a social group that has been a breadbasket for U.S. Army recruitment.

To watch this movie yourself is to realize with dawning appreciation that the director of *Bowling for Columbine* has finally learned to put his movie where his mouth is.

## "Persuasive and Passionate. *Fahrenheit 9/11* Is Both. It's Also Michael Moore's Best Film."

*San Francisco Chronicle*

MICK LASALLE, June 24, 2004

The big moment in Michael Moore's *Fahrenheit 9/11* comes midway through the documentary, and there's no mistaking it: It's the morning of Sept. 11, 2001, and the president of the United States is sitting in a little chair in a Florida classroom. His chief of staff enters and whispers in his ear that the country is under attack. And President George W. Bush just sits there for seven long minutes.

In a forceful documentary devoted to puncturing the image of the president as a take-charge leader, this will be, for many, the tipping point. At the very least, it will be the scene that everyone talks about. Moore doesn't show the whole seven minutes. Instead he lingers on the scene just long enough for the audience to daydream of Eisenhower, Reagan, Truman, Bush senior, Clinton, Nixon, or Kennedy in that situation, and to imagine any one of them standing immediately, excusing himself, and demanding to be put in touch with his national security team.

Assessing the merits of a political film is a tricky business. Obviously, its quality is partly a function of its power to persuade, but its persuasiveness is in the eye of the beholder. Yet there are other things to consider: The movie's passion. Its serious purpose. Its tone. Its mix of words and images, and the way both linger in the mind. There's the way the movie fashions its arguments, and the cumulative effect the experience provides—what you feel walking out, what you think about the next day. By all these measures, *Fahrenheit 9/11* is Michael Moore's best film.

Certainly, it's a career landmark, the film that signals his transition from political entertainer to political thinker, from propagandist to idiosyncratic journalist, from colorful gadfly to patriot. If *Bowling for Columbine* was a step, this is a leap, in which Moore vaults past Will Rogers into some territory all his own. In the 90-year history of the American feature film, there has never been a popular election-year documentary like this one.

The film, which won the Palme d'Or at this year's Cannes Film Festival, has a single unifying idea that brings together its various elements. The idea is an emotional one, namely that America has been living in a kind of nightmare for the last few years, one that began not with the events of Sept. 11, 2001, but from the moment that the networks took Florida out of the Gore column on election night 2000. Moore posits that the main source of America's nightmare has been the presidency of George W. Bush. There's anger at the core of Moore's position, but he never shows it. And while he sprinkles the film with his deadpan humor, for the most part he plays it straight, laying down facts methodically, trusting in the audience's interest and attention. The connection between the Bush family and the bin Laden family's oil interests dominates the first section of the film. Although Moore doesn't uncover anything sinister, the sheer extent of this personal and financial connection comes as a surprise, and it fuels Moore's outrage that the bin Laden family was allowed to leave the United States without interrogation following Sept. 11.

That Moore is becoming an artist is evident in the way he depicts the World Trade Center attacks. Instead of going to stock news footage, he blacks out the screen and makes us listen to the sounds of Lower Manhattan on the horrible day. It brings it all back. From there, Moore challenges the president's handling of the war on terror by bringing in experts to say that the Afghanistan war was "botched," that too few troops were sent. He details lapses in homeland security. To bolster his case that the administration has fostered a culture of fear, he goes to a tiny town in Virginia and talks to citizens on the lookout for terrorists. When asked what the terrorists might want to bomb, several locals say, "The Wal-Mart."

Moore had a camera on the ground in Iraq, and the footage he got is like nothing seen on American television. A woman sobs and screams that her family's house has been destroyed. American soldiers clown around near hooded detainees, while other soldiers express doubt about the mission. Moore's effects are manipulative in the best sense—even though the audience knows what he's up to, the moments still have power. As the president talks about the need for war, Moore shows kids playing in Baghdad. Later, he shows a boy lying in the street with his forearm barely attached to his body. On the home front, Moore shows a mother whose son was killed in Iraq, reading her son's final letter—in which he says that he hopes the president isn't re-elected.

Moore is playing for keeps. The somber tone notwithstanding, this film is on fire. It's an exhausting, shattering thing to watch, and the mood it casts lasts for days. What both exalts the experience and grounds the picture is Moore's essentially patriotic faith that a sincere, invested argument can get a hearing in America. To see *Fahrenheit 9/11* and experience its passion is to wonder why there haven't been popular political films like this since movies began, and from all points of view. It seems like such a reasonable use of cinema, and an inexpressibly worthy one.

# "*Fahrenheit 9/11* Places Real Issues in the Spotlight"

### *The Toronto Star*

### LINDA MCQUAIG, July 11, 2004

In a commentary in *Time* magazine, Andrew Sullivan lumped Michael Moore's intriguing *Fahrenheit 9/11* in with Mel Gibson's turgid *The Passion of the Christ*, dismissing both films as "deeply corrosive of the possibility of real debate and reason in our culture."

It is just downright silly to accuse Moore of corroding real debate.

Hell, the media shut down real debate long ago.

It is precisely because the debate has been so thoroughly corroded by the mainstream media—particularly in the U.S., where the extremist presidency of George W. Bush has been treated with kid gloves—that Moore's film is being so gratefully received by so many.

*Fahrenheit 9/11* appears likely to actually generate debate among ordinary Americans who have otherwise been exposed to little more than nightly TV "news" in which America fights evildoers around the world.

Moore questions the way the Bush administration has used 9/11 to justify the "war on terror," and asks what that war is really all about, starting with the fact it is being fought largely by poor people, while rich, private interests benefit.

Moore follows army recruiters into depressed areas, where recruiting prospects are hot; almost everyone already has a friend or relative in Iraq.

He then tries to get congressmen to sign up their children for war, and finds no takers, even though it was Congress that voted to go to war.

One scene shows Bush addressing a dinner of rich supporters, calling them "the haves and the have-mores."

Bush smirks: "Some people call you the elite. I call you my base."

This cozy relationship between Bush and the have-more crowd has been largely ignored by the media, which have let Bush present himself as a folksy guy.

Moore puts this coziness in the spotlight.

He also shows moving footage of black members of Congress, mostly women, blocked in their efforts to protest cases of black disenfranchisement during the 2000 presidential election.

Then there's the unforgettable footage of Bush, after being informed that a second plane has hit the World Trade Center, sitting in a Florida classroom for seven minutes while schoolchildren read a story about a pet goat.

Stuck in that classroom, with cameras on him but no one to advise him what to do, Bush is lost, confused, and utterly useless to the nation.

Should warplanes be sent up? Should buildings be evacuated? Will the little goat find a happy home? Who knows what the man at the front of the class is thinking, but, with hijacked planes still flying over the country, it seems hard to imagine this guy is capable of taking charge of anything, let alone the defence of the free world.

Which raises the question: Why did the networks never show this footage? It's been available for years on the Internet, and it's at least as interesting as the footage of Saddam Hussein's mouth being examined after his capture—which the networks never tire of running.

If the pet-goat footage had been widely shown like the Saddam-mouth footage—or the career-ending footage of Howard Dean screaming after losing a Democratic primary—Bush would have had a lot more trouble presenting himself as a tough guy defending the United States from terrorists.

He would have forever been the guy who listened to a pet-goat story while America burned—behaviour that's at least as un-presidential as screaming exuberantly in the face of defeat in the primaries.

Despite efforts to stop him, Michael Moore has managed to take some vital issues and images out of obscurity and toss them into the mainstream.

This seems more impressive than what Mel Gibson has done—take a well-known story and retell it, only this time with a great deal more violence.

Gibson's film could be said to answer the question: What does a man look like after being beaten to a pulp for hours on end?

Moore's film, on the other hand, poses the more pressing question: What might the world look like after four more years of George Bush?

# "Moore Interest in National Politics: The Liberal Film-maker Is Reshaping the 2004 U.S. Election"

*Financial Times* (London)

July 3, 2004

Every US presidential campaign produces its anti-establishment icons. Barry Goldwater, Eugene McCarthy, and the Rev. Jesse Jackson lost the popular vote but all contributed to the democratic ferment. In 2004 the insurgent to watch is Michael Moore, the maverick film director. . . .

But *Fahrenheit 9/11* has broken box-office records for feature-length documentaries. . . .

Whether this surge at the turnstiles will translate into Democratic party votes remains far from clear. Conventional wisdom argues that Mr. Moore's movie has little appeal beyond liberal activists already fired up to oust Mr. Bush from the White House. Their votes are secure. What Senator John Kerry, the presumptive Democratic party nominee, really needs is a strategy to win over disgruntled Republicans, many of whom appear to be going cool on Mr. Bush.

Mr. Kerry is doing his best to reach across the party divide by running a studiously centrist campaign. He may go further with his soon-to-be-unveiled choice of vice-presidential running mate. Mr. Kerry will want someone who can appeal well beyond his own base in liberal Massachusetts, to mid-west industrial states such as Ohio and Pennsylvania and also to the South.

Nevertheless, both Mr. Kerry and Mr. Bush would do well to take a closer look at the *Fahrenheit 9/11* phenomenon. The film's success dovetails with other evidence—notably the rash of political bestsellers, including kiss-and-tell memoirs from former senior Bush administration officials—that Americans have rediscovered their interest in national politics.

The proximate cause is Iraq. Mr. Bush has placed a huge bet that Americans will back him as a "war president" able to defend the nation against Islamic fundamentalism. Yet the chaos in Iraq and mounting U.S. casualties have steadily eroded popular support for the president, while the absence of weapons of mass destruction has undermined the original premise for war.

New polls suggest that many Americans believe the Iraq war has increased rather than decreased the threat from terrorism—the message of *Fahrenheit 9/11*. Moreover, the film's argument that Iraq was a war of choice rather than necessity is increasingly accepted, not only among liberal activists, but also by the foreign policy establishment.

Mr. Bush's counter is that this week's handover of power to the interim Iraqi government in Baghdad signals the beginning of the end of the U.S. occupation. He is betting on a long-term realignment in the Middle East. Yet there is no guarantee that Iraq will appear an unqualified success by the election date in November.

A year ago, Mr. Moore's anti-war tirade would have

been dismissed as fringe politics. Today, the big man from Flint, Michigan, has produced the biggest surprise of all with a film that has touched a chord in the nation.

This is an abridged version of a *Financial Times* leader first published on July 3, 2004.

# "Michael Moore Brings the War Home"
### It's the Stuff the Mainstream Mass Media Won't Tell You

*Sojourners Magazine*

DANNY DUNCAN COLLUM, September 2004

In the theater where I saw *Fahrenheit 9/11*, the coming attractions featured a trailer for *The Motorcycle Diaries*—an upcoming film about the early life of the Latin American revolutionary Ernesto "Che" Guevara. The trailer ended with the tag line, "If you let the world change you, you can change the world."

A good omen, I thought. But the day was filled with omens. Michael Moore's picture, and a story about his film, greeted me on the front page of the *Memphis Commercial Appeal* at breakfast. We went to lunch before the movie, and there he was again, in the café entrance, on page one of *USA Today*.

Moore's film did not disappoint those expectations. There, on the quad cinema big screen, was African-American Marine Corporal Abdul Henderson, in uniform, explaining that he won't go back to Iraq because he won't "kill other poor people" who pose no threat to our country. There, after 90 minutes in which the falsehoods behind the Iraq war were peeled away, is the explanation (from George Orwell's *1984*) that, at the end of the day, the maintenance of a hierarchical society requires war. It keeps the people at the bottom fearful and economically insecure. "The war is not meant to be won," Orwell wrote, in words that define Bush's war on terror. "It is meant to be continuous."

And that message came alongside the details of the incestuous relationship between the Saudi Kingdom and corporate America, surprising (and troubling) footage of dead and wounded Iraqi civilians, and the usually unheard voices of American soldiers left limbless and bitter by the war in Iraq. It's all the stuff the mainstream mass media won't tell you. And there it is, in *Fahrenheit 9/11*, smack dab in the middle of that mainstream. I wanted to stand and shout, "Viva!"

Many of us have made the analogy between America's Iraq invasion and the Vietnam War, and the parallels are real. But we anti-warriors would do well to remember that, compared to our predecessors at this early stage of the Vietnam disaster, we are way ahead of the game. Public opinion has already tipped against the war. During the Vietnam era, that didn't happen until 1969, four years into the full-blown conflict.

And in the 1960s, there was no Michael Moore. Well, there was, but he was a Catholic school kid in Flint, Michigan. Today he is a best-selling author of humorous political diatribes and an Oscar-winning director of popular documentary films. We are lucky to have him because, if we pay attention, he'll point us away from the mistakes and stupidities of the last great anti-war movement.

Unlike many post-Vietnam activists, Michael Moore genuinely loves his country and its common people. His patriotism is not ideological; it is rooted and local. Blue-collar Flint is his touchstone. He emerged as a celebrity-artist by telling the story of his hometown's abandonment by General Motors in *Roger & Me* ("Roger" was GM CEO Roger Smith). He comes back to Flint in the final act of *Fahrenheit 9/11*.

In this new film, Moore's sympathy is clearly with the soldiers who are forced to do the dirty work of this rich man's war, with their families back home, and with the poor and working-class kids who are the prey of military recruiters. He cares more about them than he does about any Democratic politician, or about the cookie-scarfing Fresno peaceniks we meet in a Patriot Act subplot of *Fahrenheit 9/11*.

And so should we. The soldiers who serve under America's economic draft—poor white, black, and brown, male and female—are part of the great mass of Americans disinherited and left behind by the global economy. They stream in from the bombed-out inner cities and the dying farm towns to bet their young bodies on a chance at an education and a career. They are not the enemy. They are, in the long run, the only people who can change this country.

Over the closing credits of *Fahrenheit 9/11*, we hear Neil Young's "Rockin' in the Free World." That song was originally an anthem for the overthrow of President Bush I. *Sic semper tyrannis*. And keep on rocking.

# *"Fahrenheit 9/11:* Luring TV Viewers to the Theater for News"

*Associated Press*

FRAZIER MOORE, July 14, 2004

Time was, you had to go to the movies to see the news. Then came television, which brought newsreels right into your home.

Now, in this election year a half-century later, people in huge numbers have found that getting news about the war in Iraq and the politics behind it makes a trip to the multiplex well worth the bother.

Who could have forecast such a relapse?

Could be, neither fans nor detractors of Michael Moore, whose *Fahrenheit 9/11* has uprooted couch potatoes by the carload since premiering three weeks ago.

Moore, of course, knows how to make a splash. Last year a billion viewers saw him accept his *Bowling for Columbine* best-documentary Academy Award by denouncing the war of a "fictitious president. . . . Shame on you, Mr. Bush!"

But then he elaborated on that theme with *Fahrenheit 9/11*, and the public response has been greater than anyone could have imagined, setting off shock waves even beyond its record-busting $80 million box office. His is a film that is firing up the public, both pro and con—even people who haven't seen it.

And it's done something else. In the way the film frames the presidency of George W. Bush ("Was it all just a dream?" Moore muses over images of Al Gore celebrating his short-lived win), *Fahrenheit 9/11* has managed to upstage mainstream TV journalism.

Along with his previous documentaries, a feature-film satire, and political bestsellers, Moore has engaged in made-for-TV journalism—his version of it, anyway. He headed up the prankishly muckraking *Awful Truth* on Bravo, and, before that, masterminded *TV Nation* for NBC, which billed the 1994–95 series as an "investigative comedic magazine show."

Stories on *TV Nation* included a report about Avon ladies selling makeup to natives in the Amazon wilderness and an effort by Moore to broker peace in Bosnia by getting the ambassadors of Serbia and Croatia to serenade each other with the "Barney" song.

Needless to say, *TV Nation* wasn't hatched at NBC News (where flagship newsmagazine *Dateline NBC* had been rocked by scandal a year earlier after rigging a fiery truck crash for its expose on fire risk in GM pickup trucks).

Odds are Moore could never fit the TV news mold. For instance, it's hard to picture him pinch-hitting for Stone Phillips as anchor of *Dateline NBC*. Moore is somewhat of a niche personality.

Granted, a signature personal style hasn't hurt veteran swashbuckler Geraldo Rivera of FOX News Channel, or John Stossel, the libertarian pamphleteer of ABC News.

But bulky, bluejeans-clad Moore is a committed outsider with a scruffy look and a liberal agenda. Long ago he staked his claim as a reporter-provocateur well apart from the manicured journalistic mainstream.

All the more surprising, then, that the TV-news establishment, issuing free content around the clock, could be eclipsed by an independent film that costs good money to see, and, until just weeks ago, hadn't even landed a theatrical distributor.

So what does *Fahrenheit 9/11* give its audience that newscasts thus far don't?

For starters: the video footage of recuperating U.S. soldiers, Iraqi casualties, President Bush in that classroom paralyzed for seven minutes after learning of the terrorist attacks. This is video you have likely seen nowhere else, and you emerge from the theater wondering, "Why the heck not?"

*Fahrenheit 9/11*, which won the top prize at the Cannes Film Festival in May, tackles grand themes with humor, fury, and naked partisanship that insists upon a response from the viewer.

And it provides a bracing alternative to the claims for objectivity that reign at TV news outlets (including, naturally, the "fair-and-balanced"–boasting FOX News Channel, whose lack of objectivity is probably its greatest asset). These Big Media news providers have served as Bush administration facilitators ever since his disputed election, declares Moore, a little guy whose message is unmistakably his own.

Moore has been in the public eye since his first theatrical film, *Roger & Me*, became an out-of-nowhere hit in 1989.

In the meantime, the companies that owned ABC, CBS, and CNN have been swallowed up by even larger conglomerates. NBC News and its cable-news outlet MSNBC, launched in 1996, remain under the wing of mammoth General Electric, while FOX News Channel was created in 1996 by global media giant News Corp.

Unshaken by this media upheaval, Moore remains a known quantity, a media force who charts his own path. Maybe that's another reason so many people have left their easy chairs to go see his new film. And why even people who don't go can't leave it alone.

# "*Fahrenheit 9/11* Has Recruited Unlikely Audience: U.S. Soldiers"

*The Wall Street Journal*

SHAILAGH MURRAY, July 12, 2004

FAYETTEVILLE, N.C.—John Atkins isn't the sort of person one would expect to find crowding into the Cameo Theatre here to see Michael Moore's *Fahrenheit 9/11.*

The 26-year-old U.S. Army machine gunner from Fort Bragg voted for President Bush. A graduate of the University of Colorado–Boulder, he enlisted last year "to serve my country" and expects to go to Iraq later in 2004.

"That was pretty thought-provoking," Spec. Atkins says after a showing of Mr. Moore's documentary. "I guess I'm a little disillusioned. I've got a lot more questions than answers now."

Every day since *Fahrenheit 9/11* opened here more than two weeks ago, military men and women have swarmed to the 125-seat Cameo. "Everyone thinks the military is so staunchly Republican," says Staff Sgt. Brandon Leetch, a military-intelligence specialist who spent time in Afghanistan. "What this shows," he says, looking around the theater before the movie, "is that we're not all the same."

Although a nearby suburban multiplex has started screening *Fahrenheit 9/11,* too, on two screens—

meaning Fayetteville residents have their pick of 10 shows a day—most of the tens of thousands of troops living in the area probably won't see the film. But soldiers and their families make up well over half of each audience at the Cameo, cinema owner Nasim Keunzel estimates.

That surprises Peter Feaver, a political scientist and military specialist at Duke University in North Carolina. There is a sense in the military that "the media is stabbing us in the back as they did during Vietnam" and Mr. Moore's film would seem "Exhibit A," he says.

Most viewers are coming from Fort Bragg, just up the road. But often a few Marines from Camp Lejeune, about two hours away, join them. The night Spec. Atkins attended, three soldiers arrived from South Carolina well after the 7:30 show had, as usual, sold out. The ticket seller set up chairs in an aisle.

*Fahrenheit 9/11* is a harshly satirical and controversial portrait of the Bush presidency, although it has sympathetic scenes of combat soldiers and their families. Critics say it distorts facts to make its point.

It opened in 868 theaters during the week of June 25, and is showing in more than 2,011 theaters across the country. The movie opened in the United Kingdom, Belgium, France, and Switzerland last week.

The U.S. Army and Air Force Exchange Service, which distributes films at 164 theaters on bases around the world, is trying to book *Fahrenheit 9/11*, spokesman Judd Anstey says.

"Our policy is that if a film is popular in the U.S.

and we can get our hands on a print, we'll show it," he says.

Currently, all prints are in commercial theaters. He says it took about a month to get another recent surprise hit, Mel Gibson's *The Passion of the Christ*.

## Unusual Stop

The Cameo isn't a usual stop for Fort Bragg soldiers. Ms. Keunzel and her husband turned a dilapidated downtown Fayetteville building into a two-screen theater because they loved foreign and independent films and were tired of driving to Raleigh to see them.

Ms. Keunzel didn't even advertise the opening of *Fahrenheit 9/11* in the Fort Bragg newspaper. The film's area distributor told her, "Military people won't want to see it."

But the first two scheduled shows sold out so quickly she added a midnight show. The next day, she added more screenings, for a total of five a day. They all sold out, even though the new times were never published.

Staff Sgt. Billy Alsobrook, 28, a missile repairman in a support battalion, drove to the Cameo one afternoon in his fatigues to get tickets for the evening show so he could take his wife.

"I hear they've got a lot of interviews with soldiers," says Sgt. Alsobrook, whose one-year tour in Iraq ended in February. He expects to return in September.

The Florida native said: "I want to see another point of view on Bush. It never hurts."

# "Framing Michael Moore"

*In These Times*

JOEL BLEIFUSS, June 24, 2004

What do Bill Clinton, John Kerry, and Michael Moore have in common? They have all fallen victim to Michael Isikoff's poison pen.

In the June 28 *Newsweek,* Isikoff dismissed *Fahrenheit 9/11* as "a mélange of investigative journalism, partisan commentary and conspiracy theories." He goes on to dispute three of what he calls "Moore's most provocative allegations," thereby leading the unsuspecting reader to wonder what else Moore has fabricated. More on that later. First some history about Isikoff's own "mélange of investigative journalism, partisan commentary and conspiracy theories."

In April 1989, John Kerry's Foreign Relations Subcommittee on Terrorism, Narcotics and International Operations released an exhaustive report that concluded that the Contras were involved in drug trafficking and that Reagan administration officials were aware of that involvement.

In an April 14, 1989, *Washington Post* article, Isikoff trivialized the report's findings and asserted that claims of drug trafficking by high-level contras "could not be substantiated." Subsequently *Newsweek*'s "Conventional Wisdom Watch" dubbed Kerry "a randy conspiracy buff."

The *Post* had nothing more to say on the subject until the fall of 1991, when Gen. Manuel Noriega went to trial on drug-trafficking charges in Miami. Isikoff then wrote: "Allegations that the federal government worked with known drug dealers to arm the contras have been raised for years, but congressional investigations in the late 1980s found little evidence to back charges that it was an organized activity approved by high-level U.S. officials."

That assertion was soon contradicted by the U.S. government's own witnesses against Noriega. In October 1991, Floyd Carlton Caceres testified that his smuggling operation flew U.S. guns to the contras in Nicaragua and brought cocaine into the United States on the return flight. However, federal Judge William Hoeveler, sustaining all objections from U.S. prosecutors, refused to allow Noriega's defense lawyer to press Caceres further on the subject. At one point, Hoeveler snapped, "Just stay away from it."

And in November 1991, convicted Colombian drug lord and government witness Carlos Lehder told the court that an unnamed U.S. official offered to allow him to smuggle cocaine into the United States in exchange for use of a Bahamian island that he owned as part of the contra supply route. Lehder went on to testify that the Colombian cartel had donated about $10 million to the contras.

At this point, the *Post* finally took notice. "The Kerry hearings didn't get the attention they deserved at the time," its editorial concluded. "The Noriega trial brings this sordid aspect of the Nicaraguan engagement to fresh public attention." The *Post* editorial writer might have added, "Indeed, our own reporter Michael Isikoff let us down."

Isikoff did a number on Bill and Hillary Clinton promoting the Whitewater Scandal. In a series of *Post* stories in late 1993 and early 1994, Isikoff, citing unnamed sources, offered ominous-sounding revelations about bureaucratic maneuvers ("Justice Department officials are moving forward with two separate inquiries that have been expanded") and unsubstantiated speculation from more unnamed sources ("Bill and Hillary Clinton 'could possibly have benefited from the alleged scheme' "). The press followed suit, and a publicly funded $52 million investigation turned up nothing.

In the '90s, Isikoff was also one of Washington's leading smut-rakers. He had been hot in search of a smoking presidential penis since 1994, when he was suspended from the *Post* after a dispute with his editors concerning his over-zealous flogging of Paula Jones's dubious claims against President Clinton.

But in 1998, employed at *Newsweek,* he hit the mother lode, with a little help from GOP operative Linda Tripp. That year he got the chance to write seven stories for *Newsweek* that mentioned President Clinton's semen.

"Fornigate" got its start on January 17, 1998, when scandal-monger Matt Drudge reported the following news item on "The Drudge Report," his online 'zine: "At the last minute, at 6 P.M. on Saturday evening, *Newsweek* magazine killed a story [by reporter Michael Isikoff] that was destined to shake official Washington to its foundation: A White House intern carried on a sexual affair with the President of the United States!" On the following morning, another right-wing editor, William Kristol of the *Weekly Standard,* brought up the matter on ABC's *This Week with Sam and Cokie.* On Wednesday, newspapers reported the rumors. Talk of impeachment was in the air.

Now Isikoff has turned his sights on Moore, lying in *Newsweek* and on a subsequent appearance on FOX's *The O'Reilly Factor* to make the case that Moore is not to be believed.

Isikoff contends that, contrary to the facts presented in *Fahrenheit 9/11,* the six charted airplane flights that flew the Saudis out of the United States "didn't begin until September 14, after airspace reopened." The movie says this:

> It turns out that the White House approved planes to pick up the bin Ladens and numerous other Saudis. At least six private jets and nearly two dozen commercial planes carried the Saudis and the bin Ladens out of the U.S. after September 13. In all, 142 Saudis, including 24 members of the bin Laden family, were allowed to leave the country. Indeed, the *St. Petersburg Times* reported in June that, according to Tampa International Airport records, on September 13, while most of the nation's air traffic was still grounded, a private jet landed in Tampa and picked up three young Saudi men and then left.

Isikoff also disputes the movie's claim that the Carlyle Group—a private investment firm in which both George H. W. Bush and members of the bin Laden family were involved—profited "from September 11 because it owned United Defense, a military contractor." Isikoff points out, "United Defense's $11 billion Crusader artillery rocket system developed for the U.S. army is one of the only weapons systems canceled by the Bush administration."

Again, Isikoff is twisting the truth. The Crusader contract was canceled after the Carlyle Group sold United Defense. *Fahrenheit 9/11* says this:

> September 11 guaranteed that United Defense was going to have a very good year. Just six weeks after 9/11 Carlyle filed to take United Defense public and in December made a one-day profit of $237 million."

To wit, on January 10, 2002, the *Los Angeles Times'* Mark Fineman wrote:

> On a single day last month, Carlyle earned $237 million selling shares in United Defense Industries, the Army's fifth-largest contractor. The stock offering was well timed: Carlyle officials say they decided to take the company public only after the September 11 attacks. . . . On September 26 [2001], the Army signed a $655 million modified contract with United Defense through April 2003 to complete the

Crusader's development phase. In October, the company listed the Crusader, and the attacks themselves, as selling points for its stock offering.

Of course, Isikoff doesn't even mention one of the most revealing facts presented in *Fahrenheit 9/11*. In 2004, when the White House released Bush's military records, it blacked out the name of the president's good friend James Bath. (In an original copy obtained by Moore, Bath's name had not been redacted.) The two met in the Texas Air National Guard, and both were suspended in 1972 for failing to take their medical examination. (In *Fahrenheit 9/11* the camera scans the military records as Eric Clapton's song "Cocaine" plays in the background.) In 1976, Bath was hired by the bin Laden family to manage their money in Texas. Three years later, Bath gave Bush $50,000 for a 5 percent stake in his first business, Arbusto Energy. It has long been suspected, but never proven, that the Arbusto money came directly from Salem bin Laden, head of the family and a brother of Osama bin Laden. (See "Questionable Ties: Tracking bin Laden's Money Flow Leads Back to Midland, Texas," by Wayne Madsen, November 12, 2001.)

*Fahrenheit 9/11* is an amazingly powerful documentary. Moore collects skeins of archival footage—a young George W. driving across country, Paul Wolfowitz slicking his hair back with spit as he readies for the cameras, Bush addressing a fund-raising dinner: "This is an impressive crowd, the haves and the have-mores. Some people call you the elite. I call you my base."

Moore weaves historic documents together with his

signature vignettes—two Air Force recruiters bamboo-zling youth into the military, the mourning mother whose soldier son was killed in Iraq, and members of Congress running away as he asks them to sign up and enlist their children in the war.

Through these, Moore constructs a penitential sack-cloth for a president who has no clothes, and who, come November, will, electorate willing, be out of office. Thanks, significantly, to Michael Moore.

Yes, *Fahrenheit 9/11* is propaganda, in the same way the nightly news is, or the front page of your daily paper. It's just that Moore is more upfront with the point he is trying to make. Critics contend that Moore is framing the president. Not quite. He builds his case with the president's own words, numerous damning facts, and the testimony of those most affected by the war.

What the critics of the film are really outraged about is that *Fahrenheit 9/11* could have an effect on the presidential election. After breaking records in New York, the movie opens Friday, June 25, and on Monday, June 28, MoveOn will host an evening of nationwide house parties. The parties, more than 1,000 of them, will culminate in a national online town meeting with Moore.

To fight back, some unknown person or organiza-tion hired the P.R. firm Russo, Marsh & Rogers of Sacramento, California. The company, which has strong ties to the Republican Party, set up a Web site, MoveAmericaForward.org, to attack *Fahrenheit 9/11*. The P.R. flacks who managed the site encouraged

Americans who found in Moore's movie *Fahrenheit 9/11* an attempt to undermine the war on terror, to let movie theater operators know about their objections. Think about it . . . If you walked into a Wal-Mart store and saw they were selling merchandise that attacked the military, our troops, and America's battle against Islamic terrorism, wouldn't you complain to the store manager or write a letter and ask that they not sell that product because it was undermining our national effort?

Others on the right aim to counter Moore with a movie of their own making, *Michael Moore Hates America: A Documentary That Tells the Truth about a Great Nation.*

That will be a hard sell to anyone who sees *Fahrenheit 9/11,* which makes clear that Michael Moore loves America. It's the Bush administration he can't stand.

# PART V

## Beyond *Fahrenheit 9/11*— More Writings on the Issues from the Film

# "Saving the Saudis"

*Vanity Fair*

CRAIG UNGER, October 2003

On the morning of September 13, 2001, a 49-year-old private eye named Dan Grossi got an unexpected call from the Tampa Police Department. Grossi had worked with the Tampa force for 20 years before retiring, and it was not particularly unusual for the police to recommend former officers for special security jobs. But Grossi's new assignment was very much out of the ordinary.

Two days earlier, terrorists had hijacked four airliners and carried out the worst atrocity in American history. Fifteen of the 19 hijackers had been from Saudi Arabia. "The police had been giving Saudi students protection since September 11," Grossi recalls. "They asked if I was interested in escorting these students from Tampa to Lexington, Kentucky."

Grossi was told to go to the airport, where a small charter jet would be available to take him and the Saudis on their flight. He was dubious about the prospects of accomplishing his task. "Quite frankly, I knew that everything was grounded," he says. "I never thought this was going to happen." Even so, Grossi, who'd been asked to bring a colleague, phoned Manuel Perez, a former F.B.I. agent, to put him on alert. Perez was equally unconvinced. "I said, 'Forget about it,' " Perez recalls. " 'Nobody is flying today.' "

The two men had good reason to be skeptical. Within minutes of the attacks on 9/11, the Federal Aviation Administration had sent out a special notification called a notam—a notice to airmen—ordering every airborne plane in the United States to land at the nearest airport as soon as possible, and prohibiting planes on the ground from taking off. For the next two days, commercial and private aviation throughout the entire United States ceased. Former vice president Al Gore was stranded in Austria when his flight to the U.S. was canceled. Bill Clinton postponed travel as well. Major-league baseball games were called off. For the first time in a century, American skies were nearly as empty as they had been when the Wright brothers first flew at Kitty Hawk.

Nevertheless, at 1:30 or 2 P.M. on the 13th, Dan Grossi received his phone call. He was told the Saudis would be delivered to Raytheon Airport Services, a private hangar at Tampa International Airport.

When he and Perez met at the terminal, a woman laughed at Grossi for even thinking he would be flying that day. Commercial flights had slowly begun to resume, but at 10:57 A.M. the F.A.A. had issued another notice to airmen, a reminder that private aviation was still prohibited. Three private planes violated the ban that day, and in each case a pair of jet fighters quickly forced the aircraft down. As far as private planes were concerned, America was still grounded. "I was told it would take White House approval," says Grossi.

Then one of the pilots arrived. "Here's your plane," he told Grossi. "Whenever you're ready to go."

Unbeknownst to Dan Grossi, Prince Bandar bin Sultan, the 52-year-old Saudi Arabian ambassador to the United States, had been in Washington orchestrating the exodus of about 140 Saudis scattered throughout the country who were members of, or close to, two enormous families. One was the House of Saud, the family that rules the Royal Kingdom of Saudi Arabia and that, owing to its vast oil reserves, is the richest family in the world. The other was the ruling family's friends and allies the bin Ladens, who, in addition to owning a multibillion-dollar construction conglomerate, had spawned the notorious terrorist Osama bin Laden. Thanks to the bin Ladens' extremely close relationship with the House of Saud, the family's huge construction company, the Saudi Binladin Group, had won contracts to restore the holy mosques in Mecca and Medina, two of the greatest icons in all of Islam.

The repatriation of the Saudis is far more than just a case of wealthy Arabs being granted special status by the White House under extraordinary conditions. For one thing, in the two years since September 11, a number of highly placed Saudis, including both bin Ladens and members of the royal family, have come under fire for their alleged roles in financing terrorism.

Four thousand relatives of the victims of 9/11 have filed a $1 trillion civil suit in Washington, D.C., charging the House of Saud, the bin Ladens, and hundreds of others with wrongful death, conspiracy, and racketeering for having contributed tens of millions of dollars to charities that were al-Qaeda fronts. *Newsweek* has reported that Prince Bandar's wife, perhaps unwittingly, sent thousands of dollars to charities that ended up funding the hijackers. In addition, F.B.I. documents marked "Secret" indicate that two members of the bin Laden family, which has repeatedly distanced itself from Osama bin Laden, were under investigation by the bureau for suspected associations with an Islamic charity designated as a terrorist support group.

Most recently, in July, the administration asked Congress to withhold 28 pages of its official report on 9/11. According to news reports, the classified section charges that there were ties between the hijackers and two Saudis, Omar al-Bayoumi and Osama Bassnan, who had financial relationships with members of the Saudi government. Saudi officials deny that their government was in any way linked to the attacks. The Saudis have asked that the pages be declassified so they can refute them, but President Bush has refused.

Terrorism experts say that the Saudis who were in the U.S. immediately after the attacks might have been able to shed light on the structure of al-Qaeda and to provide valuable leads for investigating 9/11. And yet, according to sources who participated in the repatriation, they left the U.S. without even being interviewed by the F.B.I.

Officially, the White House declined to comment, and a source inside asserted that the flights never took place. However, former high-level Bush-administration officials have told *Vanity Fair* otherwise.

How was it possible that, just as President Bush declared a no-holds-barred global war on terror that would send hundreds of thousands of U.S. troops to Afghanistan and Iraq, and just as Osama bin Laden became Public Enemy No. 1 and the target of a world-wide manhunt, the White House would expedite the departure of so many potential witnesses, including two dozen relatives of the man behind the attack itself?

The incident is particularly important in light of the special relationship the Saudis have long had with the United States—and the Bush family in particular. For decades, Saudi Arabia has been one of America's two most powerful allies in the Middle East, not to mention an enormous source of oil. The Bush family and the House of Saud, the two most powerful dynasties in the world, have had close personal, business, and political ties for more than 20 years. In the 80s, when the elder Bush was vice president, he and Prince Bandar became personal friends. Together, they lobbied through massive U.S. arms sales to the Saudis and participated in critical foreign policy ventures. In the 1991 Gulf War, the Saudis and the elder Bush were allies.

In the private sector, the Saudis supported Harken Energy, a struggling oil company in which George W. Bush was an investor. Most recently, former president George H. W. Bush and former secretary of state

James A. Baker III, his longtime ally, have appeared before Saudis at fund-raisers for the Carlyle Group, arguably the biggest private equity firm in the world. Today, former president Bush continues to serve as a senior adviser to the firm, whose investors allegedly include a Saudi accused of ties to terrorist support groups.

"It's always been very clear that there are deep ties between the Bush family and the Saudis," says Charles Lewis, head of the Center for Public Integrity, a Washington, D.C., foundation that examines issues of ethics in government. "It creates a credibility problem. When it comes to the war on terror, a lot of people have to be wondering why we are concerned about some countries and not others. Why does Saudi Arabia get a pass?"

On a humid July day, Nail al-Jubeir, director of information for Saudi Arabia, sits in his office in the Saudi embassy in Washington and recalls the morning of September 11, 2001. Like many people, al-Jubeir was on his way to work that morning, and as soon as he heard that a second plane had crashed into the south tower of the World Trade Center, he realized that terrorists had attacked.

Over the next few days, the Saudi embassy was in turmoil. Innocent Saudi citizens in the United States were arrested. "That created an issue," al-Jubeir says. "How do we protect the Saudis who are being rounded up? Our concern was the safety of Saudis here in the United States."

Initially, Prince Bandar had hoped that early reports

of the Saudi role in the attacks had been exaggerated—after all, al-Qaeda terrorist operatives were known to use false passports. But at 10 P.M. on the evening of September 12, about 36 hours after the attacks, a high-ranking C.I.A. official—according to *Newsweek,* it was probably C.I.A. director George Tenet—phoned Bandar and gave him the bad news: 15 of the 19 hijackers were Saudis.

After two decades as ambassador, Bandar had long been the most recognizable figure from his country in America. Widely known as "the Arab Gatsby," with his trimmed goatee and tailored double-breasted suits, Bandar embodied the contradictions of the modern, jet-setting, Western-leaning member of the royal House of Saud. He knew that public relations had never been more crucial for the Saudis.

With the help of P.R. giant Burson-Marsteller, Bandar launched an international media blitz. He placed ads in newspapers across the country condemning the attacks and disassociating Saudi Arabia from them. On TV, he hammered home the same points: Saudi Arabia would support America in its fight against terrorism. The hijackers could not even be considered real Saudis, he asserted, because "we in the kingdom, the government and the people of Saudi Arabia, refuse to have any person affiliated with terrorism to be connected to our country." That included Osama bin Laden, Bandar said, since the government had taken away his passport in response to his terrorist activities.

Osama bin Laden, however, was a Saudi, and not just any Saudi. Bandar knew the members of his prominent family well. "They're really lovely human beings," he told CNN. "[Osama] is the only one. . . . I met him only once. The rest of them are well-educated, successful businessmen, involved in a lot of charities. It is—it is tragic. . . . He's caused them a lot of pain."

The bin Laden family neatly exemplifies the dilemma the United States faces in its relations with Saudi Arabia. On the one hand, the bin Ladens are products of Wahhabi fundamentalism, a puritanical Islamic sect that has helped make Saudi Arabia a fertile breeding ground for terrorists. Contrary to popular belief, Osama was not the only member of the immense bin Laden family—there are more than 50 siblings—with ties to militant Islamic fundamentalists. As early as 1979, Mahrous bin Laden, an older half-brother of Osama's, had befriended members of the militant Muslim Brotherhood and had played, perhaps unwittingly, a key role in the Mecca Affair, a violent uprising against the House of Saud in 1979 which resulted in more than 100 deaths.

Later, the Saudi Binladin Group became part of what was known as "the Golden Chain," a list of wealthy Saudis who nurtured al-Qaeda at its inception in the late 80s, some time before it was perceived as an international threat.

On the other hand, the bin Ladens years ago had disassociated themselves from Osama and his horrific terrorist acts. These were the Saudi billionaires who banked with Citigroup, invested with Goldman Sachs and Merrill Lynch, and did business with such icons of Western culture as Disney, Snapple, and Porsche.

The young bin Ladens and members of the House of Saud who were living in the United States in September 2001 were mostly students attending high school or college and young professionals. Several bin Ladens had attended Tufts University, near Boston. Sana bin Laden had graduated from Wheelock College, in Boston. Abdullah bin Laden, a younger brother of Osama's, was a 1994 graduate of Harvard Law School and had offices in Cambridge, Massachusetts. Two bin Ladens—Mohammed and Nawaf—owned units in the Flagship Wharf condominium complex on Boston Harbor.

Wafah (sometimes spelled Waffa) Binladin, a 26-year-old graduate of Columbia Law School, lived in a $6,000-a-month loft in New York's SoHo and was considering pursuing a singing career. Partial to hip Manhattan nightspots and restaurants such as Lotus, the Mercer Kitchen, and Pravda, she happened to be in London on September 11 and did not return to the United States. Kameron bin Laden, in his 30s and a cousin of Osama's, also frequented Manhattan nightclubs and, less than two months after 9/11, reportedly spent nearly $30,000 in a single day at Prada's Fifth Avenue boutique. He elected to stay in the United States. But half-brother Khalil Binladin decided to go back to Jidda. Khalil, who has a Brazilian wife, had been appointed Brazil's honorary consul in Jidda, though he also owns a sprawling 20-acre estate in Winter Garden, Florida, near Orlando.

As for the Saudi royal family, its members were scattered across the United States. Some had gone to

Lexington, Kentucky, for the September horse auctions, which were suspended on September 11 but resumed the next day. Saudi prince Ahmed Salman, a regular in Lexington, stayed and bought two horses for $1.2 million on September 12. "I am a businessman," Salman said. "I have nothing to do with the other stuff. I feel as badly as any American."

Others felt more personally threatened. Shortly after the attacks, one of Osama bin Laden's brothers frantically called the Saudi embassy in Washington seeking protection. He was given a room at the Watergate Hotel and told not to open the door. King Fahd, the aging and infirm Saudi monarch, sent a message to his emissaries in Washington: "Take measures to protect the innocent."

If any foreign diplomat had the clout to pull strings at the White House in the midst of a grave national-security crisis, it was Prince Bandar. The Saudis were famously adept at currying favor with U.S. administrations—they have contributed to every presidential library built in the past 30 years—but no one did it better than Bandar. He had played racquetball with Colin Powell years earlier. He had run covert operations for the late C.I.A. director Bill Casey that were kept secret even from President Ronald Reagan. He was the man who had stashed away dozens of locked attaché cases that held some of the deepest secrets in the intelligence world.

But it was his intimate friendship with the Bushes that truly set him apart. When George H. W. Bush became vice president in 1981, Bandar saw him for what he was—a Texas oilman who had enormous respect for the Saudis' vast oil reserves and was not a knee-jerk defender of Israel. The two began to have lunch regularly, and in the mid-80s, at a time when the press was assailing Bush as a "wimp," Bandar staged an extravagant soiree in his honor.

After Bush became president in 1989, Bandar acted as an envoy between him and Saddam Hussein, assuring Bush that the U.S. could count on Saddam to provide a bulwark against extremist Islamic fundamentalism. In August 1990, after Iraq invaded Kuwait, Bandar joined Bush at the president's family retreat in Kennebunkport, Maine, where the two men discussed going to war together against Saddam. A few months later, at Bush's urging, Bandar persuaded King Fahd of Saudi Arabia to join Bush as an ally in the Gulf War. In 1992, Bandar took Bush's defeat by Bill Clinton as a personal loss. And after the 2000 election, Bandar flew off on his Airbus jet to go hunting in Spain with former president Bush, General Norman Schwarzkopf, and former national security adviser Brent Scowcroft.

Now, in the wake of 9/11, the Saudi-U.S. relationship was being tested, and Bandar went into overdrive. For the 48 hours after the attacks, he stayed in constant contact with Secretary of State Colin Powell and National Security Adviser Condoleezza Rice.

Before 9/11, coincidentally, President Bush had invited Bandar to come to the White House on September 13, 2001, to discuss the Middle East peace process. The meeting went ahead as scheduled, but in the wake of the terrorist attacks the political landscape had changed dramatically. According to *The New Yorker,* Bush told Bandar at the meeting that the U.S. would hand over to the Saudis any captured al-Qaeda operative who could not be made to cooperate, implying that the Saudis could use any means necessary to get suspects to talk. Nail al-Jubeir says he does not know if Prince Bandar and the president discussed getting the bin Ladens and other Saudis back to Saudi Arabia.

But the job began to get done all the same. In Tampa, on the same day that Bandar and Bush were meeting in the White House, private investigator Dan Grossi says, he and Manuel Perez waited until three Saudi men, all apparently in their early 20s, arrived. Then the pilot took Grossi, Perez, and the Saudis to a well-appointed eight-passenger Learjet. They departed for Lexington, Kentucky, at about 4:30 P.M.

Grossi did not get the names of the students he was escorting. "It happened so fast," he says. "I just knew they were Saudis. They were well connected. One of them told me his father or his uncle was good friends with George Bush Sr."

Both the *Tampa Tribune* and sources familiar with the flight say that one of the young men was either the son or nephew of Prince Sultan bin Abdul Aziz, the Saudi minister of defense and Prince Bandar's father. Another passenger was said to have been the son of a Saudi army commander. But the Saudi embassy declined to confirm their identities. The *Tribune* reported that the request to repatriate the Saudis had been made by a different Saudi royal, Prince Sultan bin Fahad.

According to Grossi, about an hour and 45 minutes after takeoff they landed at Blue Grass Airport in Lexington. There the Saudis were greeted by an American who took custody of them and helped them with their baggage. On the tarmac was a Boeing 747 with Arabic writing on it, apparently waiting to take them back to Saudi Arabia. "My understanding is that there were other Saudis in Kentucky buying race-horses at that time, and they were going to fly back together," Grossi says.

The Tampa-to-Lexington flight, which was reported in the *Tampa Tribune* in October 2001, is the only documented incident in which Saudis had been granted access to American airspace when U.S. citizens were still restricted from flying privately—access that required special government approval.

How did the phantom flight from Tampa get permission to take off? At the time, the F.A.A. denied the flight had taken place at all. "It's not in our logs," Chris White, a spokesman for the F.A.A., told the *Tampa Tribune*. "It didn't occur." On the record, the White House declined to comment, but privately a source there said the administration was confident that no secret flights took place and that there was no evidence to suggest that the White House had authorized such flights. According to Nail al-Jubeir, however, the repatriation had been approved "at the highest level of the U.S. government."

The process began in the bowels of the White House. At the time, the Bush administration was holed up in the Situation Room, a small underground suite with a plush, 18-by-18-foot conference room in the West Wing. Live links connected the room's occupants to the F.B.I., the State Department, and other relevant agencies. Vice President Dick Cheney, National Security Adviser Condoleezza Rice, and other officials hunkered down and devoured intelligence, hoping to ascertain if other terrorist attacks had been planned. The most powerful officials in the administration came and went, among them Colin Powell, C.I.A. director George Tenet, and Defense Secretary Donald Rumsfeld.

Within the cramped confines of that room, the White House terrorism czar, Richard Clarke, the head of the Counterterrorism Security Group of the National Security Council, chaired an ongoing crisis group making hundreds of decisions related to the attacks. A true Washington rarity, Clarke was a civil servant who had ascended to the highest levels of policymaking. As characterized in *The Age of Sacred Terror*, by Daniel Benjamin and Steven Simon, Clarke was a man who broke all the rules. Beholden to neither Republicans nor Democrats, he refused to attend regular National Security Council staff meetings, sent insulting e-mails to his colleagues, and regularly worked outside normal bureaucratic channels. One of only two senior directors from the administration of the elder George Bush who were kept by Bill Clinton, Clarke, abrasive as he was, had continued to rise because of his genius for knowing when and how to push the levers of power.

In the days immediately after 9/11—he doesn't remember exactly when—Clarke was approached in the Situation Room about quickly repatriating the Saudis.

"Somebody brought to us for approval the decision to let an airplane filled with Saudis, including members of the bin Laden family, leave the country," Clarke says. "My role was to say that it can't happen until the F.B.I. approves it. And so the F.B.I. was asked—we had a live connection to the F.B.I.—and we asked the F.B.I. to make sure that they were satisfied that everybody getting on that plane was someone that it was OK to leave. And they came back and said yes, it was fine with them. So we said, 'Fine, let it happen.' " Clarke, who has since left the government and now runs a consulting firm in Virginia, adds that he does not recall who initiated the request, but that it was probably either the F.B.I. or the State Department. Both agencies deny playing any role whatsoever in the episode. "It did not come out of this place," says one source at the State Department. "The likes of Prince Bandar does not need the State Department to get this done."

"I can say unequivocally that the F.B.I. had no role in facilitating these flights one way or another," says Special Agent John Iannarelli, the F.B.I.'s spokesman on counterterrorism activities.

With just three Saudis on it, the Tampa flight was hardly the only mysterious trip under way. All over the country, members of the extended bin Laden family, the House of Saud, and their associates were assembling in various locations.

According to *The New York Times*, bin Laden family members were driven or flown under F.B.I. supervision first to a secret assembly point in Texas and later to Washington. From there, the *Times* reported, they left the country when airports reopened on September 14. The F.B.I. has said the *Times* report is "erroneous."

Meanwhile, the Saudis had at least two other planes on call. Starting in Los Angeles on an undetermined date, one of them flew first to Orlando, Florida, where Khalil bin Laden boarded. From Orlando, the plane continued to Dulles International Airport, outside Washington, D.C., before going on to Boston's Logan International Airport on September 19, picking up members of the bin Laden family along the way. Other stops for the Saudis are said to have included Houston, Cleveland, and Newark. Altogether, about 140 Saudis were on the flights, according to an F.B.I. source.

By this time, the lockdown on air travel had begun to lift. The F.A.A. was allowing airlines to operate as long as they followed certain security rules. Private aviation was subject to more constraints, but even there the F.A.A. had begun to allow flights by charter-service planes when the pilots filed flight plans. The F.A.A. has given all its records of air travel during the period in question to the Department of Homeland Security. A Freedom of Information Act request has been filed, but the documents have not yet been released.

Richard Clarke's approval for repatriating the Saudis had been conditional upon the F.B.I.'s vetting them. "I asked [the F.B.I.] to make sure that no one inappropriate was leaving," he says. "I asked them if they had any objection to the entire event—to Saudis leaving the country at a time when aircraft were

banned from flying." Clarke adds that he assumed the
F.B.I. had vetted the bin Ladens prior to September
11. "I have no idea if they did a good job," he says.
"I'm not in any position to second-guess the F.B.I."

In fact, the F.B.I. had been keeping an eye on some
of the bin Ladens. A classified F.B.I. file examined by
*Vanity Fair* and marked "Secret" shows that as early as
1996 the bureau had spent nearly nine months investigating Abdullah and Omar bin Laden, who were
involved with the American branch of the World
Assembly of Muslim Youth (WAMY), a charity that has
published writings by Islamic scholar Sayyid Qutb, one
of Osama bin Laden's intellectual influences. But,
according to Dale Watson, the F.B.I.'s former head of
counterterrorism, such investigations into Saudis in the
United States were the exception. "If allegations came
up, they were looked into," he says. "But a blanket
investigation into Saudis here did not take place."

At times, the Saudis who had assembled for departure tried to get the planes to leave before the F.B.I.
had even identified who was on them. "I recall getting
into a big flap with Bandar's office about whether they
would leave without us knowing who was on the
plane," says one F.B.I. agent. "Bandar wanted the
plane to take off, and we were stressing that that plane
was not leaving until we knew exactly who was on it."

In the end, the F.B.I. decided it was simply not
practical to conduct full-blown investigations. "They
were identified," says Dale Watson, "but they were not
subject to serious interviews or interrogations." The
bureau has declined to release their identities.

Some participants in the repatriation insist that the failure to interview the Saudis was insignificant, and, indeed, a persuasive case can be made that neither the bin Ladens nor the Saudi royals would have knowingly aided terrorists. "For groups like al-Qaeda, their objective is to overthrow the Saudi government," says Nail al-Jubeir, the Saudi embassy spokesperson. "People say we pay [al-Qaeda] off, but that's simply not the case. Why would we support people who want to overthrow our own government?"

Most of those who were leaving were either students or young businessmen. The bin Ladens, moreover, had forcefully broken with Osama by issuing a statement expressing "condemnation of this sad event, which resulted in the loss of many innocent men, women, and children, and which contradicts our Islamic faith." An F.B.I. agent says that they had a right to leave and that being related to Osama did not constitute grounds for investigation.

But 9/11 was arguably the biggest crime in American history. Nearly 3,000 people had been killed. A global manhunt of unprecedented proportions was under way. Attorney General John Ashcroft had asserted that the government had "a responsibility to use every legal means at our disposal to prevent further terrorist activity by taking people into custody who have violated the law and who may pose a threat to America." All over the country Arabs were being rounded up and interrogated. By the weekend after the attacks, Ashcroft had already proposed broadening the F.B.I.'s power to arrest foreigners, wiretap them, and trace money-laundering to terrorists. Hundreds of people were detained by the government while U.S. agents performed extensive background checks. Some were held for as long as 10 months at the American naval base in Guantánamo, Cuba.

"It's a natural part of any investigation to seek out people who know the alleged suspect in the murder," says John L. Martin, who, as chief of internal security in the Criminal Division of the Justice Department, supervised the investigation and prosecution of national security offenses for 18 years. "In the case of the Kennedy assassination, Lee Harvey Oswald's family, including his wife and mother, while not culpable, were looked upon for information about his background. In the case of Timothy McVeigh, McVeigh's family became a center of attention."

How could officials bypass such an elemental and routine part of an investigation during an unprecedented national security catastrophe? At the very least, wouldn't relatives have been able to provide some information about Osama's finances, associates, or supporters?

A number of experienced investigators expressed surprise that the Saudis had not been interviewed. "Certainly it would be my expectation that they would do that," says Oliver "Buck" Revell, former associate deputy director of the F.B.I.

"Here you have an attack with substantial links to Saudi Arabia," John Martin says. "You would want to talk to people in the Saudi royal family and the Saudi government, particularly since they have pledged cooperation."

Did a simple disclaimer from the bin Laden family mean that no one in the entire family had any contacts or useful information whatsoever? Not long after 9/11, Carmen bin Laden, an estranged sister-in-law of Osama's, told ABC News that she thought members of the family might have given money to Osama. Osama's brother-in-law Mohammed Jamal Khalifa was widely reported to be an important figure in al-Qaeda and was accused of having ties to the 1993 World Trade Center bombing, to the October 2000 bombing of the U.S.S. *Cole,* and to the funding of a Philippine terrorist group. (Khalifa was rumored to be in the Philippines in September 2001.) Khalil bin Laden, who boarded a plane in Orlando that eventually took him back to Saudi Arabia, won the attention of Brazilian investigators for possible terrorist connections. According to a Brazilian paper, he had business connections in the Brazilian province of Minas Gerais, not far from the triborder region, an alleged center for training terrorists.

Then there were the secret F.B.I. documents detailing Abdullah and Omar bin Laden's involvement with the World Assembly of Muslim Youth. Indian officials and the Philippine military have both cited WAMY for funding terrorism in Kashmir and the Philippines. "WAMY was involved in terrorist-support activity," says a security official who served under George W. Bush. "There's no doubt about it."

F.B.I. officials declined to comment on the investigation, which was reported in Britain's *The Guardian,* but the documents show that the file on Abdullah and Omar was reopened on September 19, 2001, while the Saudi repatriation was still under way. "These documents show there was an open F.B.I. investigation into these guys at the time of their departure," says David Armstrong, an investigator for the Public Education Center, the Washington, D.C., foundation that obtained the documents.

In the 1980s, with the support of the American government, the House of Saud and prominent Saudi businessmen had eagerly contributed to the fight against the Soviets in Afghanistan by sending money and weapons to Islamic-fundamentalist rebels who were battling alongside local mujahideen forces. Both the Saudis and the Americans supported these militants. But after helping to expel the Soviets from Afghanistan, these guerrillas, led by Osama bin Laden, morphed into the terrorist network known as al-Qaeda. Vexing questions remain about the extent to which the Saudis continued to support militant Islamic fundamentalism after bin Laden and al-Qaeda began attacking U.S. targets in the 1990s.

During the Clinton administration, the Saudis repeatedly resisted attempts by the United States to track the funding of terrorism within the kingdom. According to Richard Clarke, who led that initiative, there were several reasons for resistance from the Saudis. "Some of them were clearly sympathetic to al-Qaeda," he says. "Some of them thought that if they allowed a certain degree of cooperation with al-Qaeda, al-Qaeda would leave them alone. And some of them were merely reacting in a knee-jerk, instinctive way to what they believed was interference in their internal affairs."

Again and again, the U.S. Treasury Department has gone after the directors of various Islamic charities for providing support to terrorists. In October 2002 the Council on Foreign Relations asserted that, more than a year after 9/11, al-Qaeda continued to raise funds from wealthy Saudi supporters.

Last November, *Newsweek* reported that thousands of dollars in charitable gifts from Princess Haifa, the wife of Prince Bandar, had indirectly ended up in the hands of two of the September 11 hijackers. And many members of the royal family, along with several members of the bin Laden family, are now defendants in the $1 trillion class-action lawsuit filed on behalf of 4,000 relatives of 9/11 victims.

Documents filed in the suit allege that Prince Bandar's father, Defense Minister Prince Sultan, has contributed at least $6 million since 1994 to four charities that finance Osama bin Laden and al-Qaeda. Sultan's own attorneys acknowledge that for 16 consecutive years he approved annual payments of about $266,000 to the International Islamic Relief Organization—a Saudi charity whose U.S. offices were raided by federal agents. Casey Cooper, an attorney for Prince Sultan, says, "The allegations have no merit." He adds that Prince Sultan authorized the grants as part of his official governmental duties and did not knowingly fund terrorism.

The allegation against Prince Sultan is just one of hundreds included in the lawsuit. In addition to

Osama bin Laden, the family company, the Saudi Binladin Group, has been named as a defendant in the suit. At the heart of the allegations is the charge that the defendants knew some of their money was going to al-Qaeda and therefore had some responsibility for the September 11 attacks.

Many of the Saudis acknowledge that they contributed to the charities in question but say they had no knowledge that the money would end up in the hands of al-Qaeda. "The biggest problem we have with Saudi charities is poor and sloppy management," says Nail al-Jubeir.

The plaintiffs' attorneys do not consider that a satisfactory answer. In addition, they believe that, by interviewing the bin Ladens and members of the royal family before they left the country, the government could have answered some key questions. "They should have been asked whether they had contacts or knew of any other Saudi contacts with Osama bin Laden," says Allan Gerson, co–lead counsel for the plaintiffs in the case. "What did they know about the financing of al-Qaeda? What did they know about the use of charitable institutions in the U.S. and elsewhere as conduits for terrorism financing? Why was the Saudi government not responsive to U.S. pleas in 1999 and 2000 that they stop turning a blind eye to terrorist financing through Saudi banks and charities?"

All of which leads to the question of who made the decision to let the Saudis go. And why? Could the long-standing relationship between the Saudis and the Bush family have influenced the administration?

National security experts such as Richard Clarke find that suggestion dubious. "Prince Bandar played a very key role during the first Gulf War," Clarke says. "He was very close to the Bush family. But I don't think it's accurate to say that he plays that role now. There's a realization that we have to work with the government we've got in Saudi Arabia. The alternatives could be far worse. The most likely replacement to the House of Saud is likely to be more hostile—in fact, extremely hostile—to the U.S. That's probably the reason the administration treats it the way it does—not any personal relationship." With the war on terror getting under way, the U.S. wanted Saudi cooperation, and repatriation was clearly a high priority at the highest levels of the kingdom.

Still, the Bush-Saudi relationship raises serious questions, if only because it is so extraordinary for two presidents to share such a long and rich personal history with any foreign power, much less one that is both as vital to U.S. economic interests and as troublesome as Saudi Arabia.

It began in the mid-70s, when two young Saudi billionaires—Salem bin Laden, Osama's older brother and the head of the Saudi Binladin Group, and Khalid bin Mahfouz, a billionaire Saudi banker—first came to Texas hoping to forge political relationships. To represent their American interests, they chose a Houston businessman named James R. Bath, who knew George W. Bush from the Texas Air National Guard. Bath invested $50,000 in Bush's new oil company, Arbusto. He denies, however, that his investment represented the Saudis' interests.

In 1986, George W. Bush sold the latest incarnation of his failing oil company to Harken Energy, an independent Texas oil company that was struggling itself, and took a seat on its board of directors. By then, Khalid bin Mahfouz had become the largest stockholder in the Bank of Commerce & Credit International, or B.C.C.I., an international bank which financed drug dealers, terrorists, and covert operations and which became known as the most corrupt financial institution in history.

Once Bush was with Harken, a phantom courtship by Khalid bin Mahfouz and B.C.C.I. began. Neither George W. Bush nor Harken ever had any direct contact with bin Mahfouz or B.C.C.I. Yet once Bush took his seat on the board, wonderful things started to happen to Harken—new investments, unexpected sources of financing, serendipitous drilling rights. Among those with links to B.C.C.I. who came to Harken's aid were the Arkansas investment bank Stephens Inc., Saudi investor Sheik Abdullah Bakhsh, and the Emir of Bahrain, who unexpectedly awarded Harken exclusive offshore drilling rights. In 1991, a *Wall Street Journal* investigation into Harken's B.C.C.I. ties concluded, "The number of B.C.C.I.-connected people who had dealings with Harken—all since George W. Bush came on board—likewise raises the question of whether they mask an effort to cozy up to a presidential son."

After George H. W. Bush and James Baker returned to the private sector in 1993, they finally began to reap the benefits of their friendship with the Saudis. That year, Baker took a position as senior counselor with the

Carlyle Group, the $16 billion private equity firm. Two years later, Bush signed on as senior adviser. In 1998, former British prime minister John Major joined the firm as well.

On several occasions, Bush, Baker, and Major flew to Saudi Arabia with Carlyle executives to meet with and speak before members of the royal family and wealthy businessmen such as the bin Ladens and the bin Mahfouzes, Saudi Arabia's richest banking family.

As world leaders who had defended the Saudis during the Gulf War, Bush, Baker, and Major had the potential to be star rainmakers for Carlyle, and the firm's practices allowed them to do so without sullying their hands by asking for money directly. "Bush's speeches are about what it's like to be a former president, and what it's like to be the father of a president," says Carlyle C.E.O. David Rubenstein. "He doesn't talk about Carlyle or solicit investors." After Bush's speeches, Rubenstein and his fund-raising team would come in for the money. "Carlyle wanted to open up doors," one observer told *The Independent*, "and they bring in Bush and Major, who saved the Saudis' ass in the Gulf War. If you got these guys coming in . . . those companies are going to have it pretty good." Rubenstein says Bush and Baker were not given special treatment in Saudi Arabia. "They were well received there, as they are throughout the world."

A source close to the Saudi government says that the royal family viewed investing in the Carlyle Group as a way to show gratitude to President Bush for defending the Saudis in the Gulf War. "George Bush or James Baker would meet with all the big guys in the royal family," the source says. "Indirectly, the message was 'I'd appreciate it if you put some money in the Carlyle Group.'"

According to *The Washington Post,* Prince Bandar was among those who invested. In 1995 the bin Ladens joined in. Khalid bin Mahfouz's sons Abdulrahman and Sultan became investors as well, according to family attorney Cherif Sedky. Abdulrahman bin Mahfouz was a director of the Muwafaq Foundation, which has been designated by the U.S. Treasury Department as "an al-Qaeda front." "Abdulrahman and Sultan made an investment in one of the Carlyle funds in 1995 which is in the neighborhood of $30 million," Sedky wrote in an e-mail. "The investment is held for their benefit by Sami Ba'arma," an investment manager who has often worked with the bin Mahfouz family. Sedky added that the bin Mahfouz family condemns terrorism and denies that funds it has given to charities have been used to finance terror. Carlyle categorically denies that the bin Mahfouzes are now or have ever been investors. Reached on vacation in Michigan, Cherif Sedky stood by his original statement. "I assume that Carlyle has records of investments from somebody on the bin Mahfouz side, whether it is with Sami Ba'arma as a nominee or someone else," he said. He added that Ba'arma was a first cousin of the bin Mahfouz brothers.

In all, Carlyle officials say that the Saudis have invested $80 million in the firm. It is unclear how much of that was raised following meetings attended by former president George Bush or James Baker. The bin Ladens put $2 million in the Carlyle Partners II Fund, a relatively small sum that was said to be part of a larger package. One family member, Shafig bin Laden, was attending an investor conference held by the Carlyle Group in Washington on September 11, 2001. But after the attacks of that day, Carlyle bought out the bin Ladens' interest. "At first I felt it was unfair to blame the other 53 half-siblings because of this guy they haven't seen in 10 years," Rubenstein says. "But then I realized, life isn't fair at times."

There is no evidence to suggest that Carlyle played any role in the repatriation of the Saudis, but public advocates argue that the Bush-Saudi ties create at least the appearance of a conflict of interest. "You would be less inclined to do anything forceful or dynamic if you are tied in with them financially," says the Center for Public Integrity's Charles Lewis. "That's common sense."

On September 18, 2001, a specially reconfigured Boeing 727 flew at least five members of the bin Laden family back to Saudi Arabia from Logan airport.

On September 19, President Bush's speechwriting team was working on a stirring address to be delivered the next day, officially declaring a global war on terror. "Our war on terror . . . will not end until every terrorist group of global reach has been found, stopped, and defeated," he would vow. At the Pentagon, planning was already under way to take this new war on terror all the way to Iraq.

That same day, the plane that had originated in Los Angeles and made stops at Orlando and Dulles airports arrived at Logan. It is unclear how many members of the bin Laden family or other Saudis had boarded prior to its arrival in Boston, but once it landed, at least 11 additional bin Laden relatives boarded the aircraft.

At the time, Logan was in chaos. The airport was reeling from criticism that its security failures had allowed the hijackings to take place. After all, the two hijacked planes that had crashed into the World Trade Center had departed from Logan. As a result, exceptional measures were now being taken. Several thousand cars were towed from the airport's parking garages. "We didn't know if they were booby-trapped or what," says Tom Kinton, director of aviation at Logan.

The F.A.A. had allowed commercial flights to resume on September 13, as long as they complied with new security measures. Logan, however, because of various security issues, did not reopen until September 15, two days later. Even then, air traffic resumed slowly. So when a call came into Logan's Emergency Operations Center in the early afternoon of September 19 saying that the charter aircraft was going to pick up members of the bin Laden family, Kinton was incredulous. "We were in the midst of the worst terrorist act in history," he says, "and here we were seeing an evacuation of the bin Ladens!"

Like Kinton, Virginia Buckingham, then the head of the Massachusetts Port Authority, which oversees Logan, was stunned. "My staff was told that a private jet was arriving at Logan from Saudi Arabia to pick up 14 members of Osama bin Laden's family living in the Boston area," she later wrote in *The Boston Globe*.

" 'Does the F.B.I. know?' staffers wondered. 'Does the State Department know? Why are they letting these people go? Have they questioned them?' This was ridiculous."

Only a few days earlier, some planes, such as the one carrying a heart to be transplanted to a deathly ill cardiac patient in Olympia, Washington, had been forced down in midflight. According to F.B.I. spokesman John Iannarelli, F.B.I. counterterrorism agents pursuing the investigation were stranded all over the country, unable to fly for several days. Yet now the same counterterrorism unit was effectively acting as a chaperone for the Saudis. Astonishingly, the repatriation was routed through Logan and Newark, two of the airports where, just a few days earlier, the hijackings had originated.

As the bin Ladens began to approach Boston, the top brass at Logan airport were agog at what was taking place. But federal law did not allow them much leeway to restrict individual flights. "I wanted to go to the highest authorities in Washington," says Tom Kinton. "This was a call for them. But this was not just some mystery flight dropping into Logan. It had been to three major airports already, and we were the last stop. It was known. The federal authorities knew what it was doing. And we were told to let it come."

Kinton and his co-workers were also told to let the other bin Ladens board and to allow the plane to leave and return to Saudi Arabia. As Virginia Buckingham put it, "Under the cover of darkness, they did."

It was an inauspicious start to the just-declared war

on terror. "What happened on September 11 was a horrific crime," says John Martin, the former Justice Department official. "It was an act of war. And the answer is no, this is not any way to go about investigating it."

# "Plane Carried 13 Bin Ladens; Manifest of Sept. 19, 2001, Flight From U.S. Is Released"

*The Washington Post*

DANA MILBANK, July 22, 2004

At least 13 relatives of Osama bin Laden, accompanied by bodyguards and associates, were allowed to leave the United States on a chartered flight eight days after the Sept. 11, 2001, attacks, according to a passenger manifest released yesterday.

One passenger, Omar Awad bin Laden, a nephew of the al Qaeda leader, had been investigated by the FBI because he had lived with Abdullah bin Laden, a leader of the World Assembly of Muslim Youth, which the FBI suspected of being a terrorist organization.

The passenger list was made public by Sen. Frank Lautenberg (D-N.J.), who obtained the manifest from officials at Boston's Logan International Airport. Lautenberg's office was given the document in recent weeks and released it before today's issuance of the final report of the commission investigating the Sept. 11 attacks.

Although much was already known about the "bin Laden flight," Lautenberg provided additional details, including the information that the plane, a 727 owned by DB Air and operated by Ryan International, began its flight in Los Angeles and made stops in Orlando, Dulles International Airport and Boston before continuing to Gander, Newfoundland; Paris; Geneva; and Jiddah, Saudi Arabia. The aircraft, tail number N521DB, has been chartered frequently by the White House for the press corps traveling with President Bush.

A staff report by the Sept. 11 commission this spring said the flight was one of six chartered flights carrying 142 people, mostly Saudi nationals, from the United States between Sept. 14 and 24 after airspace was reopened. The U.S. government had allowed, before commercial airspace was reopened, at least one domestic flight for Saudis who had feared for their safety, Lautenberg's staff said.

The commission reported that there were 23 passengers and three private security guards on the bin Laden flight. However, the manifest lists 25 passengers, plus the three guards employed by CDT Training Inc. of Elmwood Park, N.J. After a request for permission to allow the bin Ladens to leave reached Richard A. Clarke at the National Security Council, the flight departed Logan Airport in Boston at 11 P.M. on Sept. 19, 2001.

Dale Watson, former FBI counterterrorism chief,

said yesterday that FBI agents "scrubbed the people who were leaving, and I was informed none of them were anybody we needed to detain or not allow to leave."

Lautenberg, in a statement, said that Bush "needs to explain to the American people why his administration let this plane leave." White House spokesman Sean McCormack said the contentions that the flight should not have been allowed to leave have been "debunked by the facts."

Ron Ryan of Ryan International said yesterday that he is "quite confident" that the Saudi embassy arranged the flight through a Ryan partner called Sport-Hawk. He said the bin Ladens "were quite concerned for their safety," which alarmed the crew. "The Saudi embassy offered to pay more money if our crew had a concern," he said.

But he said all were reassured because "the FBI and Secret Service were heavily involved. They were in abundance every place we were."

The commission staff reported that each of the Saudi flights "was investigated by the FBI and dealt with in a professional manner prior to its departure." The staff said that 22 people on the bin Laden flight were interviewed by the FBI and that the FBI checked databases for information on the passengers. The commission said none of the passengers was on the terrorist watch list.

The flight manifest lists 13 people with the bin Laden surname and others with Brazilian, British, Indonesian and Yemeni passports. Passenger Omar

Awad bin Laden had lived with Abdullah bin Laden, a nephew of Osama bin Laden who was involved in forming the U.S. branch of the World Assembly of Muslim Youth in Alexandria. Federal agents raided the office this spring in connection with a terrorism-related investigation. The FBI has described the group as a "suspected terrorist organization."

Among the other passengers was Shafig bin Laden, a half brother of Osama bin Laden who was reportedly attending the annual investor conference of the Carlyle Group, a politically connected investment company in Washington, on Sept. 11, 2001. Also on board was Akberali Moawalla, an official with the investment company run by Yeslam bin Laden, another of Osama bin Laden's half brothers. Records show that a passenger, Kholoud Kurdi, lived in Northern Virginia with a bin Laden relative.

The bin Laden flight has received fresh publicity because it was a topic in Michael Moore's anti-Bush documentary, *Fahrenheit 9/11*.

Researcher Margot Williams and staff writer Susan Schmidt contributed to this report.

# "TIA Now Verifies Flight of Saudis"

*St. Petersburg Times*

JEAN HELLER, June 9, 2004

Two days after the Sept. 11 attacks, with most of the nation's air traffic still grounded, a small jet landed at Tampa International Airport, picked up three young Saudi men and left.

The men, one of them thought to be a member of the Saudi royal family, were accompanied by a former FBI agent and a former Tampa police officer on the flight to Lexington, Ky.

The Saudis then took another flight out of the country. The two ex-officers returned to TIA a few hours later on the same plane.

For nearly three years, White House, aviation and law enforcement officials have insisted the flight never took place and have denied published reports and widespread Internet speculation about its purpose.

But now, at the request of the National Commission on Terrorist Attacks, TIA officials have confirmed that the flight did take place and have supplied details.

The odyssey of the small LearJet 35 is part of a larger controversy over the hasty exodus from the United States in the days immediately after 9/11 of members of the Saudi royal family and relatives of Osama bin Laden.

The terrorism panel, better known as the 9/11

Commission, said in April that it knew of six chartered flights with 142 people aboard, mostly Saudis, that left the United States between Sept. 14 and 24, 2001. But it has said nothing about the Tampa flight.

The commission's general counsel, Daniel Marcus, asked TIA in a letter dated May 25 for any information about "a chartered flight with six people, including a Saudi prince, that flew from Tampa, Florida, on or about Sept. 13, 2001." He asked for the information no later than June 8.

TIA officials said they sent their reply on Monday.

The airport used aircraft tracking equipment normally assigned to a noise abatement program to determine the identity of all aircraft entering TIA airspace on Sept. 13, and found four records for the LearJet 35.

The plane first entered the airspace from the south, possibly from the Fort Lauderdale area, sometime after 3 P.M. and landed for the first time at 3:34 P.M. It took off at 4:37 P.M., headed north. It returned to Tampa at 8:23 P.M. and took off again at 8:48 P.M., headed south.

Author Craig Unger, who first disclosed the possibility of a post-9/11 Saudi airlift in his book *House of Bush, House of Saud,* said in an interview that he believes the jet came to Tampa a second time to drop off two former law enforcement agents from Tampa who accompanied three young Saudis to Lexington for security purposes.

The Saudis asked the Tampa Police Department to escort the flight, but the department handed off the assignment to Dan Grossi, a former member of the force, Unger said. Grossi recruited Manuel Perez, a retired FBI agent, to accompany him. Both described the flight to Unger as somewhat surreal.

"They got the approval somewhere," Perez is quoted as telling Unger. "It must have come from the highest levels of government."

While there is no manifest for those aboard the Lear flight to Kentucky, Unger says the foreign nationals left Lexington for London aboard a Boeing 727. That manifest lists eight Saudis, two Sudan nationals, one Tunisian, one Philippine citizen, one Egyptian and two British subjects.

Of those, three listed residences on Normandy Trace Drive in Tampa, and all of them held Florida driver's licenses. They are Ahmad Al Hazmi, then 19; Fahad Al Zeid, then 20; and Talal M. Al Mejrad, then 18, all male Saudis.

It is not known which, if any, is a Saudi prince.

Perez, the former FBI agent on the flight, could not be located this week, and Grossi declined to talk about the experience.

"I'm over it," he said in a telephone interview. "The White House, the FAA and the FBI all said the flight didn't happen. Those are three agencies that are way over my head, and that's why I'm done talking about it."

Grossi did say that Unger's account of his participation in the flight is accurate.

The FAA is still not talking about the flights, referring all questions to the FBI, which isn't answering anything, either. Nor is the 9/11 Commission.

Unger's book criticizes the Bush administration for

allowing so many Saudis, including the relatives of bin Laden, to leave the country without being questioned thoroughly about the terrorist attacks.

Fifteen of the 19 men who hijacked four airlines on Sept. 11 were Saudi, as is bin Laden.

The 9/11 Commission, which has said the flights out of the United States were handled appropriately by the FBI, appears concerned with the handling of the Tampa flight.

"What information, if any, do you have about the screening by law enforcement personnel—including law enforcement personnel affiliated with the airport facility—of individuals on this flight?" the commission asked TIA.

The TIA Police Department said a check of its records indicated no member of its force screened the Lear's passengers.

Despite evidence that the flight occurred, several new questions have arisen.

Raytheon Aircraft is the only facility at TIA that services general aviation, which includes charter flights. When appropriate, Raytheon collects landing fees from those aircraft for TIA and reports to TIA on the flights.

According to airport records, Raytheon collected landing fees from only two aircraft on Sept. 13, one of them a Lear 35. But according to the record, the registration on the Lear is 505RP, a tail number which, according to the latest federal records, is assigned to a Cessna Citation based in Kalamazoo, Mich., and Oskar Rene Poch.

Poch confirmed Tuesday that he owns a Citation with that tail number and did before the terrorist attacks.

"Somebody must have gotten the registration number wrong in Tampa," he said.

TIA spokeswoman Brenda Geoghagan said it is believed the Lear's Sept. 13 journey began in Fort Lauderdale, possibly at a charter company called Hop-a-Jet Inc. The fact that the four trips in and out of Tampa all carried the flight designation "HPJ32" lends support to that idea.

But an official of Hop-a-Jet who wouldn't identify himself said the company does not own an aircraft with the registration number 505RP. Furthermore, he said, if that tail number is assigned to a Cessna Citation, the company doesn't own any Citations, either.

Most of the aircraft allowed to fly in U.S. airspace on Sept. 13 were empty airliners being ferried from the airports where they made quick landings on Sept. 11. The reopening of the airspace included paid charter flights, but not private, nonrevenue flights.

"Whether such a [LearJet] flight would have been legal hinges on whether somebody paid for it," said FAA spokesman William Shumann. "That's the key."

# "A Princely Sum Will Help Bail Out Euro Disney; Tourism: Nephew of Saudi King Fahd Comes to Rescue of the Troubled Amusement Park with Pledge of up to Half a Billion Dollars"

*Los Angeles Times*

JESUS SANCHEZ, June 2, 1994

*"Someday, my prince will come . . ."*

—SNOW WHITE, 1937

Someday was Wednesday for Walt Disney Co. and its partners in Euro Disney, as a Saudi Arabian prince pledged to invest up to $500 million in a plan designed to rescue the deeply troubled theme park.

Prince Al-Waleed bin Talal Ibn Abdulaziz al Saud, who also owns large stakes in Citicorp and Saks Fifth Avenue, agreed to buy 13% to 24% of Euro Disney through a new stock offering that is the heart of a $1 billion bailout by investors and bankers aimed at turning around the money-losing park.

In addition, Al-Waleed agreed to put up $100 million in financing for a convention center being considered near the park 20 miles east of Paris. Such a center could attract additional visitors to the park and its hotels, particularly during midweek and the off-season, Euro Disney said.

Walt Disney Co., which owns 49% of Euro Disney, could see its stake reduced to 36% by a sale of shares to Al-Waleed.

"This significant investment and financing commitment by Prince Al-Waleed means that there is a strong, sophisticated new partner who shares our view of Euro Disney's future and whose involvement enhances Disney's major contribution to the Euro Disney financial restructuring package," Disney Chairman Michael D. Eisner said in a statement.

Despite becoming one of Europe's most popular destinations, Euro Disney has piled up nearly $4 billion in debt and posted mounting losses since it opened more than two years ago. The park's backers blame a European recession and lower-than-expected visitor spending for its financial problems.

As part of a financial restructuring announced last month, Disney would forgo until 1998 royalties it is supposed to receive on the sale of tickets and merchandise at Euro Disney and inject more than $526 million into the park from proceeds of the new stock sale. In return, 61 creditor banks would forgive 18 months of interest payments.

Disney is required to sell Al-Waleed up to $178 million worth of its new shares if the prince cannot buy a sufficient amount of the new shares from other shareholders.

"Becoming a partner in the Euro Disney project is consistent with my strategy to invest significant amounts of capital in association with superior management teams around the world," Al-Waleed said in a statement.

The 37-year-old prince, a nephew of Saudi Arabia's King Fahd, has attracted attention in the past for his investments in well-known U.S. companies. In 1991, he became the largest single investor in banking giant Citicorp by purchasing $800 million worth of company stock. Last year, he bought an 11% share of retailer Saks Fifth Avenue.

Analysts said Al-Waleed's participation will ensure the completion of Euro Disney's financial restructuring, which is expected later this summer.

Still, the theme park's future is not yet secured.

"The bigger issues are on the operating side," said entertainment industry analyst Jeffrey Logsdon of Seidler Cos. in Los Angeles. "How do you increase attendance and increase per-capita spending? That's a big challenge."

## "Bush Blew It the Morning of 9/11"

New York *Daily News*

BILL MAHER, August 12, 2004

John Kerry has waded into an issue raised by Michael Moore in his film *Fahrenheit 9/11*, namely, President Bush's sitting for seven minutes in a Florida classroom after being told "the country is under attack."

Republicans are waxing indignant, of course. But the criticism is richly deserved.

The fact that Bush wasted 27 minutes that day—not only the seven minutes reading to kids but 20 more at a photo op afterward—was, in my view, the most outrageous thing a President has done since Franklin Roosevelt tried to pack the Supreme Court.

Watergate was outrageous but it still did not carry the possibility of utter devastation, like a President's freezing at the very moment we needed his immediate focus on an attack on the United States.

This is an issue about the ultimate presidential duty, acting in an emergency. If nothing else in Washington is nonpartisan, this should be.

But it is not. Republicans are tying themselves in knots trying to defend Bush's actions that morning. The excuses they put forward are absurd:

He was "gathering his thoughts." This was a moment a President should have imagined a thousand times. There is no time in the nuclear age for a President to sit like Forrest Gump "gathering thoughts" after an attack has begun. Gathering information is what he should have been doing.

From the White House press secretary: "The President felt he should project strength and calm until he could better understand what was happening." I agree that gaining a better understanding of what was happening should have been his goal. What I don't get is how that goal was reached by just sitting there instead of getting up and talking to people. Is he a psychic? Was he receiving the information telepathically?

"He didn't want to scare the children." Vice President Cheney has said of Kerry, "The senator from Massachusetts has given us ample reason to doubt the judgment he brings to vital issues of national security." So Kerry's judgment is suspect, but at a moment of national crisis, Bush's judgment was: Better not to scare 20 children momentarily than to react immediately to an attack on the country!

If he had just said, "Hey, kids, gotta go do some President business—be good to your moms and dads, bye!" my guess is the kids would have survived.

I cannot see how someone who considers himself a conservative can defend George Bush's inaction. Conservatives pride themselves on being clear-eyed and decisive. They don't do nuance, and they respect toughness.

But Bush choked at the most important moment a President could have. We're lucky Al-Qaeda had done its worst by the time he pulled himself away from the photo op. Next time, it might not be that way.

Maher is the host of HBO's *Real Time with Bill Maher*.


The Project for the New American Century (PNAC) is a powerful neoconservative think tank that advocates a hawkish foreign policy. Its chairman, William Kristol, is a prominent hawk with close ties to the Bush administration and an analyst for FOX News. Below is a letter that PNAC wrote to President Bill Clinton in

January 1998. It was signed by several prominent hawks who later became key members of the Bush administration: Defense Secretary Donald Rumsfeld, Deputy Defense Secretary Paul Wolfowitz, and White House envoy Elliott Abrams, to name a few. The letter called for the removal of Saddam Hussein and provides a now all-too-obvious clue about how they planned to invade Iraq from Day One. . . .

http://www.newamericancentury.org/iraqclintonletter.htm

January 26, 1998

The Honorable William J. Clinton
President of the United States
Washington, DC

Dear Mr. President:

We are writing you because we are convinced that current American policy toward Iraq is not succeeding, and that we may soon face a threat in the Middle East more serious than any we have known since the end of the Cold War. In your upcoming State of the Union Address, you have an opportunity to chart a clear and determined course for meeting this threat. We urge you to seize that opportunity, and to enunciate a new strategy that would secure the interests of the U.S. and our friends and allies around the world. That strategy should aim, above all, at the removal of Saddam

Hussein's regime from power. We stand ready to offer our full support in this difficult but necessary endeavor.

The policy of "containment" of Saddam Hussein has been steadily eroding over the past several months. As recent events have demonstrated, we can no longer depend on our partners in the Gulf War coalition to continue to uphold the sanctions or to punish Saddam when he blocks or evades UN inspections. Our ability to ensure that Saddam Hussein is not producing weapons of mass destruction, therefore, has substantially diminished. Even if full inspections were eventually to resume, which now seems highly unlikely, experience has shown that it is difficult if not impossible to monitor Iraq's chemical and biological weapons production. The lengthy period during which the inspectors will have been unable to enter many Iraqi facilities has made it even less likely that they will be able to uncover all of Saddam's secrets. As a result, in the not-too-distant future we will be unable to determine with any reasonable level of confidence whether Iraq does or does not possess such weapons.

Such uncertainty will, by itself, have a seriously destabilizing effect on the entire Middle East. It hardly needs to be added that if Saddam does acquire the capability to deliver weapons of mass destruction, as he is almost certain to do if we continue along the present course, the safety of American troops in the region, of our friends and allies like Israel and the moderate Arab states, and a significant portion of the world's supply of oil will all be put at hazard. As you have rightly declared, Mr. President, the security of the world in the first part of the 21st century will be determined largely by how we handle this threat.

Given the magnitude of the threat, the current policy, which depends for its success upon the steadfastness of our coalition partners and upon the cooperation of Saddam Hussein, is dangerously inadequate. The only acceptable strategy is one that eliminates the possibility that Iraq will be able to use or threaten to use weapons of mass destruction. In the near term, this means a willingness to undertake military action as diplomacy is clearly failing. In the long term, it means removing Saddam Hussein and his regime from power. That now needs to become the aim of American foreign policy.

We urge you to articulate this aim, and to turn your Administration's attention to implementing a strategy for removing Saddam's regime from power. This will require a full complement of diplomatic, political, and military efforts. Although we are fully aware of the dangers and difficulties in implementing this policy, we believe the dangers of failing to do so are far greater. We believe the U.S. has the authority under existing UN resolutions to take the necessary steps, including military steps, to protect our vital interests in the Gulf. In any case, American policy cannot continue to be crippled by a misguided insistence on unanimity in the UN Security Council.

We urge you to act decisively. If you act now to end the threat of weapons of mass destruction against the U.S. or its allies, you will be acting in the most fundamental national security interests of the country. If we accept a course of weakness and drift, we put our interests and our future at risk.

Sincerely,

Elliott Abrams    Richard L. Armitage
William J. Bennett    Jeffrey Bergner    John Bolton
Paula Dobriansky    Francis Fukuyama
Robert Kagan    Zalmay Khalilzad
William Kristol    Richard Perle    Peter W. Rodman
Donald Rumsfeld  William Schneider Jr.
Vin Weber    Paul Wolfowitz    R. James Woolsey
Robert B. Zoellick

## "They Knew . . ."

### Despite the Whitewash, We Now Know That the Bush Administration Was Warned Before the War That Its Iraq Claims Were Weak

*In These Times*

DAVID SIROTA AND CHRISTY HARVEY,
August 3, 2004

If desperation is ugly, then Washington, D.C. today is downright hideous.

As the 9/11 Commission recently reported, there was "no credible evidence" of a collaborative relationship between Iraq and al Qaeda. Similarly, no weapons of mass destruction have been found in Iraq. With U.S. casualties mounting in an election year, the White House is grasping at straws to avoid being held accountable for its dishonesty.

The whitewash already has started: In July, Republicans on the Senate Intelligence Committee released a controversial report blaming the CIA for the mess. The panel conveniently refuses to evaluate what the White House did with the information it was given or how the White House set up its own special team of Pentagon political appointees (called the Office of Special Plans) to circumvent well-established intelligence channels. And Vice President Dick Cheney continues to say without a shred of proof that there is "overwhelming evidence" justifying the administration's pre-war charges.

But as author Flannery O'Connor noted, "Truth does not change according to our ability to stomach it." That means no matter how much defensive spin spews from the White House, the Bush administration cannot escape the documented fact that it was clearly warned before the war that its rationale for invading Iraq was weak.

Top administration officials repeatedly ignored warnings that their assertions about Iraq's supposed Weapons of Mass Destruction (WMD) and connections to al Qaeda were overstated. In some cases, they were told their claims were wholly without merit, yet they went ahead and made them anyway. Even the Senate report admits that the White House "misrepresented" classified intelligence by eliminating references to contradictory assertions.

In short, they knew they were misleading America.

And they did not care.

### They knew Iraq posed no nuclear threat

There is no doubt even though there was no proof of Iraq's complicity, the White House was focused on Iraq within hours of the 9/11 attacks. As CBS News reported, "barely five hours after American Airlines Flight 77 plowed into the Pentagon, Defense Secretary Donald H. Rumsfeld was telling his aides to come up with plans for striking Iraq." Former Bush counterterrorism czar Richard Clarke recounted vividly how, just after the attack, President Bush pressured him to find an Iraqi connection. In many ways, this was no surprise—as former Treasury Secretary Paul O'Neill and another administration official confirmed, the White House was actually looking for a way to invade Iraq well before the terrorist attacks.

But such an unprovoked invasion of a sovereign country required a public rationale. And so the Bush administration struck fear into the hearts of Americans about Saddam Hussein's supposed WMD, starting with nuclear arms. In his first major address on the "Iraqi threat" in October 2002, President Bush invoked fiery images of mushroom clouds and mayhem, saying, "Iraq is reconstituting its nuclear weapons program."

Yet, before that speech, the White House had intelligence calling this assertion into question. A 1997 report by the U.N.'s International Atomic Energy Agency (IAEA)—the agency whose purpose is to prevent nuclear proliferation—stated there was no indication Iraq ever achieved nuclear capability or had any physical capacity for producing weapons-grade nuclear material in the near future.

In February 2001, the CIA delivered a report to the White House that said: "We do not have any direct evidence that Iraq has used the period since Desert Fox to reconstitute its weapons of mass destruction programs." The report was so definitive that Secretary of State Colin Powell said in a subsequent press conference, Saddam Hussein "has not developed any significant capability with respect to weapons of mass destruction."

Ten months before the president's speech, an intelligence review by CIA Director George Tenet contained not a single mention of an imminent nuclear threat—or capability—from Iraq. The CIA was backed up by Bush's own State Department: Around the time Bush gave his speech, the department's intelligence bureau said that evidence did not "add up to a compelling case that Iraq is currently pursuing what [we] consider to be an integrated and comprehensive approach to acquiring nuclear weapons."

Nonetheless, the administration continued to push forward. In March 2003, Cheney went on national television days before the war and claimed Iraq "has reconstituted nuclear weapons." He was echoed by State Department spokesman Richard Boucher, who told reporters of supposedly grave "concerns about Iraq's potential nuclear programs."

Even after the invasion, when troops failed to uncover any evidence of nuclear weapons, the White House refused to admit the truth. In July 2003, Condoleezza Rice told PBS's Gwen Ifill that the administration's nuclear assertions were "absolutely supportable." That same month, White House spokesman Scott McClellan insisted: "There's a lot of evidence showing that Iraq was reconstituting its nuclear weapons program."

### They knew the aluminum tubes were not for nuclear weapons

To back up claims that Iraq was actively trying to build nuclear weapons, the administration referred to Iraq's importation of aluminum tubes, which Bush officials said were for enriching uranium. In December 2002, Powell said, "Iraq has tried to obtain high-strength aluminum tubes which can be used to enrich uranium in centrifuges for a nuclear weapons program." Similarly, in his 2003 State of the Union address, Bush said Iraq "has attempted to purchase high-strength aluminum tubes suitable for nuclear weapons production."

But, in October 2002, well before these and other administration officials made this claim, two key agencies told the White House exactly the opposite. The State Department affirmed reports from Energy Department experts who concluded those tubes were ill-suited for any kind of uranium enrichment. And according to memos released by the Senate Intelligence Committee, the State Department also warned Powell not to use the aluminum tubes hypothesis in the days before his February 2003 U.N. speech. He refused and used the aluminum tubes claim anyway.

The State Department's warnings were soon validated by the IAEA. In March 2003, the agency's director stated, "Iraq's efforts to import these aluminum tubes were not likely to be related" to nuclear weapons deployment.

Yet, this evidence did not stop the White House either. Pretending the administration never received any warnings at all, Rice claimed in July 2003 that "the consensus view" in the intelligence community was that the tubes "were suitable for use in centrifuges to spin material for nuclear weapons."

Today, experts agree the administration's aluminum tube claims were wholly without merit.

### They knew the Iraq-uranium claims were not supported

In one of the most famous statements about Iraq's supposed nuclear arsenals, Bush said in his 2003 State of the Union address, "The British government has learned that Saddam Hussein recently sought significant quantities of uranium from Africa." The careful phrasing of this statement highlights how dishonest it was. By attributing the claim to an allied government, the White House made a powerful charge yet protected itself against any consequences should it be proved false. In fact, the president invoked the British because his own intelligence experts had earlier warned the White House not to make the claim at all.

In the fall of 2002, the CIA told administration officials not to include this uranium assertion in presidential speeches. Specifically, the agency sent two memos to the White House and Tenet personally called top national security officials imploring them not to use the claim. While the warnings forced the White House to remove a uranium reference from an October 2002 presidential address, they did not stop the charge from being included in the 2003 State of the Union.

Not surprisingly, evidence soon emerged that forced the White House to admit the deception. In March 2003, IAEA Director Mohammed El Baradei said there was no proof Iraq had nuclear weapons and added "documents which formed the basis for [the White House's assertion] of recent uranium transactions between Iraq and Niger are in fact not authentic." But when Cheney was asked about this a week later, he said, "Mr. El Baradei frankly is wrong."

Bush and Rice both tried to blame the CIA for the failure, saying the assertion "was cleared by the intelligence services." When the intelligence agency produced the memos it had sent to the White House on the subject, Rice didn't miss a beat, telling *Meet the Press* "it is quite possible that I didn't" read the memos at all—as if they were "optional" reading for the nation's top national security official on the eve of war. At about this time some high-level administration official or officials leaked to the press that Ambassador Joseph Wilson's wife was an undercover CIA agent—a move widely seen as an attempt by the administration to punish Wilson for his

July 6, 2003, *New York Times* op-ed that stated he had found no evidence of an Iraqi effort to purchase uranium from Niger.

In recent weeks, right-wing pundits have pointed to new evidence showing the Iraq uranium charge may have flirted with the truth at some point in the distant past. These White House hatchet men say the administration did not manipulate or cherry-pick intelligence. They also tout the recent British report (a.k.a. *The Butler Report*) as defending the president's uranium claim. Yet, if the White House did not cherry-pick or manipulate intelligence, why did the president trumpet U.S. intelligence from a foreign government while ignoring explicit warnings not to do so from his own? The record shows U.S. intelligence officials explicitly warned the White House that "the Brits have exaggerated this issue." Yet, the administration refused to listen. Even *The Butler Report* itself acknowledges the evidence is cloudy. As nonproliferation expert Joseph Cirincione of the Carnegie Endowment for International Peace recently pointed out, "The claim appears shaky at best—hardly the stuff that should make up presidential decisions."

But now, instead of contrition, Republicans are insisting the White House's uranium charge was accurate. Indeed, these apologists have no option but to try to distract public attention from the simple truth that not a shred of solid evidence exists to substantiate this key charge that fueled the push for war.

## *They knew there was no hard evidence of chemical or biological weapons*

In September 2002, President Bush said Iraq "could launch a biological or chemical attack in as little as 45 minutes after the order is given." The next month, he delivered a major speech to "outline the Iraqi threat," just two days before a critical U.N. vote. In his address, he claimed without doubt that Iraq "possesses and produces chemical and biological weapons." He said that "Iraq has a growing fleet of manned and unmanned aerial vehicles (UAVs) that could be used to disperse chemical or biological weapons" and that the government was "concerned Iraq is exploring ways of using these UAVs for missions targeting the United States."

What he did not say was that the White House had been explicitly warned that these assertions were unproved.

As the *Washington Post* later reported, Bush "ignored the fact that U.S. intelligence mistrusted the source" of the 45-minute claim and, therefore, omitted it from its intelligence estimates. And Bush ignored the fact that the Defense Intelligence Agency previously submitted a report to the administration finding "no reliable information" to prove Iraq was producing or stockpiling chemical weapons. According to *Newsweek*, the conclusion was similar to the findings of a 1998 government commission on WMD chaired by Rumsfeld.

Bush also neglected to point out that in early October 2002, the administration's top military experts told the

White House they "sharply disputed the notion that Iraq's Unmanned Aerial Vehicles were being designed as attack weapons." Specifically, the Air Force's National Air and Space Intelligence Center correctly showed the drones in question were too heavy to be used to deploy chemical/biological-weapons spray devices.

Regardless, the chemical/biological weapons claims from the administration continued to escalate. Powell told the United Nations on February 5, 2003, "There can be no doubt that Saddam Hussein has biological weapons and the capability to rapidly produce more, many more." As proof, he cited aerial images of a supposed decontamination vehicle circling a suspected weapons site.

According to newly released documents in the Senate Intelligence Committee report, Powell's own top intelligence experts told him not to make such claims about the photographs. They said the vehicles were likely water trucks. He ignored their warnings.

On March 6, 2003, just weeks before the invasion, the president went further than Powell. He claimed, "Iraqi operatives continue to hide biological and chemical agents."

To date, no chemical or biological weapons have been found in Iraq.

### They knew Saddam and bin Laden were not collaborating

In the summer of 2002, *USA Today* reported White House lawyers had concluded that establishing an Iraq–al Qaeda link would provide the legal cover at the

United Nations for the administration to attack Iraq. Such a connection, no doubt, also would provide political capital at home. And so, by the fall of 2002, the Iraq–al Qaeda drumbeat began.

It started on September 25, 2002, when Bush said, "you can't distinguish between al Qaeda and Saddam." This was news even to members of Bush's own political party who had access to classified intelligence. Just a month before, Sen. Chuck Hagel (R-Neb.), who serves on the Senate Foreign Relations Committee, said, "Saddam is not in league with al Qaeda. I have not seen any intelligence that would lead me to connect Saddam Hussein to al Qaeda."

To no surprise, the day after Bush's statement, *USA Today* reported several intelligence experts "expressed skepticism" about the claim, with a Pentagon official calling the president's assertion an "exaggeration." No matter, Bush ignored these concerns and that day described Saddam Hussein as "a man who loves to link up with al Qaeda." Meanwhile, Rumsfeld held a press conference trumpeting "bulletproof" evidence of a connection—a sentiment echoed by Rice and White House spokesman Ari Fleischer. And while the *New York Times* noted, "the officials offered no details to back up the assertions," Rumsfeld nonetheless insisted his claims were "accurate and not debatable."

Within days, the accusations became more than just "debatable"; they were debunked. German Defense Minister Peter Stuck said the day after Rumsfeld's press conference that his country "was not aware of any connection" between Iraq and al Qaeda's efforts to acquire chemical weapons. *The Orlando Sentinel* reported that terrorism expert Peter Bergen—one of the few to actually interview Osama bin Laden—said the connections between Iraq and al Qaeda are minimal. In October 2002, Knight Ridder reported, "a growing number of military officers, intelligence professionals and diplomats in [Bush's] own government privately have deep misgivings" about the Iraq–al Qaeda claims. The experts charged that administration hawks "exaggerated evidence." A senior U.S. official told *The Philadelphia Inquirer* that intelligence analysts "contest the administration's suggestion of a major link between Iraq and al Qaeda."

While this evidence forced British Prime Minister Tony Blair and other allies to refrain from playing up an Iraq–al Qaeda connection, the Bush administration refused to be deterred by facts.

On November 1, 2002, President Bush claimed, "We know [Iraq has] got ties with al Qaeda." Four days later, Europe's top terrorism investigator Jean-Louis Bruguiere reported: "We have found no evidence of links between Iraq and al Qaeda. If there were such links, we would have found them. But we have found no serious connections whatsoever." British Foreign Secretary Jack Straw, whose country was helping build the case for war, admitted, "What I'm asked is if I've seen any evidence of [Iraq–al Qaeda connections]. And the answer is: 'I haven't.'"

Soon, an avalanche of evidence appeared indicating the White House was deliberately misleading America. In January 2003, intelligence officials told the *Los*

*Angeles Times* that they were "puzzled by the administration's new push" to create the perception of an Iraq–al Qaeda connection and said the intelligence community has "discounted—if not dismissed—information believed to point to possible links between Iraq and al Qaeda." One intelligence official said, "There isn't a factual basis" for the administration's conspiracy theory about the so-called connection.

On the morning of February 5, 2003, the same day Powell delivered his U.N. speech, British intelligence leaked a comprehensive report finding no substantial links between Iraq and al Qaeda. The BBC reported that British intelligence officials maintained "any fledgling relationship [between Iraq and al Qaeda] foundered due to mistrust and incompatible ideologies." Powell, nonetheless, stood before the United Nations and claimed there was a "sinister nexus between Iraq and al Qaeda." A month later, Rice backed him up, saying al Qaeda "clearly has had links to the Iraqis." And in his March 17, 2003, speech on the eve of war, Bush justified the invasion by citing the fully discredited Iraq–al Qaeda link.

When the war commenced, the house of cards came down. In June 2003, the chairman of the U.N. group that monitors al Qaeda told reporters his team found no evidence linking the terrorist group to Iraq. In July 2003, the *Los Angeles Times* reported the bipartisan congressional report analyzing September 11 "undercut Bush administration claims before the war that Hussein had links to al Qaeda." Meanwhile, the *New York Times* reported, "Coalition forces have not brought to light any significant evidence demonstrating the bond between Iraq and al Qaeda." In August 2003, three former Bush administration officials came forward to admit pre-war evidence tying al Qaeda to Iraq "was tenuous, exaggerated, and often at odds with the conclusions of key intelligence agencies."

Yet, the White House insisted on maintaining the deception. In the fall of 2003, President Bush said, "There's no question that Saddam Hussein had al Qaeda ties." And Cheney claimed Iraq "had an established relationship to al Qaeda." When the media finally began demanding proof for all the allegations, Powell offered a glimmer of contrition. In January 2004, he conceded that there was no "smoking gun" to prove the claim. His admission was soon followed by a March 2004 Knight Ridder report that quoted administration officials conceding "there never was any evidence that Hussein's secular police state and Osama bin Laden's Islamic terror network were in league."

But Powell's statement was the exception, not the norm. The White House still refuses to acknowledge wrongdoing, and instead resorts to the classic two-step feint, citing sources but conveniently refusing to acknowledge those sources' critical faults.

For instance, Cheney began pointing reporters to an article in the right-wing *Weekly Standard* as the "best source" of evidence backing the Saddam–al Qaeda claim, even though the Pentagon had previously discredited the story. Similarly, in June, the Republicans' media spin machine came to the aid of the White House and promoted a *New York Times* article about a document showing failed efforts by bin Laden to work with Iraq in the mid-'90s against Saudi Arabia. Not surprisingly, the spinners did not mention the article's key finding—a Pentagon task force found that the document "described no formal alliance being reached between Mr. bin Laden and Iraqi intelligence."

When the 9/11 Commission found "no credible evidence" of a collaborative relationship between Iraq and al Qaeda, the White House denials came as no surprise. Cheney defiantly claimed there was "overwhelming evidence" of a link, provided no evidence, and then berated the media and the commission for having the nerve to report the obvious. Bush did not feel the need to justify his distortions, saying after the report came out, "The reason I keep insisting that there was a relationship between Iraq and Saddam and al Qaeda is because there was a relationship between Iraq and al Qaeda."

That was the perfect answer from an administration that never lets the factual record impinge on what it says to the American public.

### They knew there was no Prague meeting

One of the key pillars of the Iraq–al Qaeda myth was a White House–backed story claiming 9/11 hijacker Mohammed Atta met with an Iraqi spy in April 2001. The tale originally came from a lone Czech informant who said he saw the terrorist in Prague at the time. White House hawks, eager to link al Qaeda with Saddam, did not wait to verify the story, and instead immediately used it to punch up arguments for a pre-emptive attack on Iraq. On November 14, 2001, Cheney claimed Atta was "in Prague in April of this year, as well as earlier." On December 9, 2001, he went further, claiming without proof that the Atta meeting was "pretty well confirmed."

Nine days later, the Czech government reported there was no evidence that Atta met with an Iraqi intelligence agent in Prague. Czech Police Chief Jiri Kolar said there were no documents showing Atta had been in Prague that entire year, and Czech officials told *Newsweek* that the uncorroborated witness who perpetuated the story should have been viewed with more skepticism.

By the spring of 2002, major news publications such as the *Washington Post*, the *New York Times*, *Newsweek* and *Time* were running stories calling the "Prague connection" an "embarrassing" mistake and stating that, according to European officials, the intelligence supporting the claim was "somewhere between 'slim' and 'none.'" The stories also quoted administration officials and CIA and FBI analysts saying that on closer scrutiny, "there was no evidence Atta left or returned to the United States at the time he was supposed to be in Prague." Even FBI Director Robert S. Mueller III, a Bush political appointee, admitted in April 2002, "We ran down literally hundreds of thousands of leads and checked every record we could get our hands on, from flight reservations to car rentals to bank accounts," but found nothing.

But that was not good enough for the administration,

which instead of letting the story go, began trying to manipulate intelligence to turn fantasy into reality. In August 2002, when FBI case officers told Deputy Defense Secretary Paul Wolfowitz that there was no Atta meeting, *Newsweek* reported Wolfowitz "vigorously challenged them." Wolfowitz wanted the FBI to endorse claims that Atta and the Iraqi spy had met. FBI counterterrorism chief Pat D'Amuro refused.

In September 2002, the CIA handed Cheney a classified intelligence assessment that cast specific, serious doubt on whether the Atta meeting ever occurred. Yet, that same month, Richard Perle, then chairman of Bush's Defense Policy Board, said, "Muhammad Atta met [a secret collaborator of Saddam Hussein] prior to September 11. We have proof of that, and we are sure he wasn't just there for a holiday." In the same breath, Perle openly admitted, "The meeting is one of the motives for an American attack on Iraq."

By the winter of 2002, even America's allies were telling the administration to relent: In November, British Foreign Secretary Jack Straw said he had seen no evidence of a meeting in Prague between Atta and an Iraqi intelligence agent.

But it did not stop. In September 2003, on *Meet the Press*, Cheney dredged up the story again, saying, "With respect to 9/11, of course, we've had the story that's been public out there. The Czechs alleged that Mohammed Atta, the lead attacker, met in Prague with a senior Iraqi intelligence official five months before the attack." He provided no new evidence, opted not to mention that the Czechs long ago had withdrawn the allegations, and ignored new evidence that showed the story was likely untrue.

Even today, with all of the intelligence firmly against him, Cheney remains unrepentant. Asked in June about whether the meeting had occurred, he admitted, "That's never been proven." Then he added, "It's never been refuted." When CNBC's Gloria Borger asked about his initial claim that the meeting was "pretty well confirmed," Cheney snapped, "No, I never said that. I never said that. Absolutely not."

His actual words in December 2001: "It's been pretty well confirmed that [Atta] did go to Prague and he did meet with a senior official of the Iraqi intelligence service."

In other words, Cheney hit a new low. He resorted not only to lying about the story, but lying about lying about the story.

### Conclusion: They knew they were misleading America

In his March 17, 2003 address preparing America for the Iraq invasion, President Bush stated unequivocally that there was an Iraq–al Qaeda nexus and that there was "no doubt that the Iraq regime continues to possess and conceal some of the most lethal weapons ever devised."

In the context of what we now know the White House knew at the time, Bush was deliberately dishonest. The intelligence community repeatedly told the White House there were many deep cracks in its case for war. The president's willingness to ignore such warnings and make these unequivocal statements proves the administration was intentionally painting a black-and-white picture when it knew the facts merited only gray at best.

That has meant severe consequences for all Americans. Financially, U.S. taxpayers have shelled out more than $166 billion for the Iraq war, and more will soon be needed. Geopolitically, our country is more isolated from allies than ever, with anti-Americanism on the rise throughout the globe.

And we are less secure. A recent U.S. Army War College report says "the invasion of Iraq was a diversion from the more narrow focus on defeating al Qaeda." U.N. envoy Lakhdar Brahimi put it this way: "The war in Iraq was useless, it caused more problems than it solved, and it brought in terrorism."

These statements are borne out by the facts: The International Institute of Strategic Studies in London reports al Qaeda is now 18,000 strong, with many new recruits joining as a result of the war in Iraq. Not coincidentally, the White House recently said the American homeland faces an imminent threat of a terrorist attack from a still-active al Qaeda operation in Afghanistan. Yet, the administration actually moved special forces out of Afghanistan in 2002 to prepare for an invasion of Iraq. Because of this, we face the absurd situation whereby we have no more than 20,000 troops in Afghanistan hunting down those who directly threaten us, yet have 140,000 troops in Iraq—a country that was not a serious menace before invasion.

Of course, it is those troops who have it the worst. Our men and women in uniform are bogged down in a quagmire, forced to lay down life and limb for a lie.

To be sure, neoconservative pundits and Bush administration hawks will continue to blame anyone but the White House for these deceptions. They also will say intelligence gave a bit of credence to some of the pre-war claims, and that is certainly true.

But nothing can negate the clear proof that President Bush and other administration officials vastly overstated the intelligence they were given. They engaged in a calculated and well-coordinated effort to turn a war of choice in Iraq into a perceived war of imminent necessity.

And we are all left paying the price.

# "Advocates of War Now Profit from Iraq's Reconstruction; Lobbyists, Aides to Senior Officials and Others Encouraged Invasion and Now Help Firms Pursue Contracts. They See No Conflict."

*Los Angeles Times*

WALTER F. ROCHE JR. AND KEN SILVERSTEIN,
July 14, 2004

In the months and years leading up to the U.S.-led invasion of Iraq, they marched together in the vanguard of those who advocated war.

As lobbyists, public relations counselors, and confidential advisors to senior federal officials, they warned against Iraqi weapons of mass destruction, praised exiled leader Ahmad Chalabi, and argued that toppling Saddam Hussein was a matter of national security and moral duty.

Now, as fighting continues in Iraq, they are collecting tens of thousands of dollars in fees for helping business clients pursue federal contracts and other financial opportunities in Iraq. For instance, a former Senate aide who helped get U.S. funds for anti-Hussein exiles who are now active in Iraqi affairs has a $175,000 deal to advise Romania on winning business in Iraq and other matters.

And the ease with which they have moved from advocating policies and advising high government officials to making money in activities linked to their policies and advice reflects the blurred lines that often exist between public and private interests in Washington. In most cases, federal conflict-of-interest laws do not apply to former officials or to people serving only as advisors.

Larry Noble, executive director of the Center for Responsive Politics, said the actions of former officials and others who serve on government advisory boards, although not illegal, can raise the appearance of conflicts of interest. "It calls into question whether the advice they give is in their own interests rather than the public interest," Noble said.

Michael Shires, a professor of public policy at Pepperdine University, disagreed. "I don't see an ethical issue there," he said. "I see individuals looking out for their own interests."

Former CIA Director R. James Woolsey is a prominent example of the phenomenon, mixing his business interests with what he contends are the country's strategic interests. He left the CIA in 1995, but he remains a senior government advisor on intelligence and national security issues, including Iraq. Meanwhile, he works for two private companies that do business in Iraq and is a partner in a company that invests in firms that provide security and antiterrorism services.

Woolsey said in an interview that he was not directly involved with the companies' Iraq-related ventures. But as a vice president of Booz Allen Hamilton, a consulting firm, he was a featured speaker in May 2003 at a conference co-sponsored by the company at which about 80 corporate executives and others paid up to $1,100 to hear about the economic outlook and business opportunities in Iraq.

Before the war, Woolsey was a founding member of the Committee for the Liberation of Iraq, an organization set up in 2002 at the request of the White House to help build public backing for war in Iraq. He also wrote about a need for regime change and sat on the CIA advisory board and the Defense Policy Board, whose unpaid members have provided advice on Iraq and other matters to Defense Secretary Donald H. Rumsfeld.

Woolsey is part of a small group that shows with unusual clarity the interlocking nature of the way the insider system can work. Moving in the same social circles, often sitting together on government panels and working with like-minded think tanks and advocacy groups, they wrote letters to the White House urging military action in Iraq, formed organizations that pressed for invasion and pushed legislation that authorized aid to exile groups.

Since the start of the war, despite the violence and instability in Iraq, they have turned to private enterprise.

The group, in addition to Woolsey, includes:

- Neil Livingstone, a former Senate aide who has served as a Pentagon and State Department advisor and issued repeated public calls for Hussein's overthrow. He heads a Washington-based firm, GlobalOptions, that provides contacts and consulting services to companies doing business in Iraq.
- Randy Scheunemann, a former Rumsfeld advisor who helped draft the Iraq Liberation Act of 1998 authorizing $98 million in U.S. aid to Iraqi exile groups. He was the founding president of the Committee for the Liberation of Iraq. Now he's helping former Soviet Bloc states win business there.
- Margaret Bartel, who managed federal money channeled to Chalabi's exile group, the Iraqi National Congress, including funds for its prewar intelligence program on Hussein's alleged weapons of mass destruction. She now heads a Washington-area consulting firm helping would-be investors find Iraqi partners.
- K. Riva Levinson, a Washington lobbyist and public relations specialist who received federal funds to drum up prewar support for the Iraqi National Congress. She has close ties to Bartel

and now helps companies open doors in Iraq, in part through her contacts with the Iraqi National Congress.

Other advocates of military action against Hussein are pursuing business opportunities in Iraq. Two ardent supporters of military action, Joe Allbaugh, who managed President Bush's 2000 campaign for the White House and later headed the Federal Emergency Management Agency, and Edward Rogers Jr., an aide to the first President Bush, recently helped set up two companies to promote business in postwar Iraq. Rogers's law firm has a $262,500 contract to represent Iraq's Kurdistan Democratic Party.

Neither Rogers nor Allbaugh has Woolsey's high profile, however.

Soon after the Sept. 11 attacks, he wrote an opinion piece in the *Wall Street Journal* saying a foreign state had aided Al Qaeda in preparing the strikes. He named Iraq as the leading suspect. In October 2001, Deputy Secretary of Defense Paul D. Wolfowitz sent Woolsey to London, where he hunted for evidence linking Hussein to the attacks.

At the May 2003 Washington conference, titled "Companies on the Ground: The Challenge for Business in Rebuilding Iraq," Woolsey spoke on political and diplomatic issues that might affect economic progress. He also spoke favorably about the Bush administration's decision to tilt reconstruction contracts toward U.S. firms.

In an interview, Woolsey said he saw no conflict

between advocating for the war and subsequently advising companies on business in Iraq.

Booz Allen is a subcontractor on a $75 million telecommunications contract in Iraq and also has provided assistance on the administration of federal grants. Woolsey said he had had no involvement in that work.

Woolsey was interviewed at the Washington office of the Paladin Capital Group, a venture capital firm where he is a partner. Paladin invests in companies involved in homeland security and infrastructure protection, Woolsey said.

Woolsey also is a paid advisor to Livingstone's GlobalOptions. He said his own work at the firm did not involve Iraq.

Under Livingstone, GlobalOptions "offers a wide range of security and risk management services," according to its website.

In a 1993 opinion piece for *Newsday*, Livingstone wrote that the United States "should launch a massive covert program designed to remove Hussein."

In a recent interview, Livingstone said he had second thoughts about the war, primarily because of the failure to find weapons of mass destruction. But he has been a regular speaker at Iraq investment seminars.

While Livingstone has focused on opportunities for Americans, Scheunemann has concentrated on helping former Soviet Bloc states.

Scheunemann runs a Washington lobbying firm called Orion Strategies, which shares the same address as that of the Iraqi National Congress's Washington spokesman and the now-defunct Committee for the Liberation of Iraq.

Orion's clients include Romania, which signed a nine-month, $175,000 deal earlier this year. Among other things, the contract calls for Orion to promote Romania's "interests in the reconstruction of Iraq."

Scheunemann has also traveled to Latvia, which is a former Orion client, and met with a business group to discuss prospects in Iraq.

Few people advocated for the war as vigorously as Scheunemann. Just a week after Sept. 11, he joined with other conservatives who sent a letter to Bush calling for Hussein's overthrow.

In 2002, Scheunemann became the first president of the Committee for the Liberation of Iraq, which scored its biggest success last year when 10 Eastern European countries endorsed the U.S. invasion. Known as the "Vilnius 10," they showed that "Europe is united by a commitment to end Saddam's bloody regime," Scheunemann said at the time.

He declined to discuss his Iraq-related business activities, saying, "I can't help you out there."

Scheunemann, Livingstone and Woolsey played their roles in promoting war with Iraq largely in public. By contrast, Bartel and Levinson mostly operated out of the public eye.

In early 2003, Bartel became a director of Boxwood Inc., a Virginia firm set up to receive U.S. funds for the intelligence program of the Iraqi National Congress.

Today, critics in Congress say the Iraqi National Congress provided faulty information on Hussein's efforts to develop weapons of mass destruction and his ties to Osama bin Laden.

Bartel began working for the Iraqi National Congress in 2001. She was hired to monitor its use of U.S. funds after several critical government audits. After the war began, Bartel established a Virginia company, Global Positioning. According to Bartel, the firm's primary purpose is to "introduce clients to the Iraqi market, help them find potential Iraqi partners, set up meetings with government officials . . . and provide on-the-ground support for their business interests."

Bartel works closely with Levinson, a managing director with the Washington lobbying firm BKSH & Associates. Francis Brooke, a top Chalabi aide, said BKSH received $25,000 a month to promote the Iraqi National Congress, and Levinson "did great work on our behalf."

In 1999, Levinson was hired by the Iraqi National Congress to handle public relations. She said her contract with the congress ended last year. Before the invasion and in the early days of fighting in Iraq, Chalabi and the congress enjoyed close relations with the Bush administration, but the relationship has cooled.

Levinson told the *Times:* "We see no conflict of interest in using our knowledge and contacts in Iraq that we developed through our previous work with the INC to support economic development in Iraq. As a matter of fact, we see this as complementary to a shared goal to build a democratic country."

# "Profits of War"

*The Guardian*—excerpted from
*The Halliburton Agenda*

DAN BRIODY, July 22, 2004

On January 12, 1991, Congress authorised President George HW Bush to engage Iraq in war. Just five days later, Operation Desert Storm commenced in Kuwait. As with the more recent war in the Gulf, it did not take long for the US to claim victory—it was all over by the end of February—but the clean-up would last longer, and was far more expensive than the military action itself. In a senseless act of desperation and defeat, Iraqi troops set fire to more than 700 Kuwaiti oil wells, resulting in a constant fog of thick, black smoke that turned day into night.

It was thought the mess would take no less than five years to clean up, as lakes of oil surrounding each well blazed out of control, making it nearly impossible to approach the burning wells, let alone extinguish them. But with the fighting over, Halliburton angled its way into the clean-up and rebuilding effort that was expected to cost around $200bn (£163bn) over the next 10 years.

The company sent 60 men to help with the firefighting effort. Meanwhile, its engineering and construction subsidiary Kellogg Brown & Root (KBR) won an additional $3m contract to assess the damage that the invasion had done to Kuwait's infrastructure—a contract whose value had multiplied seven times by the end of KBR's involvement. More significantly still, KBR won a contract to extract troops from Saudi Arabia after their services were no longer needed in the Gulf. Halliburton was back in the army logistics business in earnest for the first time since Vietnam. The end of the Gulf war saw nothing less than the rebirth of the military outsourcing business.

Military outsourcing was not new. Private firms had been aiding in war efforts since long before KBR won its first naval shipbuilding contract. But the nature of military outsourcing has changed dramatically in the last decade. The trend towards a "downsized" military began because of the "peace dividend" at the end of the cold war, and continued throughout the 1990s. This combination of a reduced military but continued conflict gave rise to an unprecedented new industry of private military firms. These firms would assist the military in everything from weapons procurement and maintenance to training of troops and logistics.

In the decade after the first Gulf war, the number of private contractors used in and around the battlefield increased tenfold. It has been estimated that there is now one private contractor for every 10 soldiers in Iraq. Companies such as Halliburton, which became the fifth largest defence contractor in the nation during the 1990s, have played a critical role in this trend.

The story behind America's "super contract" begins in 1992, when the department of defence, then headed by Dick Cheney, was impressed with the work Halliburton did during its time in Kuwait. Sensing the need to bolster its forces in the event of further conflicts of a similar nature, the Pentagon asked private contractors to bid on a $3.9m contract to write a report on how a private firm could provide logistical support to the army in the case of further military action.

The report was to examine 13 different "hot spots" around the world, and detail how services as varied as building bases to feeding the troops could be accomplished. The contractor that would potentially provide the services detailed in the report would be required to support the deployment of 20,000 troops over 180 days. It was a massive contingency plan, the first of its kind for the American military.

Thirty-seven companies tendered for the contract; KBR won it. The company was paid another $5m later that year to extend the plan to other locations and add detail.

The KBR report, which remains classified to this day, convinced Cheney that it was indeed possible to create one umbrella contract and award it to a single firm. The contract became known as the Logistics Civil Augmentation Programme (Logcap) and has been called "the mother of all service contracts." It has been used in every American deployment since its award in 1992—at a cost of several billion dollars (and counting). The lucky recipient of the first, five-year Logcap contract was the very same company hired to draw up the plan in the first place: KBR.

The Logcap contract pulled KBR out of its late

1980s doldrums and boosted the bottom line of Halliburton throughout the 1990s. It is, effectively, a blank cheque from the government. The contractor makes its money from a built-in profit percentage, anywhere from 1% to 9%, depending on various incentive clauses. When your profit is a percentage of the cost, the more you spend, the more you make.

Before the ink was dry on the first Logcap contract, the US army was deployed to Somalia in December 1992 as part of Operation Restore Hope. KBR employees were there before the army even arrived, and they were the last to leave. The firm made $109.7m in Somalia. In August 1994, they earned $6.3m from Operation Support Hope in Rwanda. In September of that same year, Operation Uphold Democracy in Haiti netted the company $150m. And in October 1994, Operation Vigilant Warrior made them another $5m.

In the spirit of "refuse no job," the company was building the base camps, supplying the troops with food and water, fuel and munitions, cleaning latrines, even washing their clothes. They attended the staff meetings and were kept up to speed on all the activities related to a given mission. They were becoming another unit in the US army.

The army's growing dependency on the company hit home when, in 1997, KBR lost the Logcap contract in a competitive rebid to rival Dyncorp. The army found it impossible to remove Brown & Root from their work in the Balkans—by far the most lucrative part of the contract—and so carved out the work in that theatre to keep it with KBR. In 2001, the company won the

Logcap contract again, this time for twice the normal term length: 10 years.

To the uninitiated, the appointment of Cheney to the chairman, president, and chief executive officer positions at Halliburton in August 1995 made little sense. Cheney had almost no business experience, having been a career politician and bureaucrat. Financial analysts downgraded the stock and the business press openly questioned the decision.

Cheney has been described by those who know him as everything from low-key to downright bland, but the confidence he inspired and the loyalty he professed made him an indispensable part of Donald Rumsfeld's rise to power. In the 1970s, Rumsfeld became Gerald Ford's White House chief of staff, with Cheney as his deputy. In those days, Cheney was assigned a codename by the secret service that perfectly summed up his disposition: "Backseat."

But Halliburton understood Cheney's value. With him as CEO, the company gained considerable leverage in Washington. Until Cheney's appointment in the autumn of 1995, Halliburton's business results had been decent. After a loss of $91m in 1993, the company had returned to profitability in 1994 with an operating profit of $236m. With the new revenue coming in from Logcap, Halliburton and its prize subsidiary, KBR, were back on track. Though Logcap was producing only modest revenues, it was successful in reintegrating KBR into the military machine.

The big opportunity came in December 1995, just two months after Cheney assumed the post of CEO, when the US sent thousands of troops to the Balkans as a peace-keeping force. As part of Operation Joint Endeavour, KBR was dispatched to Bosnia and Kosovo to support the army in its operations in the region. The task was massive in scope and size.

One example of the work KBR did in the Balkans was Camp Bondsteel. The camp was so large that the US general accounting office (GAO) likened it to "a small town." The company built roads, power generation, water and sewage systems, housing, a helicopter airfield, a perimeter fence, guard towers, and a detention centre. Bondsteel is the largest and most expensive army base since Vietnam. It also happens to be built in the path of the Albanian-Macedonian-Bulgarian Oil (Ambo) Trans-Balkan pipeline, the pipeline connecting the oil-rich Caspian Sea region to the rest of the world. The initial feasibility project for Ambo was done by KBR.

KBR's cash flow from Logcap ballooned under Cheney's tenure, jumping from $144m in 1994 to more than $423m in 1996, and the Balkans was the driving force. By 1999, the army was spending just under $1bn a year on KBR's work in the Balkans. The GAO issued a report in September 2000 charging serious cost-control problems in Bosnia, but KBR retains the contract to this day.

Meanwhile, Cheney was busy developing Halliburton's business in other parts of the world. "It is a false dichotomy that we have to choose between our commercial and other interests," he told the [public policy research foundation] Cato Institute in 1998, speaking out against economic sanctions levied by the Clinton administration against countries suspected of terrorist activity. "Our government has become sanctions-happy," he continued.

In particular, Cheney objected to sanctions against Libya and Iran, two countries with which Halliburton was already doing business regardless. Even more disconcerting, though, was the work the company did in Iraq. Between his stints as secretary of defence and vice-president, Cheney was in charge of Halliburton when it was circumventing strict UN sanctions, helping to rebuild Iraq and enriching Saddam Hussein.

In September 1998, Halliburton closed a $7.7bn stock merger with Dresser Industries (the company that gave George HW Bush his first job). The merger made Halliburton the largest oilfield services firm in the world. It also brought with it two foreign subsidiaries that were doing business with Iraq via the controversial Oil for Food programme. The two subsidiaries, Dresser Rand and Ingersoll Dresser Pump Co, signed $73m worth of contracts for oil production equipment.

Cheney told the press during his 2000 run for vice-president that he had a "firm policy" against doing business with Iraq. He admitted to doing business with Iran and Libya, but "Iraq's different," he said. Cheney told ABC TV: "We've not done any business in Iraq since UN sanctions were imposed on Iraq in 1990, and I had a standing policy that I wouldn't do that."

Three weeks later, Cheney was forced to admit the business ties, but claimed ignorance. He told reporters that he was not aware of Dresser's business in Iraq, and that besides, Halliburton had divested itself of both companies by 2000. In the meantime, the companies had done another $30m worth of business in Iraq before being sold off.

The Dresser merger was, it appeared, the crowning achievement of the Cheney years at Halliburton. But Cheney left Halliburton several other legacies. David Gribbin, Cheney's former chief of staff, became Halliburton's chief lobbyist in Washington. Admiral Joe Lopez, a former commander of the sixth fleet, was hired to be KBR's governmental operations expert. Together, Cheney's team made Halliburton one of the top government contractors in the country. KBR had nearly doubled its government contracts, from $1.2bn in the five years prior to his arrival, to $2.3bn during his five years as CEO. Halliburton soared from 73rd to 18th on the Pentagon's list of top contractors.

After 9/11, KBR went to work on the war on terrorism, building the 1,000 detention cells at Guantánamo Bay, Cuba, for terrorist suspects, at a cost of $52m. The work had to feel familiar to KBR: it had done the exact same job 35 years earlier in Vietnam. When troops were deployed to Afghanistan, so was KBR. It built US bases in Bagram and Kandahar for $157m. As it had done in the past, KBR had men on the ground before the first troops even arrived in most locations. They readied the camps, fed the troops, and hauled away the waste. And they did it like the military would have done it: fast, efficient, and effective. It was good work, solid revenues, but nothing like the windfall the company had experienced in the Balkans.

In addition, Halliburton won the contract for restoring the Iraqi oil infrastructure—a contract that was not competitively bid. It was given to Halliburton out of convenience, because it had developed the plan for fighting oil fires (all, by this time, extinguished). Despite the new business, the fortunes of Halliburton and its subsidiary have not prospered. The stock that Cheney cashed in near its peak, when he renewed his political career in 2000, has since plummeted. The main culprit was the 1998 merger with Dresser, which saddled the company with asbestos liabilities that ultimately led to two Halliburton subsidiaries—one of them KBR—having to file for bankruptcy.

When Cheney left to become Bush's running mate, he took a golden parachute package—in addition to the stock options he was obliged to sell for $30m. In September 2003, Cheney insisted: "Since I've left Halliburton to become George Bush's vice-president, I've severed all my ties with the company, gotten rid of all my financial interests. I have no financial interest in Halliburton of any kind and haven't now for over three years."

The Congressional Research Service (CRS), a non-partisan agency that investigates political issues at the request of elected officials, says otherwise. Cheney has been receiving a deferred salary from Halliburton in the years since he left the company. In 2001, he received $205,298. In 2002, he drew $162,392. He is scheduled to receive similar payments through 2005, and has an insurance policy in place to protect the payments in the event that Halliburton should fold. In addition, Cheney still holds 433,333 unexercised stock options in Halliburton. He has agreed to donate any profits to charity.

## "Here's New Face of U.S. Military: Lynndie England"

*The New York Observer*

PHILIP WEISS, May 31, 2004

The condemnation of Lynndie England, the abuser of prisoners, in some ways echoes the exaltation a year ago of Jessica Lynch. Both young women come from small West Virginia towns. The privileged who offer such strong opinions about them are not their peers; they would never make the decision to enlist that these young women did. Notwithstanding the livid horror of Abu Ghraib, there is something condescending and unconvincing about the portrayals of the poor people who are fighting the war for the rest of us.

The class issue has shadowed the war from the start but has lately been getting more attention. It is the impetus for several initiatives on Capitol Hill and a theme of Michael Moore's anti-war documentary, *Fahrenheit 9/11*. "It's a poverty draft," said Rick Jahnkow, who does anti-military recruiting in California. "The vast number of people in this country who are escaping this draft are not elites. They're middle-class or upper-middle-class people."

The issue started percolating politically last year.

"We were looking at casualties from Texas on the Department of Defense Web site and it struck us that 'Gee, these kids are coming from towns in Texas that we never heard of,' " said Robert G. Cushing, a retired sociology professor in Austin who works with the Austin *American-Statesman*. "Not just small towns. But small towns not even close to metropolitan areas."

The newspaper undertook a study of the numbers and found that while one in five Americans live in non-metropolitan counties, nearly one out of three casualties in Iraq have come from these counties. These are places that do not have a city over 50,000 people and are not within commuting distance of a big city. The paper's interviews with enlistees from these places have shown that they can't find good jobs in their communities and feel that a university education is out of their reach—they couldn't afford to move to a community near a state school.

Representative Ike Skelton of Missouri, the ranking minority member on the House Armed Services Committee, was even more emphatic. Last fall he stated that 43.5 percent of the soldiers killed in Iraq came from rural cities and towns with a population below 20,000.

These kids tend to be rural white. The others who have been disproportionately affected are blacks and Hispanics from the inner city.

"I've heard people say, 'These kids want to fight, they

volunteered,' " said Charles Rangel, the longtime Harlem congressman. "But I saw these kids go off to camp and then to Iraq, and I'll tell you, they need the sense of importance of a uniform. And they're torn. They say, 'Congressman, continue to fight against this war, but don't worry about me. I'm going to make you proud, I'm going to be a good goddamn staff sergeant.'"

Representative Rangel came out for the draft as a more equitable means of sharing the risk. He promptly heard from Senator Ernest Hollings of South Carolina.

"Fritz Hollings said, 'My rednecks are catching hell,' " Representative Rangel recalled. "In these small towns, you're a big shot if you have a couple of stripes on your shoulder or bars on your collar."

The issue took on a special poignancy in South Carolina last year after three young men from one small town high school, Orangeburg-Wilkinson, died in Iraq, sowing disturbance in that community.

How many high schools in Westchester or Montgomery County, Md., have similar records? None; we'd have heard about it.

While the draft proposal has gone nowhere on Capitol Hill, the larger issue of fairness has gained a following in the "red" districts, to cite the red/blue divide of the last Presidential election. One conservative Republican, Sen. James Inhofe, of Oklahoma, has endorsed the call for a draft, while another, Chuck Hagel of Nebraska, has called for a national debate over the question. In the meantime, Mr. Skelton has called on the General Accounting Office to study the socio-economic composition of the military.

Michael Moore has also showed up on Capitol Hill. In a scene in his new documentary, the filmmaker and provocateur approaches three congressmen outside the Capitol, trying to recruit their children to the military. According to people who have seen the film, the congressmen walk away flabbergasted or blathering.

The issue goes well beyond Congress. Anti-recruiter Rick Jahnkow points out that Junior ROTC's can be found in every high school in San Diego except for the three high schools on the affluent north side of town.

The same exemption goes for the big Northeastern cities. The most startling statistic produced by a Defense Department human-resources contractor (humrro.org/poprep2002) is that at the end of the Vietnam era, the Northeast provided 22 percent of the people in the military. Today that number has sunk to 14 percent. Over the same period, the percentage of enlistment from the South has risen. Enter Jessica Lynch.

"In so many communities the choices seem to be, here go work at Burger King or go into the Army where you can have a career path, and get money for college, get training for a career,'" said Nancy Lessin, a member of the anti-war group Military Families Speak Out.

The obvious response to this imbalance is that the military has always functioned in this manner, as a bridge for powerless groups to rise into the middle class. It served that role for white ethnics during World War II and for blacks in the last generation. The poor will always be over-represented at the front lines;

the educated will almost always find jobs as paper-pushers.

Yet the difference in Iraq is that the selection of the poor is purer than ever. Yes, multitudes of affluent people got out of the draft during Vietnam. This time around they don't even have to worry about it. When Representative Susan Tauscher, a moderate Democrat serving the affluent hill communities outside Oakland, called for an increase of forces in Iraq and introduced legislation seeking more aggressive recruitment, she could be confident that those numbers won't be coming from her soccer-mom constituency.

And while the left often asserts that Iraq is recapitulating Vietnam, the big improvement from the military's standpoint is the passivity of those who oppose the war. Poll numbers suggest that opposition is widespread. But the campuses are quiet. There haven't been big anti-war demonstrations.

"All the demonstrations are on the telephone," said Emile Milne, an aide to Congressman Rangel.

For all their vehemence against the war, the affluent aren't waking up with nightmares about their children. If privileged youth were called upon to make the greatest sacrifice that a society demands of its citizens, this war would probably be ended in an instant. "The decisions about this war are being made by people with no personal stake," said Nancy Lessin (who said that on three occasions her organization tried to speak to John Kerry about the war, and on three occasions he could not make time for them).

Or as Congressman Rangel said, "It's easy to make the decision to go to war if you don't expect an uproar."

The poverty draft reflects the great divide in the new economy. The college-educated would regard it as a waste if their children were to join the military. No, they must be trained to the highest degree for participation in the global economy. Meanwhile, high risk can be outsourced, to the new immigrant from Guatemala or the ghetto kid who can't find employment. And to ice the deal, the military offers bonuses of tens of thousands of dollars to those who enlist, while editorialists who favor a larger military involvement call for "better incentives" and "better marketing" to enlistees.

There's got to be a better way to define citizenship. Representative Rangel served (and froze) in Korea, and while he didn't see the mission that time either, he has never forgotten the democratic lessons the military taught him: "We had the ability then to bring people of different classes and races together, and force their asses to respect each other."

The Iraq war has replaced that sense of a democratic collective with disrespect for those who can't participate in the new economy. And don't think that the citizens of Arab oligarchies don't see that. We like to think that we're exporting democracy. So far we're exporting ruthless capitalism.

Originally this space was going to be used to print an article from the *New York Times*.

On May 26, 2004, in an unprecedented admission about their Iraq coverage, the *New York Times* admitted some of their "coverage was not as rigorous as it should have been." They also admitted a failure in their reporting about the key source on Iraq's WMD program and its links to al Qaeda:

"The *Times* never followed up on the veracity of this source or the attempts to verify his claims."

I wanted to print their mea culpa here. You would think that if the *Times* felt truly sorry for the way they banged Bush's war drum, they'd allow me to print it here. Instead they denied permission because, as George W. Bush knows, it is hard to say you are sorry. Especially when you were wrong.

# "Why the Media Owe You an Apology on Iraq"

*The Free Lance–Star* (Fredericksburg, Virginia)

RICK MERCIER, March 28, 2004

The media are finished with their big blowouts on the anniversary of the invasion of Iraq, and there's one thing they forgot to say: We're sorry.

Sorry we let unsubstantiated claims drive our coverage.

Sorry we were dismissive of experts who disputed White House charges against Iraq.

Sorry we let a band of self-serving Iraqi defectors make fools of us.

Sorry we fell for Colin Powell's performance at the United Nations.

Sorry we couldn't bring ourselves to hold the administration's feet to the fire before the war, when it really mattered.

Maybe we'll do a better job next war.

Of course it's absurd to receive this apology from a person so low in the media hierarchy. You really ought to be getting it from the editors and reporters at the agenda-setting publications, such as the *New York Times* and the *Washington Post*. It's the elite print media that failed you the most, because they're the institutions you have to rely on to keep tabs on the politicians in Washington (television news cannot do the kind of in-depth or investigative reporting that print media can do—when they're doing their job properly).

In the past several months, the *Times,* the *Post,* and other print media have gotten around to asking questions about the quality of prewar intelligence on Iraq and about whether the administration might have misused that intelligence to sell the war to Americans and the rest of the world.

Most of these media outlets, however, also need to conduct self-examinations. From the horrendously distorted coverage of *Times* reporter Judith Miller (her sins in many ways were far worse than those of plagiarist/fabricator Jayson Blair) to the bewildering (and biased?) news judgment of the *Post*'s editors, journalists at America's most influential publications helped ensure that a majority of you would be misinformed about Iraq and the nature of the threat it posed to you.

## Stenographers or journalists?

The main reason you were misinformed is that the major print media were too willing to take the White House at its word. A study released earlier this month by the University of Maryland's Center for International Security Studies concluded that much of the prewar coverage about Iraq and weapons of mass destruction "stenographically reported the incumbent administration's perspective" and provided "too little critical examination of the way officials framed the events, issues, threats, and policy options." Too few stories, the study said, included perspectives that challenged the official line.

A study published last month in *The New York Review of Books* reached a similar conclusion. "In the period before the war, U.S. journalists were far too reliant on sources sympathetic to the administration. Those with dissenting views—and there were more than a few—were shut out," writes Michael Massing, a *Columbia Journalism Review* contributing editor who authored the study.

Even much of the prewar enterprise or investigative reporting was shaped by the assumption that pro-war sources were above serious scrutiny. This was particularly the case with Iraqi defectors, on whom both the administration and media relied heavily for painting a picture of the Iraqi threat.

As Massing observes, there was vigorous debate inside intelligence circles about the veracity of many of the defectors' claims, but not much of this reached readers. Instead, the print media were repeatedly duped by defectors on the Pentagon's payroll who were busily slipping credulous reporters the same disinformation they were peddling to the administration.

Knight Ridder journalists Jonathan Landay and Tish Wells reported earlier this month that the main Iraqi exile group, the Iraqi National Congress, fed the *Times*, the *Post*, the Associated Press (the primary source of world and national news for this newspaper), and other print media numerous unsubstantiated allegations about the Iraqi regime that resulted in over 100 articles worldwide.

Those articles, the Knight Ridder correspondents found, made assertions that still have not been substantiated but that helped build the administration's case for invasion. They included claims that Iraq had mobile biological weapons facilities; that it had Scud missiles loaded with poison that were ready to strike Israel; that Saddam was aggressively pursuing nuclear weapons and that he had collaborated with al-Qaida.

The *Times*' diva of disinformation, Judith Miller, had a particularly uncritical fondness for the INC and its leader, Ahmed Chalabi. Last spring, *Post* media columnist Howard Kurtz obtained an internal *Times* e-mail in which she wrote: "I've been covering Chalabi for about 10 years. He has provided most of the front-page exclusives on WMD to our paper."

It's hard to imagine a more damning admission, not only in the light of hindsight but also because of the questions many intelligence analysts (both inside and outside the government) had before the invasion about the quality of the INC's information.

The *Times* cannot argue that it was impossible to get dissenting views from those inside the U.S. intelligence establishment. Knight Ridder was able to develop sources among career intelligence officers who were dismayed by many of the administration's claims. In an interview with Massing for his study, Knight Ridder Washington bureau chief John Walcott explained the news service's decision to use these "blue collar" sources:

"These people were better informed about the details of the intelligence than the people higher up in the food chain, and they were deeply troubled by what they regarded as the administration's deliberate misrepresentation of intelligence, ranging from overstating the case to outright fabrication."

Knight Ridder produced some accurate, balanced reporting as a result of their approach, but mid-level intelligence experts remained a missing piece of the puzzle in most print-media coverage.

### Powell's really big show

There were other important pieces of the puzzle to which the media had access but downplayed or ignored.

Take Hussein Kamel, Saddam's son-in-law, who was Iraq's weapons chief until his defection in 1995. He was cited by Vice President Dick Cheney, Secretary of State Colin Powell, and just about every other invasion supporter as an important source of intelligence on Saddam's arsenal. However, while he was describing all of Saddam's awful weapons during his post-defection debriefings, Kamel added one little thing that the administration and its mouthpieces forgot to mention: All of Iraq's prohibited weapons had been destroyed.

*Newsweek* obtained the transcript of the interview in which Kamel made this assertion and reported on it about two weeks before the start of the invasion, but the magazine did not give the story the prominence it deserved.

Elsewhere in the U.S. print media, only the *Post* and the *Boston Globe* picked up the story, according to the media watchdog group Fairness and Accuracy in Reporting. Both of these papers placed the news deep inside their A sections.

The Kamel example illustrates a common problem with prewar coverage: Even when reporters did good investigative work, it often got buried. *Post* staff writer Walter Pincus told Massing that his paper's editors "went through a whole phase in which they didn't put things on the front page that would make a difference."

It's not clear from Massing's article when that phase might have been, but at least some of it must have fallen in the period after Powell's presentation to the United Nations and before the beginning of the invasion.

The day after Powell's big show, an editorial in the *Post* titled "Irrefutable" declared it "hard to imagine how anyone could doubt that Iraq possesses weapons of mass destruction." The *Post*'s news pages, and those of other elite publications, seemed to have been operating under that assumption for months, but Powell's performance sealed the deal.

Yet there was plenty to question about Powell's case: the ammunition depot that supposedly stored prohibited weapons; the alleged mobile bioweapons labs; the aluminum tubes that were said to have been bought to further Iraq's nuclear-weapons program; and the claims of a Saddam/al-Qaida connection. Even the recorded conversations between Iraqi military personnel that Powell presented as evidence of the regime's trying to hide banned weapons raised skepticism among some experts who had knowledge of Iraqi security protocol. (See the Robert Greenwald documentary

*Uncovered: The Whole Truth About the Iraq War* for a full dissection of Powell's presentation.)

But most mass media weren't interested in drawing too much attention to these weaknesses in Powell's case or in doing further investigative work to scrutinize the secretary of state's claims. Instead, they played it safe and geared up for war.

### "We were taken for a ride"

Earlier this month, the president of Poland, which has over 2,000 troops in Iraq, said "We were taken for a ride" by the administration in the run-up to the war. It's now clear that the major media helped navigate for the White House during that long, strange trip.

Yet a couple of things should be said in the media's defense.

First, it's not easy to ask tough questions amid war hysteria, and those who do a good job of it will be attacked by the überpatriots. (I can attest from personal experience that some may even clamor for your head.)

Second, there were a few mainstream journalists who did ask the tough questions when it counted. But there were too many reporters who weren't asking them, and there were some who acted as little more than cogs in the White House propaganda machine.

Most disturbing of all, some of these journalists still don't get it. When Massing asked the *Times'* Miller—an investigative reporter covering intelligence—why she didn't include more comments in her stories by experts who contested White House assertions, she replied: "My job isn't to assess the government's information and be an independent intelligence analyst myself. My job is to tell readers of *The New York Times* what the government thought about Iraq's arsenal."

But even a cub reporter should know that if the government tells her the sky is blue, it's her job to check whether it might not be red or gray or black. And skepticism must be exercised most strongly when the matter at hand is whether the nation will go to war.

By neglecting to fully employ their critical-thinking faculties, Miller and many of her colleagues in the elite print media not only failed their readers during the countdown to the Iraq invasion, they failed our democracy.

And there's no excusing that failure. The only thing that can be said is, Sorry.

Rick Mercier is a writer and editor for *The Free Lance–Star*. He can be reached at rmercier@freelancestar.com.

# "Why the Media Failed Us in Iraq"

### ORVILLE SCHELL

When, on May 26, 2004, the editors of the *New York Times* published a mea culpa for the paper's one-sided reporting on weapons of mass destruction and the Iraq war, they admitted to "a number of instances of coverage that was not as rigorous as it should have been." They also commented that they had since come to "wish we had been more aggressive in re-examining claims" made by the Bush administration. But we are still left to wonder why the *Times*, like many other major media outlets in this country, was so lacking in skepticism toward administration rationales for war? How could such a poorly thought through policy, based on spurious exile intelligence sources, have been so blithely accepted, even embraced, by so many members of the media? In short, what happened to the press's vaunted role, so carefully spelled out by the Founding Fathers, as a skeptical "watchdog" over government?

There's nothing like seeing a well-oiled machine clank to a halt to help you spot problems. Now that the Bush administration is in full defensive mode and angry leakers in the Pentagon, the CIA, and elsewhere in the Washington bureaucracy are slipping documents, secrets, and charges to reporters, our press looks more recognizably journalistic. But that shouldn't stop us from asking how an "independent" press in a "free" country could have been so paralyzed for so long. It not only failed to seriously investigate administration rationales for war, but little took into account the myriad voices in the on-line, alternative, and world press that sought to do so. It was certainly no secret that a number of our Western allies (and other countries), administrators of various NGOs, and figures like Mohamed El Baradei, head of the International Atomic Energy Agency, and Hans Blix, head of the UN's Monitoring, Verification and Inspections Commission, had quite different pre-war views of the "Iraqi threat."

Few in our media, it seemed, remembered I. F. Stone's hortatory admonition, "If you want to know about governments, all you have to know is two words: Governments lie." Dissenting voices in the mainstream were largely buried on back pages, ignored on op-ed pages, or confined to the margins of the media, and so denied the kinds of "respectability" that a major media outlet can confer.

As reporting on the lead-up to war, the war itself, and its aftermath vividly demonstrated, our country is now divided into a two-tiered media structure. The lower-tier—niche publications, alternative media outlets, and Internet sites—hosts the broadest spectrum of viewpoints. Until the war effort began to unravel in spring 2004, the upper-tier—a relatively small number of major broadcast outlets, newspapers, and magazines— had a far more limited bandwidth of critical views, regularly deferring to the Bush Administration's vision of the world. Contrarian views below rarely bled upwards.

As Michael Massing pointed out recently in the *New York Review of Books,* Bush administration insinuations that critics were unpatriotic—White House Press Secretary Ari Fleischer infamously warned reporters as war approached, "People had better watch what they say"—had an undeniably chilling effect on the media. But other forms of pressure also effectively inhibited the press. The President held few press conferences and rarely submitted to truly open exchanges. Secretive and disciplined to begin with, the administration adeptly used the threat of denied access as a way to intimidate reporters who showed evidence of independence. For reporters, this meant no one-on-one interviews, special tips, or leaks, being passed over in press conference question-and-answer periods, and exclusion from select events as well as important trips.

After the war began, for instance, Jim Wilkinson, a 32-year-old Texan who ran Centcom's Coalition Media Center in Qatar, was, according to Massing, known to rebuke reporters whose copy was deemed insufficiently "supportive of the war," and "darkly warned one correspondent that he was on a 'list' along with two other reporters at his paper." In the play-along world of the Bush administration, critical reporting was a quick ticket to exile.

## A media world of faith-based truth

The impulse to control the press hardly originated with George W. Bush, but his administration has been less inclined than any in memory to echo Thomas

Jefferson's famous declaration that, "The basis of our government being the opinion of the people, the very first object should be to keep that right; and were it left to me to decide whether we should have a government without newspapers or newspapers without government, I should not hesitate a moment to prefer the latter."

The Bush Administration had little esteem for the watchdog role of the press, in part because its own quest for "truth" has been based on something other than empiricism. In fact, it enthroned a new criterion for veracity, "faith-based" truth, sometimes corroborated by "faith-based" intelligence. For officials of this administration (and not just the religious ones either), truth seemed to descend from on high, a kind of divine revelation begging no further earthly scrutiny. For our president this was evidently literally the case. The Israeli paper *Ha'aretz* reported him saying to Mahmoud Abbas, the Palestinian Prime Minister of the moment, "God told me to strike Al Qaeda and I struck, and then he instructed me to strike Saddam, which I did."

It is hardly surprising, then, that such a president would eschew newspapers in favor of reports from other more "objective sources," namely, his staff. He has spoken often of trusting "visceral reactions" and acting on "gut feelings." For him as for much of the rest of his administration, decision-making has tended to proceed not from evidence to conclusion, but from conclusion to evidence. Reading, facts, history, logic and the complex interaction between the electorate, the media, and the government have all been relegated to subsidiary roles in what might be called "fundamentalist" policy formation.

Just as the free exchange of information plays little role in the relationship between a fundamentalist believer and his or her God, so it has played a distinctly diminished role in our recent parallel world of divine political revelation. After all, if you already know the answer to a question, of what use is the media, except to broadcast that answer? The task at hand, then, is never to listen but to proselytize the political gospel among non-believers, thereby transforming a once interactive process between citizen and leader into evangelism.

Although in the Bush political universe, freedom has been endlessly extolled in principle, it has had little utility in practice. What possible role could a free press play when revelation trumps fact and conclusions are preordained? A probing press is logically viewed as a spoiler under such conditions, stepping between the administration and those whose only true salvation lies in becoming part of a nation of true believers. Since there was little need, and less respect, for an opposition (loyal or otherwise), the information feedback loops in which the press should have played a crucial role in any functioning democracy, ceased operating. The media synapses which normally transmit warnings from citizen to government froze shut.

Television networks continued to broadcast and papers continued to publish, but, dismissed and ignored, they became irrelevant, except possibly for their entertainment value. As the press has withered, the government, already existing in a self-referential and self-deceptive universe, was deprived of the ability to learn of danger from its own policies and thus make course corrections.

### A universe in which news won't matter

Karl Rove, the president's chief political advisor, bluntly declared to *New Yorker* writer Ken Auletta that members of the press "don't represent the public any more than other people do. I don't believe you have a check-and-balance function." Auletta concluded that, in the eyes of the Bush Administration, the press corps had become little more than another special-interest lobbying group. Indeed, the territory the traditional media once occupied has increasingly been deluged by administration lobbying, publicity, and advertising—cleverly staged "photo ops," carefully produced propaganda rallies, preplanned "events," tidal waves of campaign ads, and the like. Afraid of losing further "influence," access, and the lucrative ad revenues that come from such political image-making, major media outlets have found it in their financial interest to quietly yield.

What does this downgrading of the media's role say about how our government views its citizens, the putative sovereigns of our country? It suggests that "we the people" are seen not as political constituencies conferring legitimacy on our rulers, but as consumers to be sold policy the way advertisers sell product. In the storm of selling, spin, bullying, and "discipline" that has been the Bush signature for years, traditional news outlets found themselves increasingly drowned out, ghettoized, and cowed. Attacked as "liberal" and "elitist," disesteemed as "trouble makers" and "bashers" (even when making all too little trouble), they were relegated to the sidelines, increasingly uncertain and timid about their shrinking place in the political process.

Add in a further dynamic (which intellectuals from Marxist-Leninist societies would instantly recognize): Groups denied legitimacy and disdained by the state tend to internalize their exclusion as a form of culpability, and often feel an abject, autonomic urge to seek reinstatement at almost any price. Little wonder, then, that "the traditional press" has had a difficult time mustering anything like a convincing counter-narrative as the administration herded a terrified and all-too-trusting nation to war.

Not only did a mutant form of skepticism-free news succeed—at least for a time—in leaving large segments of the populace uninformed, but it corrupted the ability of high officials to function. All too often they simply found themselves looking into a fun-house mirror of their own making and imagined that they were viewing reality. As even the conservative *National Review* noted, the Bush administration has "a dismaying capacity to believe its own public relations."

In this world of mutant "news," information loops have become one-way highways; and a national security advisor, cabinet secretary, or attorney general, a well-managed and programmed polemicist charged to "stay on message," the better to justify whatever the government has already done, or is about to do. Because these latter-day campaigns to "dominate the media environment," as the Pentagon likes to say, employ all the sophistication and technology developed by communications experts since Edward Bernays, nephew of Sigmund Freud, first wed an understanding of psychology to the marketing of merchandise, they are far more seductive than older-style news. Indeed, on Fox News, we can see the ultimate marriage of news and PR in a fountainhead of artful propaganda so well-packaged that most people can't tell it from the real thing.

For three-plus years we have been governed by people who don't view news, in the traditional sense, as playing any constructive role in our system of governance. At the moment, they are momentarily in retreat, driven back from the front lines of faith-based truth by their own faith-based blunders. But make no mistake, their frightening experiment will continue if Americans allow it. Complete success would mean not just that the press had surrendered its essential watchdog role, but—a far darker thought—that, even were it to refuse to do so, it might be shunted off to a place where it would not matter.

As the war in Iraq descended into a desert quagmire, the press belatedly appeared to awaken and adopt a more skeptical stance toward an already crumbling set of Bush administration policies. But if a bloody, expensive, catastrophic episode like the war in Iraq is necessary to remind us of the important role that the press plays in our democracy, something is gravely amiss in the way our political system has come to function.

Mr. Schell is dean of the Graduate School of Journalism at the University of California, Berkeley. This piece is adapted from the preface to a collection of *New York Review of Books* articles on the media's coverage of the war in Iraq by Michael Massing. It has been published as a short book, *Now They Tell Us* (The New York Review of Books, 2004).

## "Not Again"

### Indian Writer Arundhati Roy Argues That It Is the Demands of Global Capitalism That Are Driving the West to War with Iraq

*Manchester Guardian Weekly*

ARUNDHATI ROY, October 9, 2002

Recently, those who have criticised the actions of the US government (myself included) have been called "anti-American." Anti-Americanism is in the process of being consecrated into an ideology. The term is usually used by the American establishment to discredit and, not falsely—but shall we say inaccurately—define its critics. Once someone is branded anti-American, the chances are that he or she will be judged before they're heard and the argument will be lost in the welter of bruised national pride.

What does the term mean? That you're anti-jazz? Or that you're opposed to free speech? That you don't delight in Toni Morrison or John Updike? That you have a quarrel with giant sequoias? Does it mean you don't admire the hundreds of thousands of American citizens who marched against nuclear weapons, or the thousands of war resisters who forced their government to withdraw from Vietnam? Does it mean that you hate all Americans?

This sly conflation of America's music, literature, the breathtaking physical beauty of the land, the ordinary pleasures of ordinary people with criticism of the US government's foreign policy is a deliberate and extremely effective strategy. It's like a retreating army taking cover in a heavily populated city, hoping that the prospect of hitting civilian targets will deter enemy fire.

To call someone anti-American, indeed, to be anti-American, is not just racist, it's a failure of the imagination. An inability to see the world in terms other than those that the establishment has set out for you: If you don't love us, you hate us. If you're not good, you're evil. If you're not with us, you're with the terrorists.

Last year, like many others, I too made the mistake of scoffing at this post–September 11 rhetoric, dismissing it as foolish. I've realised that it's not. It's actually a canny recruitment drive for a misconceived, dangerous war. Every day I'm taken aback at how many people believe that opposing the war in Afghanistan amounts to supporting terrorism.

Uppermost on everybody's mind, of course, particularly in the US, is the horror of what has come to be known as 9/11. Nearly 3,000 civilians lost their lives in that lethal terrorist strike. The grief is still deep. The rage still sharp. And a strange, deadly war is raging around the world. Yet, each person who has lost a loved one surely knows that no war, no act of revenge, will blunt the edges of their pain or bring their own loved ones back. War cannot avenge those who have died. War is only a brutal desecration of their memory.

To fuel yet another war—this time against Iraq—by manipulating people's grief, by packaging it for TV specials sponsored by corporations selling detergent or running shoes, is to cheapen and devalue grief, to drain it of meaning. We are seeing a pillaging of even the most private human feelings for political purpose. It is a terrible, violent thing for a state to do to its people.

The US government says that Saddam Hussein is a war criminal, a cruel military despot who has committed genocide against his own people. That's a fairly accurate description of the man. In 1988 he razed hundreds of villages in northern Iraq and killed thousands of Kurds. Today, we know that that same year the US government provided him with $500m in subsidies to buy American farm products. The next year, after he had successfully completed his genocidal campaign, the US government doubled its subsidy to $1bn. It also provided him with high-quality germ seed for anthrax, as well as helicopters and dual-use material that could be used to manufacture chemical and biological weapons.

It turns out that while Saddam was carrying out his worst atrocities, the US and British governments were his close allies. So what changed?

In August 1990 Saddam invaded Kuwait. His sin was not so much that he had committed an act of war, but that he acted independently, without orders from his masters. This display of independence was enough to upset the power equation in the Gulf. So it was decided that Saddam be exterminated, like a pet that has outlived its owner's affection.

What if Iraq does have a nuclear weapon? Does that justify a pre-emptive US strike? The US has the largest arsenal of nuclear weapons in the world. It's the only country in the world to have actually used them on civilian populations. If the US is justified in launching a pre-emptive attack on Iraq, why, any nuclear power is justified in carrying out a pre-emptive attack on any other. India could attack Pakistan, or the other way around.

Recently, the US played an important part in forcing India and Pakistan back from the brink of war. Is it so hard for it to take its own advice? Who is guilty of feckless moralising? Of preaching peace while it wages war? The US, which George Bush has called "the most peaceful nation on earth," has been at war with one country or another every year for the past 50 years.

Wars are never fought for altruistic reasons. They're usually fought for hegemony, for business. And then, of course, there's the business of war. In his book on globalisation, *The Lexus and the Olive Tree*, Tom Friedman says: "The hidden hand of the market will never work without a hidden fist. McDonald's cannot flourish without McDonnell Douglas. And the hidden fist that keeps the world safe for Silicon Valley's technologies to flourish is called the U.S. Army, Air Force, Navy and Marine Corps." Perhaps this was written in a moment of vulnerability, but it's certainly the most succinct, accurate description of the project of corporate globalisation that I have read.

After September 11 and the war against terror, the hidden hand and fist have had their cover blown—and we have a clear view now of America's other weapon—the free market—bearing down on the developing world, with a clenched, unsmiling smile. The Task That Never Ends is America's perfect war, the perfect vehicle for the endless expansion of American imperialism.

As the disparity between the rich and poor grows, the hidden fist of the free market has its work cut out. Multinational corporations on the prowl for "sweetheart deals" that yield enormous profits cannot push them through in developing countries without the active connivance of state machinery. Today, corporate globalisation needs an international confederation of loyal, corrupt, preferably authoritarian governments in poorer countries, to push through unpopular reforms and quell the mutinies. It needs a press that pretends to be free. It needs courts that pretend to dispense justice. It needs nuclear bombs, standing armies, sterner immigration laws, and watchful coastal patrols to make sure that it is only money, goods, patents and services that are globalised—not the free movement of people, not a respect for human rights, not international treaties on racial discrimination or chemical and nuclear weapons, or greenhouse gas emissions, climate change, or, God forbid, justice. It's as though even a gesture towards international accountability would wreck the whole enterprise.

Close to one year after the war against terror was officially flagged off in the ruins of Afghanistan, in country after country freedoms are being curtailed in the name of protecting freedom, civil liberties are being suspended in the name of protecting democracy. All kinds of dissent is being defined as "terrorism." The US secretary of defence, Donald Rumsfeld, said that his mission in the war against terror was to persuade the world that Americans must be allowed to continue their way of life. When the maddened king stamps his foot, slaves tremble in their quarters. So, it's hard for me to say this, but the American way of life is simply not sustainable. Because it doesn't acknowledge that there is a world beyond America.

Fortunately, power has a shelf life. When the time comes, maybe this mighty empire will, like others before it, overreach itself and implode from within. It looks as though structural cracks have already appeared.

Soviet-style communism failed, not because it was intrinsically evil but because it was flawed. It allowed too few people to usurp too much power: 21st-century market-capitalism, American-style, will fail for the same reasons.

# PART VI

## Cartoons and Photographs

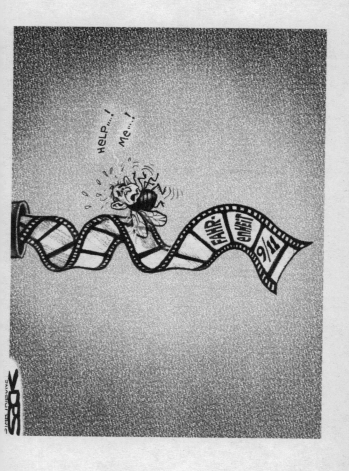

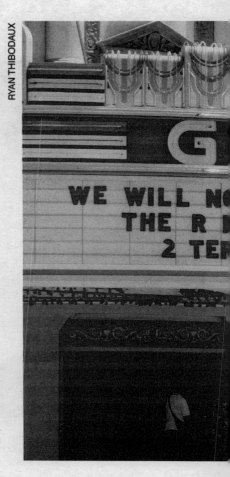

Here's the marquee of the Grand Lake
Theater in Oakland, California. The theater's
owner refused to enforce the R rating.

**What a great story!**
A group of friends was
so moved after seeing
the film that they all
chipped in and rented
a prop plane to drag
this message over the
beaches of Delaware
and Maryland on the
July Fourth weekend.

GET YOUR

GET YOUR HEAD OUT OF THE SAND–SEE FAHRENHEIT 9/11

OF THE SAND–SEE FAHRENHEIT 9/11

Sunday 10p.m.    Still packed.    Ft. Lauderdale, FL

Even on a beautiful night in Ft. Lauderdale, moviegoers were lined up the block in hopes of catching the film on its opening weekend.

Folks were standing in line for hours waiting for tickets that first weekend, causing a shortage that brought on what might have been the first scalping of a movie ticket in history.

A crowded opening-weekend day outside
the Westwood Crest Theater in L.A.

A crowded opening-weekend night outside
the Westwood Crest Theater in L.A.

# PERMISSIONS ACKNOWLEDGMENTS

All works reprinted with permission.

"TIA Now Verifies Flight of Saudis" by Jean Heller. Copyrigh
*St. Petersburg Times* 2004.

"Moore's Message Delivered, Big-Time" by Denis Hamill. New
York *Daily News*, L.P. Reprinted with permission.

"Persuasive and Passionate. *Fahrenheit 9/11* Is Both" by Mich
LaSalle. *San Francisco Chronicle*.

"Michael Moore Brings the War Home" by Danny Duncan Collum
Reprinted with permission from *Sojourners Magazine*, (800) 714
7474, http://www.sojo.net.

"*Fahrenheit 9/11*: Luring TV Viewers to the Theater for News" by
Frazier Moore. Reprinted with permission of The Associated Press.

"*Fahrenheit 9/11* Has Recruited Unlikely Audience: U.S. Soldiers"
by Shailagh Murray. Reprinted by permission of the *Wall Stree
Journal*. Copyright © 2004 Dow Jones & Company, Inc. All Rights
Reserved Worldwide. License number 1056581051946.

"Framing Michael Moore" by Joel Bleifuss. *In These Times*
http://inthesetimes.com.

"They Knew . . ." by David Sirota and Christy Harvey. *In These
Times*, http://inthesetimes.com.

*The Halliburton Agenda* by Dan Briody. Copyright © 2004 Danie
Briody. Reprinted with permission of John Wiley & Sons, Inc.

"*Fahrenheit 9/11*: Connecting with a Hard Left" by Desson
Thomson. Copyright © 2004, *The Washington Post*.

"Plane Carried 13 Bin Ladens" by Dana Milbank. Copyright ©
2004, *The Washington Post*.

"Moore Interest in National Politics." This is an abridged version of
a *Financial Times* leader first published on July 3, 2004.

## ABOUT THE AUTHOR

Michael Moore has won an Oscar (*Bowling for Columbine*), an Emmy (*TV Nation*), a Palme d'Or at Cannes (*Fahrenheit 9/11*), and the British Book of the Year 2003 award (*Stupid White Men*). He was an Eagle Scout, a seminarian, and the first eighteen-year-old elected to public office. He has never bowled over 200.